Lecture Notes in
Fixed Income
Fundamentals

World Scientific Lecture Notes in Finance

ISSN: 2424-9955

Series Editor: Professor Itzhak Venezia

Published:

Vol. 1   Lecture Notes in Introduction to Corporate Finance
  *by Ivan E. Brick (Rutgers Business School at Newark and
  New Brunswick, USA)*

Vol. 2   Lecture Notes in Fixed Income Fundamentals
  by Eliezer Z. Prisman (York University, Canada)

Forthcoming Titles:

Lecture Notes in Behavioral Finance
  by Itzhak Venezia (The Hebrew University of Jerusalem, Israel)

Lecture Notes in Market Microstructure and Trading
  by Peter Joakim Westerholm (The University of Sydney, Australia)

Lecture Notes in Risk Management
  *by Zvi Wiener and Yevgeny Mugerman (The Hebrew University of
  Jerusalem, Israel)*

World Scientific Lecture Notes in Finance – **Vol. 2**

Lecture Notes in Fixed Income Fundamentals

Eliezer Z Prisman

Schulich School of Business
York University, Canada

 **World Scientific**

NEW JERSEY · LONDON · SINGAPORE · BEIJING · SHANGHAI · HONG KONG · TAIPEI · CHENNAI · TOKYO

Published by

World Scientific Publishing Co. Pte. Ltd.

5 Toh Tuck Link, Singapore 596224

USA office: 27 Warren Street, Suite 401-402, Hackensack, NJ 07601

UK office: 57 Shelton Street, Covent Garden, London WC2H 9HE

Library of Congress Cataloging-in-Publication Data
Names: Prisman, Eliezer Z., author.
Title: Lecture notes in fixed income fundamentals / Eliezer Z. Prisman (York University, Canada).
Description: New Jersey : World Scientific, [2016] |
    Series: World scientific lecture notes in finance | Includes index.
Identifiers: LCCN 2016035725| ISBN 9789813149755 | ISBN 9789813149762 (pbk)
Subjects: LCSH: Fixed-income securities.
Classification: LCC HG4650 .P75 2016 | DDC 332.63/2044--dc23
LC record available at https://lccn.loc.gov/2016035725

British Library Cataloguing-in-Publication Data
A catalogue record for this book is available from the British Library.

Desk Editor: Shreya Gopi

Typeset by Stallion Press
Email: enquiries@stallionpress.com

Printed in Singapore

Preface

This book is the hard copy version of the eBook *Fixed Income Fundamentals: An interactive e-book powered by Maple*, see http://www.yorku.ca/eprisman. As such, it contains all the Maple commands that are used to calculate the examples. The Maple programming language is very intuitive and at the level used in this book is very much like a pseudo code. The commands are self-explanatory, so that the purpose of each calculation is apparent, even to a reader not familiar with Maple. Where there was a need to use a more complicated calculation/algorithm a procedure was written. The procedure's name, the input parameters, the output and the goal of the procedure are all explained in the body of the text. Hence again the reader of the hardcopy version will find the material very intuitive.

To distinguish the text from the Maple commands, lines containing Maple commands start with $>$. The hard copy version is thus equivalent to the eBook and therefore the rest of the preface that was written for the eBook applies as well to the hardcopy version. The only exception is that the eBook allows interactive interaction as explained henceforth.

The topic of fixed income securities has advanced tremendously in the last decade or so. Simultaneously, the use of sophisticated Mathematics needed to fully grasp this material has grown exponentially. The term "fixed income securities", historically a synonym for bonds (as they promise deterministic fixed cash flows to be paid at fixed deterministic times), no longer accurately describes this field. Bonds that now incorporate many options-like features and financial contracts that are contingent on interest rates are very popular, thereby rendering the "term fixed income securities" obsolete.

Bonds and the behavior of interest rates are not as detached as they were, a few years ago, from the topics of valuation and derivative securities. In fact the topic of interest rate derivative securities (contingent claims) is more complex than equity derivatives. Yet many books, maybe even most books in this area, try to teach students the basics of fixed income securities together with interest rate derivative securities.

The complexity of the quantitative methods needed in this field stemmed mostly from the need to model the evolution of the term structure of interest rates (TS). Modern books in this area tend to attempt (and they may be justified in doing so) to encompass the frontier of the field and thus speak about options, interest rate contingent claims, the evolution of the TS and thereby present a very daunting task to beginners in this field. The result could be an overwhelming amount of material for a beginner and consequently the student may fail to grasp a deep understanding of fixed income securities. At the same time they may not fully comprehend the derivative securities aspect.

Yet, there is a lot that can be done in this field without modelling the evolution of the TS by using only the "yield curve" or the current realization of the TS. The basic understanding of the no arbitrage condition (NA), its relation to the existence and estimation of the TS and to valuation of various instruments (swapes, forward rate agreements etc.) can be mastered and well explained without reference to the evolution of the TS. Such an approach would allow the student to grasp the philosophy behind the NA and its use.

This is exactly what this book aims to achieve. It is meant to equip novices to this area with a solid and intuitive understanding of the NA, its link to the existence and estimation of the term structure of interest rates and to valuation of financial contracts. The book uses the modern approach of arbitrage arguments and addresses only positions and contracts that do not require the knowledge of the evolution of the TS. As such, the book removes a barrier to entry to this field (at the cost of being only an introduction to this subject). We believe that this trade off is well justified and will provide the readers of this book with good intuition for the TS, the NA, the bond market and certain financial contracts.

This book concentrates on understanding and explaining the pillars of fixed income markets using the modern finance approach as stipulated and implied by the 'no free lunch condition'. The book focuses on a conceptual understanding so that the readers will be familiar with the tools needed to analyze bond markets. Institutional information is covered only to the extent that such is needed to get a full appreciation of the concepts. It follows the philosophy that institutional details are much easier to understand and are readily available from different sources unlike the core ideas and ways of thinking about fixed income markets. Furthermore these institutional details might be slightly different from country to country, thus concentrating on conceptual issues will help to maintain a universal book that can be used anywhere.

The book is written for an undergraduate first course in fixed income securities, bonds, interest rates and related financial contracts. It assumes that readers are familiar with the concept of "time value of money", even though it is reviewed in the first chapter. The book assumes a certain mathematical maturity but not much above what is sometimes referred to as "finite mathematics". Calculus or optimization is used in a very small fraction of the material. Its use however is hidden (in appendixes or suppressed) and readers lacking this knowledge can read the complete book without difficulties. Thus the book will also be of interest to anybody who seeks an introduction to the subjects of bonds, interest rates and financial contracts the valuation of which depends on interest rates.

The book is tailored for beginners in this area and as such it does not attempt to teach students about fixed income derivative securities and the evaluation of the term structure of interest rates. Rather it focuses on cementing the core and fundamental points of fixed income securities. The valuation of different positions and financial contracts is covered as long as it can be done by using only the current term structure of interest rates (and not its evolution). Thereby we believe that we will expose the student to the way of thinking and analyzing situations utilizing the NA condition (without the complicated issues of the evolution of the term structure).

The book starts by reviewing the concept of time value of money. It continues by underlying the basic framework of government bond markets, the role of the NA (no free lunch condition), and its relation to the TS and discount factors. Next the estimation of the TS is addressed followed by the valuations of swaps and futures (forwards) in a one-period setting. A variety of instruments, the valuation of which depends on the TS (in a multi-period framework), are explored. The book also covers interest rate risk management, immunization strategies, and matched cash flow. It also touches on interest rate options (mainly utilizing a binomial-based model) and credit derivatives.

This book is tailored to an introductory (undergraduate) course spanning 12–15 weeks of lectures or a short graduate course of about 6 weeks. After taking a course based on this book, the students will know how to value different financial contracts that require the current realization of the TS ("yield curve") as an input. However we believe they will appreciate and acquire a full understanding of the implications and applications of the NA in bond markets. The book presents a universal view of bond markets which could be applied anywhere. We believe that our goals can be accomplished requiring only the very basic course of introduction to finance that exists in almost all business schools and most economics departments. After completing a course based on this book students will be ready to obtain the needed mathematical modelling of the evolution of the TS and move to this next step.

The e-book presents an interactive and dynamic friendly environment allowing readers to learn through hands-on experience. The book can only be read with the Maple software. We have chosen Maple because of its symbolic computation ability as well as its visualization capability and the structure of its files that allows embedding commands within the text. This e-book is a series of Maple worksheets connected by hyperlinks and a Table of Contents which has links to each worksheet. It presents an Interactive Dynamic Environment for Advanced Learning (IDEAL) which is supported by a collection of procedures — a Maple package.

A reader who follows the book on-screen, will find the commands are already typed in the appropriate files. The reader should merely re-execute the printed commands while reading. The technology allows readers to learn through immediate application of theory and concepts, while avoiding the frustration of tedious calculations. Readers can use the prepared Maple files, follow the text on-screen, and explore different numerical examples with no prior programming knowledge. In fact, readers can keep generating their own examples, verifying and investigating different situations not addressed in the book. Learning is enhanced by altering the parameters of the commands, varying them at will, in order to experiment with applications of the concepts and different (reader-generated) examples, in addition to the ones already in the prepared file. It is this interaction and experimentation, making use of Maple together with the ability to bring to life on the screen the theoretical material of the chapter, which provides a unique, powerful, and entertaining way to be introduced to the fundamentals of fixed income securities.

Copyright and Disclaimer

The copyright holder retains ownership of the Maple code included with this e-book. U.S. Copyright law prohibits you from mailing (making) a copy of this e-book for any reason without written permission, only copying files for personal research, teaching, and communication excepted.

The author makes no warranties or representations, either expressed or implied, concerning the information contained in the copyright material including its quality, merchantability, or fitness for a particular use, and will not be liable for damages of any kind whatsoever arising out of the use or inability to use the e-book. The author makes no warranty or representation, either expressed or implied, with respect to this e-book, including its quality, merchantability, or fitness for particular purpose. In no event will the author be liable for direct, indirect, special, incidental, or consequential damages arising out of the use or inability to use the e-book, even if the author has been advised of the possibility of such damages.

To the extent permissible under applicable laws, no responsibility is assumed by the author for any injury and/or damage to persons or property as a result of any actual or alleged libellous statements, infringement of intellectual property or privacy rights, or products liability, whether resulting from negligence or otherwise, or from any use or operation of any ideas, instructions, procedures, products or methods contained in the material therein.

Suggested Settings

Verify the following the first time you open Maple:

From the Tools menu, select Options. (On an Apple computer click Maple 2016 on the top left and go to 'Preferences')

In the Options dialog, click the Display tab.

Ensure that: the 'Input display' shows Maple Notation, the 'Output display' shows 2-D Math Notation, and the 'Show equation labels' feature is not selected. Save your settings globally so they will be set for every session, not just the current one. Otherwise make sure you reset it every time you read the book.

Contents

About the Author

Dr. Eliezer Z. Prisman, a Professor of Finance at the Schulich School of Business (SSB) York University, Toronto, was the developer and the director of the Financial Engineering Diploma. Dr. Prisman's background is Economics, Statistics and Operations Research. While at SSB he taught graduate and undergraduate courses, published in refereed journals, authored books/eBooks and consulted in various aspects of Finance. He works in the areas of Investment, Financial Engineering, Risk Management, applications of Financial Risk Models to Medicine and Historical Finance. He is also interested in the use of symbolic and numerical computations and eLearning of financial Models (http://www.mymathapps.com and http://www.maplesoft.com/products/thirdparty/main.aspx).

Chapter 1

Introduction and Review of Simple Concepts

One of the most basic concepts of finance is *"time value of money"*. Dollars, like quantities in physics, also have a measure of units other than the magnitude measure. This unit measure is the time at which the magnitude of money is available to you to be used. Financial markets offer investors the opportunity to invest their money rather than "keeping it idle". If you have a certain amount of money, for example $1000, that you do not need now but only in a year, this money can be invested for a year. In most of this book we are concerned with risk-less investments, which means that there are no uncertainties about the return of the investment. It is fixed at the time the investment is made, and the likelihood that it will not be realized as promised is zero. While we shall touch on the meaning of "risk-free" investment in the next section, for now let us just take it for granted. The existence of such risk-free investment possibilities introduces the second dimension (unit) of monies, which is time. Assume that one can get r for each dollar invested for a year. If r for example is 10%, then $1000 today will grow to be $1000(1.10)$ or in general to $1000 + 1000\,r$. Therefore $1000 today is not equivalent to $1000 a year from today. If one needs $1000 in a year, one only needs to have $1000\,(1+r)^{-1}$. Given $1000\,(1+r)^{-1}$ today and investing it for a year generates $[1000\,(1+r)^{-1}](1+r) = 1000$ which is the required amount. We see therefore that $X in a year is equivalent to $\dfrac{X}{1+r}$ today. $\dfrac{X}{1+r}$ is termed the present value of X. Similarly Y dollars today is equivalent to $Y(1+r)$ in a year and the latter is termed the future value of Y. The conversion of dollars of a year from now to dollars of today is done by multiplying by $(1+r)^{-1}$, which is termed a *discount factor*. It is usually denoted by d with a sub index of the time. It is a discount factor for a year from now and will be denoted by d_1. The future value of a dollar in a year can thus be written also as $\dfrac{1}{d_1}$.

A feature of financial markets therefore is the *"opportunity cost"* of monies and this is why if one borrows money, one pays for using other peoples' money. Money can be invested and it increases its value. Hence borrowing \$1000 for a year will require returning $1000 + 1000\,r$. In this introduction we assume a very simplistic model whereby borrowing and lending money is done at the same rate and everybody can borrow and lend at the same risk-free rate. Of course the return on the investment depends on the duration of the investment. Obviously a dollar invested for a year will yield less than a dollar invested for two years. Similarly, borrowing for a year will require less interest payments than borrowing for two years. We again start with a simplistic assumption, which will be relaxed very soon, that the interest charge is r per year regardless of the duration the money is either borrowed or invested. This means that if a dollar is invested for a year it will grow to $1 + r_1$, and we use r_1 for the interest rate received over a year. If a dollar is invested for 2 years it will grow to $1 + r_2$ and the relation between r_1 and r_2 is such that $1 + r_2 = (1 + r_1)(1 + r_1)$. The interest rate r_2 is also referred to as the simple interest earned over a period of 2 years. The expression $(1 + r_1) \cdot (1 + r_1)$ is referred to as *compound interest*. It can be interpreted as if the dollar was invested first for a year to grow to $(1 + r_1)$, and then this amount is invested again for a year, at the same rate, to grow to $(1 + r_1) \cdot (1 + r_1)$. Thus at the end of the second year interest is paid also on the interest earned over the first year, and hence the term compound. It is not necessarily the case in the market place that the simple interest rate paid over k years, r_k, satisfies $(1 + r_1)^k = 1 + r_k$. However, r_2 must be bigger than r_1. If this is the not case, i.e., if $r_1 > r_2$ then it implies that $d_2 = (1 + r_2)^{-1}$ will be bigger than $d_1 = (1 + r_1)^{-1}$. One can thus borrow \$ d_2 to be returned in 2 years which means that \$1 should be paid in 2 years. Obtaining the \$ d_2 one would then invest it for a year to receive $d_2(1 + r_1) = \dfrac{d_2}{d_1}$ which is more than a dollar. Thus one reaches the end of year one with an amount $1 < \dfrac{d_2}{d_1}$. At the beginning of the second year, the interest rate that will prevail in the market at the end of year one, for an investment of one year, is not known. However, it will be a positive number say, $0 < x$. Thus, investing the $\dfrac{d_2}{d_1}$ at the end of year

one for one year will generate $\dfrac{d_2(1+x)}{d_1}$ which is for sure greater than 1.

Paying back the loan one would pocket $0.0 < \dfrac{d_2(1+x)}{d_1} - 1.0$.

Clearly, such situations cannot exist in real markets. Such an investment strategy that produces profit with no risk and no out-of-pocket money is called *arbitrage*. We shall see it in more detail and adapted to more realistic situations in the following chapters. If such a situation exists, investors, being rational, will go for it and as a result will produce demand and supply for money invested and borrowed for different periods. In the above example all investors would demand to borrow money to be returned in 2 years. Since interest rates can be thought of as the price of money, the interest rate charge for a loan for two years will increase due to the demand. Similarly, the interest rate for money over a period of one year will decrease, as there will be excess supply of money in the market. This arbitrage opportunity thus will never last very long. Hence the simple interest r_2 will always be greater than r_1 or in general $r_i < r_j$ for $i < j$. Nevertheless, we would like to compare the interest charge over a loan of m years to a loan of n years, but we know that $r_m < r_n$ if $m < n$. Hence we calculate the compound rate per year that is equivalent to a simple rate of m years and to a simple rate of n years, i.e., $(1+r_n)^{\left(\frac{1}{n}\right)} - 1$ and $\sqrt[m]{1+r_m} - 1$ respectively. In fact this is how interest rates are usually quoted (even though the quoted compounding period is not always a year). That is, if the rate of a loan for k years is reported to be r_k it means that borrowing a dollar for k years requires a return of payment of $(1+r_k)^k$. Thus one can define a function $r(t)$ which equals the interest rate paid for an investment or a loan over t years. The simple rate paid over t years will be $(1+r(t))^t - 1$. The function $r(t)$ is termed the *"term structure of interest rates"*. If the function is $r(t) = r$ for every t, like the simplistic assumption we made here, we say that the term structure is *flat* — since graphing it will generate a line parallel to the x-axis. On the other hand, if we were to graph the discount factor function $d(t)$, with or without the assumption of a flat term structure, the function $d(t)$ will be a decreasing function. If the assumption of a flat term structure is adapted then $d(t) = (1+r)^{-t}$ for some value of $0 < r$.

Examples

Let us see how some of the concepts mentioned above can be calculated with Maple.

```
> 1000*1.12;
```

$$1120.0$$

```
> 1/1.12;
```

$$0.8928571429$$

```
> 1000*(1+r);
```

$$1000 + 1000\,r$$

```
> subs(r=0.03,%);
```

$$1030.0$$

```
> subs(r=0.10,%%);
```

$$1100.0$$

Assume the simple 2-year rate is 4%, it will be reported based on an annual compounding as r that solves $(1+r)^2 = 1.04 \lor \sqrt{1.04} - 1$

```
> sqrt(1+0.04)-1;
```

$$0.019803903$$

```
> (1+%)^2;
```

$$1.040000001$$

```
> solve((1+r)^2 = 1+0.04);
```

$$0.01980390272, \; -2.019803903$$

```
> r:=r->0.02;
```

$$r := r \mapsto 0.02$$

```
> plot(r(t),t=0..10);
```

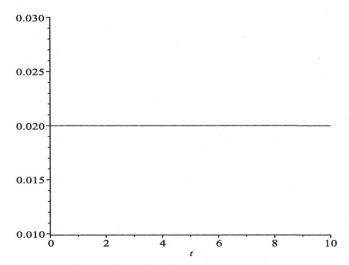

```
> d:=t->(1+r(t))^(-t);
```

$$d := t \mapsto (1+r(t))^{-t}$$

```
> d(1);
```

$$0.9803921569$$

```
> d(2);
```

$$0.9611687812$$

```
> d(3);
```

$$0.9423223345$$

```
> plot(d(t),t=0..50);
```

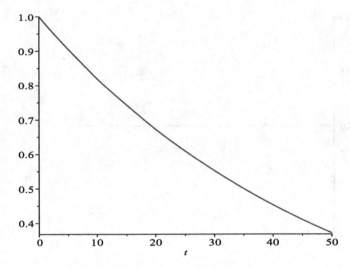

Assume that $d(1)=\dfrac{49}{50}$ but $d(2)=\dfrac{99}{100}$. This means that the simple rate for one year is

```
> solve((1+r)^(-1)=98/100);
```

$$1/49$$

and the simple rate for 2 years is

```
> solve((1+r)^(-1)=99/100);
```

$$\frac{1}{99}$$

Thus investing for a year is more profitable than investing for 2 years.

This implies that borrowing for 2 years is a "good deal" while investing for one year is not.

How can we capitalize on this situation?

Let us borrow an amount that requires paying back $1 in 2 years, that is

```
> solve(1=x*(1+1/99));
```

$$\frac{99}{100}$$

investing the borrowed amount for a year will generate

```
> 99/100*(1+1/49);
```

$$\frac{99}{98}$$

Thus after a year we can pay back the the loan that is due only in a year. This is because $\dfrac{99}{100} < \dfrac{99}{98}$

```
> 99/98-99/100;
```

$$\frac{99}{4900}$$

Note that when we took the 2-year loan we did not know what the one year rate in a year would be. However this rate must be a positive number. Hence investing the amount received after the one year, $\dfrac{99}{98}$, for a year will be even larger than $\dfrac{99}{98}$. Thus we can repay the loan after a year and we will pocket the difference which will be at least $\dfrac{99}{4900}$

```
> evalf(99/4900);
```

$$0.02020408163$$

If instead of borrowing for 2 years $\dfrac{99}{100}$ we will borrow 990000

```
> 1000000*99/100;
```

$$990000$$

we will pocket at least

```
> 990000*99/4900.0;
```

$$20002.04082$$

In the next chapters we will see that the information about the term structure is implicit in market prices and we will learn how to impute (estimate) the term structure from market data. In the rest of this chapter we assume that the term structure is given to us and that it is flat. The rest of this chapter reviews how, with the aid of the term structure, we can calculate the value of a few financial contracts or instruments. Valuing these

instruments will accomplish two goals: introduce some financial instruments that perhaps the reader is not familiar with, and cement the idea of
arbitrage. There are some financial instruments for which the need to use
the term structure in valuing them is not so apparent. We will also introduce such instruments here but only in the context of a one-period time.

1.1   Annuities, perpetuities and mortgages

Given the term structure of interest rates, it is possible to find the present
value of different profiles of cash flows. As we progress through this book
we will better understand that the value at which a future stream of cash
flow is being sold or purchased is its present value. For now we are just
going to take it for granted. Given the above, it is a standard exercise in
introductory finance courses to calculate the present value of certain types
of cash flows. Assuming a flat term structure, most of these calculations are
based on, or derived from, the sum of a geometric sequence. Henceforth
we will review some of these cases and will present a few as exercises at
the end of this chapter. A sequence of the form $aq, aq^2, \ldots, aq^N$ is called a
geometric sequence and its sum is calculated as follows.

Let $PV = \sum_{i=1}^{N} aq^i$ thus $qPV = PV - aq + aq^{N+1}$ and hence $PV = \dfrac{aq(1 - q^{(N+1)})}{1 - q}$.

If $-1 < q < 1$ the sum of such an infinite sequence converges and it
equals $\dfrac{aq}{1 - q}$.

An annuity is a cash flow of a fixed amount of money that is received at
the end of every year for N years. Let a be the amount obtained at the end
of each year and let r be the interest rate per year. Thus the present value
of such an annuity (at the beginning of the first year) is:

$$\sum_{i=1}^{N} \frac{a}{(1 + r)^i},$$

and the closed form solution of it is obtained by substituting $q = (1 + r)^{-1}$
in $\dfrac{-aq + aq^{N+1}}{q - 1}$ which yields

$$\frac{a((1+r)^N - 1)}{(r(1+r))^N}.$$

A perpetuity is an annuity that continues in perpetuity and again its present value is obtained by the substitution of $q = (1+r)^{-1}$ in $\dfrac{aq}{1-q}$ and yields $\dfrac{a}{r}$. A mortgage is a loan taken against an asset and usually is paid back by installments of the same amount every period, say every year. Consider taking a mortgage of $\$X$ for N years at an interest of r. The yearly payment therefore will be solved by finding the a such that the present value of the payment equals the amount of the loan. Hence a is the solution to

$$\frac{a((1+r)^N - 1)}{(r(1+r))^N} = X$$

Examples

```
> solve({q*PV = PV-a*q+aq^(N+1)},{PV});
```

$$\left\{ PV = \frac{-aq + aq^{N+1}}{q-1} \right\}$$

If $-1 < q < 1$ the sum of such an infinite sequence converges and it equals $\dfrac{aq}{1-q}$.

```
> sum(a*q^i,i=1..infinity);
```

$$-\frac{aq}{q-1}$$

```
> solve(sum(a*(1+0.03)^(-i),i=1..20)=100000);
```

$$6721.570760$$

```
> sum(6721.570760*(1+0.03)^(-i),i=1..20);
```

$$100000.0$$

```
> solve({sum(a*(1+r)^(-i),i=1..N)=X},{a});
```

$$\left\{ a = -\frac{Xr}{-1 + \left((1+r)^{-1}\right)^{N+1} r + \left((1+r)^{-1}\right)^{N+1}} \right\}$$

```
> op(%);
```

$$a = -\frac{Xr}{-1 + \left((1+r)^{-1}\right)^{N+1} r + \left((1+r)^{-1}\right)^{N+1}}$$

```
> simplify(rhs(%));
```

$$-\frac{Xr}{\left((1+r)^{-1}\right)^{N} - 1}$$

```
> solve({a*((1+r)^N-1)/(r*(1+r)^N) = X},{a});
```

$$\left\{ a = \frac{Xr(1+r)^{N}}{(1+r)^{N} - 1} \right\}$$

Clearly therefore the yearly payment a is divided differently between payment towards interest and payment towards the reduction of the principal (the loan amount). This becomes clear as after a year the interest due is $X(1+r)$ hence, $a - X(1+r)$ is paid toward a reduction of the principal. Thus the amount of the loan over the second year is $X - a + X(1+r)$ and consequently the interest due after a year is $[X - (a - X(1+r)](1+r)$ and $a - [X - a + X(1+r)](1+r)$ is paid toward reduction of the principal. There is however a more elegant way of finding the portion of a that is paid towards the principal and towards the interest payment. After $k - 1$ years of payments one owes the present value of the remaining payments, i.e.,

$$a \sum_{i=1}^{N-k+1} (1+r)^{-i}$$

and after k years one owes

$$a \left(\sum_{i=1}^{N-k} (1+r)^{-i} \right).$$

Hence the amount by which the kth payment reduces the principal is

$$a \left(\sum_{i=1}^{N-k+1} (1+r)^{-i} \right) - a \sum_{i=1}^{N-k} (1+r)^{-i} = (a(1+r))^{-N+k-1}.$$

and consequently the portion of a, in the the kth payment, that is paid toward interest is $a - (a(1+r))^{-N+k-1}$.

The exercises at the end of the chapter introduce modifications of the above cash flow, most of which can be calculated with the aid of the geometric sequence formula.

1.2 Forward Contracts

A forward contract is a binding agreement between two parties. The parties to this agreement are obligated to a transaction, which will take place in the future for a price agreed upon now, but no transfer of money occurs in the present time. The seller and the buyer agree on the price at which a particular transaction involving a specified commodity or a financial security will take place in the future. The price at which the transaction will take place is fixed now but will be paid in the future. Not surprisingly, these types of contracts are called futures or forward contracts. There is a distinction between a futures contract and a forward contract. However, in the setting of the one-period model (where only two points in time are considered, now and the future) these contracts are identical. We shall revisit these issues in a multi-period context and at that time will clarify the difference between futures and forward contracts. The agreed-upon price for future delivery of the specified asset is called the futures or forward price. Forward agreements are mostly transacted between two parties, sometimes with the help of a financial institution. Futures contracts are standardized and traded on exchanges such as the Chicago Board of Trade (CBOT). Both contracts are not default free and forward contracts are subject to a much higher risk. This is due to the fact that futures contracts are standardized and guaranteed by the CBOT. The analysis below will ignore this risk. The forward agreement can be regarding buying a good, a financial security, or a foreign currency. This is a non-exhaustive list of possible underlying assets for forward and futures contracts. The possibilities are limited only by the imagination of the parties involved in the transaction and by their willingness to agree to exchange the asset at the agreed-upon terms. Forward and futures contracts are agreements that introduce another market for goods and securities. The investor has at least two markets in which to trade these assets or commodities: the spot market and the forward market. The spot market is the usual and familiar market. Assets are exchanged on the spot and delivered immediately. In the forward market, assets or commodities are bought and sold for future delivery. Assume that at time t_0 you wish to ensure that you will receive a certain stock, say XXY, at time t_1 at a fixed price. Thus you are interested in a contract obligating your counterparty to deliver to you security XXY, at t_1 for a fixed amount, say, F, that you will pay at t_1. No cash is exchanged at the initial time t_0. Note that both parties to this agreement have obligated themselves to a transaction that will take place in the future for a price agreed upon in the current time period. What fixed amount, F, should be paid at $t = 1$? Consider the following strategy for the seller of the security. At time t_0 the seller buys security XXY but finances it with a loan. Assume that the price of XXY at time t_0 is P and that the interest rate for a loan taken from time t_0 to t_1 is r. Thus the seller will have to pay $P(1+r)$ at t_1 but the seller's net cash flow at time t_0 is zero. No money was taken out of the seller's pocket. At time t_1 the seller delivers to the buyer the security, which the seller purchased at time t_0. The buyer of the forward contract pays \$F at this time and in return receives security XXY. Hence at time t_1 the cash flow to the buyer is the value of security XXY at time t_1 less \$F. The seller receives \$F from the buyer of the contract, and closes (repays) the loan. Hence the cash flow to the seller at time t_1 is $F - P(1+r)$. If $0 < F - P(1+r)$ the seller will make money with no risk and no out of pocket investment, clearly an arbitrage opportunity. To show why if $F - P(1+r) < 0$ there are arbitrage opportunities, we need to explain the meaning of a short position. This will also be explained and reviewed again in the context of bond markets in the next Chapter. A short position in a security involves selling a security one does not own (but borrowed from a broker) and buying it back, paying market price, to return it to the broker. Taking a short position in a security thus generates positive proceeds. The short seller receives the price of the security being shorted in exchange for the commitment to pay back the value of that security when the transaction is being closed — whatever that value may end up being. Such a position produces profit when the price of the security decreases. Hence if $F - P(1 + r) < 0$ the buyer will enter such an agreement and will do the following. Take a short position in XXY at time t_0 and hence receive a cash flow of P, which is going to be invested until time t_1. At time t_1 the buyer will pay F and receive the security and close the short position. Thus the cash flow to the buyer is $P(1 + r) - F$ which is positive since $F - P(1 + r) < 0$. The buyer will make money with no risk and no out of pocket investment, clearly an arbitrage opportunity. Therefore, there will be no arbitrage opportunities to either one if and only if $F = P(1 + r)$. That is, F is the future value of P. Since calculating the value of F in this way involves buying the security and holding it until delivery, this argument is known as the *cost-of-carry model*.

Forward Contract on the Exchange Rate

Different countries use different currencies as their local denomination. Naturally a market has developed for the exchange of currencies. Exchange rates are quoted in terms of the amount of domestic currency needed to buy one unit of the foreign currency. Thus, in Canada, for example, an exchange rate of 1.38/USD means that each U.S. dollar costs 1.38 Canadian dollars. Notice that if one unit of a foreign currency costs $F0$ units of the domestic currency, then one unit of the domestic currency costs $F0^{-1}$ units of the foreign currency. There are two types of markets which deal in foreign exchange: the spot market and the forward market, as explained above. In the forward market currency is bought and sold for future delivery. Assume that at time t_0 the (spot) exchange rate between the foreign and domestic currencies is $F0$ of the domestic currency per one unit of the foreign currency. Consider a contract, written at time t_0, which obligates two counterparties to exchange, at time t_1, 1000 units of the foreign currency for FR units of the domestic currency per unit of the foreign currency payable at time t_1. What should the value of FR be? We can again use the cost-of-carry model to answer this question. If an investor is obligated to deliver a particular asset at a future time say t_1, the investor buys it now and stores it until that future time period. Thus the investor ensures having it on hand in order to make delivery. When the deliverable good is money, the storage costs involved are negative. An investor can make money while storing money via interest earned. Thus there is a need to have on hand, now, an amount that is smaller than the amount to be delivered in the future time period. The investor buys the present value of the deliverable amount and invests it at the risk-free rate of interest in the currency to be delivered. Thus the investor ensures the availability of the amount to be delivered at the delivery time in the future. Assume that the domestic and foreign interest rate from time t_0 to t_1 is r and r_f, respectively. Hence to have 1000 units of the foreign currency at time t_1 one needs only the present value of it, e.g., $1000(1+r_f)^{-1}$. Since at time t_0 the exchange rate is $F0$ to have $1000(1+r_f)^{-1}$ of the foreign currency one needs $F0(1000(1+r_f)^{-1})$ of the local currency.

Let us also consider the following strategy of the currency seller: At t_0 borrow $F0(1000(1+r_f)^{-1})$ units of the local currency to be repaid at time t_1. The amount to be paid back is $(1+r)F0(1000(1+r_f)^{-1})$. Convert this amount from the local currency to the foreign currency to receive $1000(1+r_f)^{-1}$. Invest the received amount in the foreign market until time t_1. The net cash flow of the seller at time t_0 is thus zero. At time t_1 the amount $1000(1+r_f)^{-1}$ in the foreign currency that was invested at time t_0 will grow to 1000. Deliver the 1000, receive FR and repay $(1+r)F0(1000(1+r_f)^{-1})$ in the local currency to close the loan. The net cash flow of the seller at time t_1 is thus $FR-(1+r)F0(1000(1+r_f)^{-1})$.

The reader may realize by now that the absence of arbitrage means, "the price is right". The seller thus managed to deliver the required good (foreign currency in this case) at a cost of zero (at time t_0). It must mean that the amount the seller receives at time t_1 is also zero. Thus to avoid arbitrage

$$FR-(1+r)F0(1000(1+r_f)^{-1}) = 0$$

so the forward exchange rate per one unit of the foreign currency is $FF = (1+r)\left(\dfrac{F0}{1+r_f}\right)$. Thus we have that

$$\frac{FF}{F0} = \frac{1+r}{1+r_f},$$

a relation that is termed the *interest rate parity condition*. An exercise at the end of this chapter asks the reader to show how arbitrage will result if this relation is violated.

1.3 Swaps

A swap contract is an agreement made at the current time t_0, between two parties to exchange securities, currencies, or some payments at some point in the future, t_1. There are a variety of swap contracts possible. Here we make use of the one period model and the present value concept in order to introduce the reader to the valuation of equity swaps. An equity swap is an agreement to exchange the return on an index (a variable cash flow) or on a specific security with, for example, a fixed rate of interest. The variable cash flow is a random variable, which depends on the realized rate of return of the agreed upon index (or security) from t_0 to t_1. The two swapped cash flows depend on some principal amount, say $N, called the notional principal as only the returns are swapped. The fixed cash flow is N_r, where r is the relevant rate of interest between t_0 and t_1. The variable cash flow depends on the return on an agreed-upon index or security. Denoted by N_{t_1} the realized value of $N = N_{t_0}$ that is invested in the index from time t_0 to t_1. The variable cash flow is given by $r_i N$, where r_i solves $N(1+r_i) = N_{t_1}$, hence $r_i = \frac{N_{t_1} - N_{t_0}}{N_{t_0}}$. Note that the agreement is made at time t_0 and at this time Nr is known but not Nr_i as r_i depends on the value of N_{t_1} which will be known only at time t_1. It might surprise the reader to find that even though Nr_i is not known at time t_0, we can, at this time, devise an investment strategy, independent of the realized value of r_i, that guarantees to produce Nr_i. Hence we can determine at time t_0 if such a swap is fair, e.g. if the present values of the two swapped cash flows are the same. By now it should be clear that the present value of Nr is $\frac{Nr}{1+r}$. To determine the present value of $N_{t_0} r_i$ we take a slightly different approach, which still has it origins in the absence of arbitrage. This approach is termed the replication approach. Its essence is that the present value of Nr_i is the cost at time t_0 of replicating this return. One of the exercises at the end of the chapter asks the reader to stipulate the arbitrage strategies if this relation is not satisfied. Here is how it goes: At t_0 borrow $\$\dfrac{N}{1+r}$ to be returned at t_1 and invest $\$N$ in the index. Thus, the out-of-pocket cost of this strategy is: $N - \dfrac{N}{(1+r)} = \$\dfrac{N \cdot r}{(1+r)}$. At t_1 sell the investment in the index, receive $\$N_{t_1}$ and payback $\$N$ to close the loan. Thus the net cash flow at time t_1 is $N_{t_1} - N$. Recall that $N_{t_1} = N(1 + r_i)$, hence $N_{t_1} - N_{t_0} = N r_i$. Thus the cost of generating the cash flow of $N r_i$ is $\left(\dfrac{N \cdot r}{1+r}\right)$ and therefore it is also its present value.

It follows that the present values of the two swapped cash flows are the same and hence that such a swap is fair. Thus at time t_0 when the agreement is done, neither side has to pay any money to the other side.

1.4 Conclusions

This chapter reviewed the concept of present value and its use in a variety of situations. We were introduced to the notion of arbitrage and how it is utilized, in a one period model, to value financial contracts that their values depend on the interest rate. The next chapter enhances the notation of arbitrage in a multi-period model of bond markets and relaxes some of the assumptions made in this chapter regarding the term structure.

1.5 Questions and problems

1. An amount of 10,000 is deposited into a savings account that pays interest at a rate of 7%. If 10 equal annual withdrawals are made from the account starting one year after the money was deposited, how much can be withdrawn so that in the fifth year, one would also be able to withdraw an additional $1,000 and the account will be depleted after 10 years?

2. A person has a 10-year contract to receive a base salary of $25,000 a year and an increase of 5% every year starting from the second year. The person purchases a luxury item now for $43,000. The interest rate is 4% per year and the person would like to arrange a loan such that an equal amount of money will be available for

consumption in each of the next 10 years. Calculate the amount to be borrowed and the amount to be paid back each year. The person cannot borrow money if he/she cannot afford to pay it back.

3. Show that if the relation $\dfrac{FR}{FO} = \dfrac{(1+r)}{(1+r_f)}$ is violated, arbitrage opportunities exist. Stipulate the arbitrage strategy in the case where $\dfrac{FR}{FO} < \dfrac{(1+r)}{(1+r_f)}$ and in the case where $\dfrac{FR}{FO} > \dfrac{(1+r)}{(1+r_f)}$.

4. Show that if the cost at t_0 to generate the amount Nr at time t_1, where N is the notional principal, r_i is the rate of return on a certain index and r_f is the risk free rate, is not $\dfrac{Nr_i}{(1+r_f)}$ arbitrage exists. Stipulate the arbitrage strategies.

5. Two parties enter a swap agreement with a notional principal of $10,000 to be exchanged in a year. The interest rate in the market is 6%. The party that pays the fixed rate also pays $100 at initiation. How, if at all, does this payment change the fixed rate to be paid at the end of the year?

6. Your uncle promised you the following cash flow over the next five years: at the end of each of the next four years 13.58 and 113.58 at the end of the fifth year. However you have a loan of $165.94 to pay at the end of the fourth year. The current annual interest rate is 11%. Will you be able to pay your loan with the money promised to you by your uncle? How much will you be able to pay toward the loan if the interest rate is 9.5, 10.5, 11.5, 12.5? Can you explain the results?

7a. Given the latest Canadian and USA treasury bill's rates in http://www.financialpost.com/markets/data/money-yields-can_us.html for 1-month, 3-month and 6-month and the spot exchange rate between the Canadian and USA dollars in http://www.financialpost.com/markets/currencies/index.html utilize the interest rate parity relation to find the forward 1-month, 3-month and 6-month exchange rate.

7b. Assume that the forward exchange rate for 1 month is 10% above the value you calculated. Assume that your credit rating allows you borrow up to 100$CA that you can use to exploit this deviation from the correct value. Stipulate the transactions you will take to exploit it, and state the arbitrage profit that can be obtained.

Note: Treasury bills are priced at a discount and their yield is quoted as an annual percentage. The return to the investor is the difference between the purchase price and the par value. The rate of return (yield) is calculated by dividing this difference by the purchase price, and expressing the result as an annual percentage rate, using a 365-day year.

For example, a price of $990.13 per $1,000 of face amount for a 91-day bill would produce an annualised rate of return equal to $\sim$4.00 percent, computed as follows:

$$\frac{(1000 - 990.13)}{990.13} \cdot \frac{365}{91}$$

> (365/91)*(1000-990.13)/(990.13);

0.03998309468

Chapter 2

A Basic Model of Bond Markets

In Chapter 1 we revisited the concept of time value of money and its relation to opportunity cost, but over a one period model. We did touch upon multi period models but only under the assumption that the interest rate from period to period is the same: a phenomena referred to as a flat term structure of interest rate.

In this chapter we expand our model to a more realistic situation of a multi period time and relax our assumption about a flat term structure. Rather, here we will look into the prices of bonds in the market and infer the term structure of interest rate for these prices. As before, our guideline for the inferences is the stratification of the no arbitrage condition. However, in this multi period model the formulation of the no arbitrage condition and the consequences of its satisfaction are somewhat different and more structured than our presentation of the one period model. We start with some basic notation and definitions so that we can be in a position to formulate the no arbitrage condition.

2.1 Setting the Framework

The *debt market*, as its name implies, is a market in which debts are bought and sold. This market is also referred to as the *bond market*. A bond is a security issued by a particular entity which promises to pay the holder of the bond a fixed amount of money at fixed times in the future, t_1, t_2 ,...., t_k. At each of the payment times except the last one, t_k, the bond pays the same amount of money which we will denote by c. On the last payment date, referred to as the *maturity* of the bond, the bond pays an amount equal to $c + F$. The amount F is referred to as the *principal* or the *face value* of the bond and the payments of the amount c are called *coupon payments*.

The value of c is a certain percentage of the face value, F, and is called the *coupon rate*. The coupon rate is specified when the bond is issued and remains fixed for the life of the bond. Thus for example, a bond may pay $5 every year for the next three years and at the end of the three years pay $(100+5). Such a bond has a maturity of three years and a face value of $100 and the annual coupon payments are $5 each. One immediately recognizes that the cash flow from a bond is like a repayment of a loan that was taken for three years at an interest rate of 5 percent, paid annually. Indeed, buying a bond is giving a loan to the issuer. Such a bond, as in our example, is called a 5 percent bond since it is like a loan taken at 5 percent. In most countries though, the payments from a bond are made semiannually: a 5 percent bond will pay 2.5 percent of the face value every six months.

The coupon rate at which the bond is issued depends, of course, on the interest rate that prevails at the time of issue in the market. In order to induce investors to buy the bond (lend their money), the bond must offer a competitive interest rate. Similarly, after the bond has been issued, it can also be bought and sold in the market (called the *secondary market*). The price in the secondary market will reflect current market conditions with respect to the interest rate prevailing at that time.

Consider the bond in our example that was issued with a coupon rate of 5 percent. An investor holding the bond for the first six months and then selling it in the secondary market may get more or less than $100 when it is sold. Buying a bond six months after the bond was issued is like giving a loan of $100 to the issuer for 2.5 years. If at that time the interest rate prevailing in the market for loans over 2.5 years is, for example, 4 percent, the bond will not be sold for $100. If the bond did sell for $100, it would constitute a lending at an interest rate higher than the one prevailing in the market. The holder of this bond will not like to pass such good deal to others. Furthermore, the owner realizes that the bond will attract buyers if it will offer a rate competitive with the current market rate. Hence the bond will be sold at a price, say P, such that

```
> P=5*(1+0.04)^(-0.5)+5*(1+0.04)^(-1.5)
+105*(1+0.04)^(-2.5);
```

$$P = 104.8104389 \tag{1.1.1}$$

In such an environment, the bond will sell for more than its face value. Such a bond is called a *premium bond*.

Suppose instead that interest rates rise to 8 percent. The competitive forces in the market will alter the price of the bond in such a way that

```
> P=5*(1+0.08)^(-0.5)+5*(1+0.08)^(-1.5)
+105*(1+0.08)^(-2.5);
```

$$P = 95.88845520 \tag{1.1.2}$$

Thus, the bond will be sold at less than its face value. Such a bond is called a *discount bond*. We thus see that there is an *inverse relationship between the price of a bond and the level of interest rates*. Therefore, implicit in the prices of bonds in the market is some information about the interest rates in the market. This information can be uncovered using a technique that we will soon introduce.

Moreover, recovering information about interest rates implicit in bond prices is intimately related to the no-arbitrage condition. A condition with which we have already familiarized ourselves in the simplistic model and of the former chapter.

The fuzzy term we just used ("competitive forces in the market") will soon be seen to be the force of investors seeking arbitrage opportunities. Consequently, these investors affect the market so that prevailing prices eliminate such opportunities. Stating it differently, prices in the market satisfy the no-arbitrage condition. Furthermore, an explanation of the way the condition was formulated in the former Chapter will make it adaptable to a realistic model of the bond market. As well, the discount factors of the former Chapter will be replaced with a function of discount factor — the term structure of interest rates in the market.

We limit our focus, almost throughout this Chapter, to national government bonds. These securities are regarded as risk-free securities, since governments do not usually default on their obligations.[1] Bonds, as we

---

[1] Note, however, that the government can act in a number of different ways which essentially reduce the value of its obligations. Examples include printing too much money and opting for strategies which increase inflation. This however is beyond the scope of our

see, represent fixed payment amounts which are paid at fixed, deterministic times. For this reason, bonds are also referred to as *fixed income securities*. Thus, if an investor holds a bond to its maturity, the amount of the payments and their timing are certain, provided that the issuer does not default on some payments. Hence, national government bonds are considered non-risky securities.

A bond which is issued by a less creditworthy issuer must offer a higher interest rate, in comparison to a government bond, in order to compensate the investor for taking the risk of the issuer defaulting on the bond. The lower the creditworthiness of the issuer, the higher the interest rate the bond must offer. Indeed, we observe this in the market for corporate bonds (issued by corporations) which offer higher interest rates than government-issued bonds. Agencies exist in the market which engage in rating the creditworthiness of different issuers. The lower the rating is, the higher the interest rate they must offer on their bonds. There are other factors that may affect the interest rate at which the bond is issued.

Certain bonds have features that affect the interest rate. For example, some bonds, called *callable bonds*, allow the issuer to call the bond back prior to its maturity. The issuer can pay the holder the principal plus a certain amount and so buy back the bond, at certain times subject to certain conditions. If interest rates decrease it might be advantageous to the issuer to "call" the bond. If it is advantageous to the issuer, it is disadvantageous to the holder of the bond. The investor holding such a bond would require compensation for this callable feature. The compensation is in terms of a higher interest rate offered on the bond. Bonds with no extra features are sometimes referred to as *straight bonds*.

Studying the interest rate structure is conducted in the market for national government bonds and includes only straight bonds. In this market, the interest rate implicit in the prices of these bonds does not include compensation for risk. It reflects only the economic competitive conditions in the market. For this reason we limit our attention to the government bond market and, for the time being, to straight bonds. As we proceed we will discover that there are a few rates in the market and that what we referred to as the "interest rate" in the market is a more complicated structure of interest rates.

---

analysis. We will assume that the inflation rate is zero.

2.2 Arbitrage in the Debt Market

Consider a government bond market with n bonds where P_i denotes the price[2] of bond i, $i = 1,...,n$. These bonds have been issued at various times in the past and thus offer different coupon rates and pay coupons on different days. For example, a bond that was issued three years ago with a maturity of six years on February 2, will pay on the second of February and the second of August of each year until it matures on the second of February three years from now. On that last date it will pay the final coupon and will repay the principal (face value) to the holder of the bond. The payment dates of a bond that was issued two years ago on the second of February, with a maturity of two years, will coincide with the dates of the earlier bond, but will mature earlier (almost immediately).

Assume that the collection of outstanding bonds in the market pays on N distinct days and define a_{ij} to be the payment from bond i on date j, $j = 1,...,N$. Note that since N is the collection of the dates on which the bonds make payments, for a given bond, there might be many dates j for which a_{ij} is zero; i.e., bond i_0 does not pay on some of the dates in $\{1, 2, ..., N\}$.

Thus an investor pays the price P_i for bond i now and in so doing purchases a certain sequence of cash flows to be paid in the future at specified times, the amount a_{ij} to be paid at the future times j, $j = 1,...,N$. Let us look at an example in which we have a market with three bonds that pay on three distinct payment dates, and for simplicity we assume these dates are equally spaced in time.[3] The prices and payments from the bond are summarized in Table (2.1).

Our simple market is assumed to be a "perfect market" or frictionless market. It is a stylized market in which there are no transaction costs, no

---

[2]See the discussion of clean and dirty prices in the next section.

[3]Indeed, in a realistic market this is not the case, and typically the number of payment dates is about two or three times the number of bonds. Also the payment dates are not necessarily equally spaced. The user may decide to adopt a smaller time unit to accommodate other structures of payments. One may choose the smallest time period between two consecutive payment dates, from any outstanding bonds, as the time unit. They will accommodate any structure of payments at the expense of having more variables (the d's) although the cash flow from the bonds would include many zeros (be very sparse). We shall come back to these assumptions and either relax them or examine how to treat such markets.

Table 2.1   A Simple Bond Market Specification.

Price/Time	1	2	3	Security
$94.5	$105	$0	$0	Bond 1
$97	$10	$110	$0	Bond 2
$89	$8	$8	$108	Bond 3

margin requirements, no taxes, and no limit on short sales.

Consider buying a portfolio in this market of *B1* units of bond 1, *B2* of bond 2, and *B3* of the bond 3. We interpret positive values of *B1*, *B2* and *B3* as buying the securities, or taking a long position, and negative values as short positions.

Taking a short position in a security generates positive proceeds. The short seller receives the price of the security being shorted at time zero, when the transaction is initiated. In exchange, the short seller is committed to pay back the value of that security when the position is closed, whatever that value may end up being, and to make the coupon payments until the position is closed. In most cases we will deal only with a position that is being held until the maturity of the bond. Such positions are called "buy and hold" and thus a short position in a bond will require the seller to pay the future coupons of the bond and as well as its face value at maturity.

Taking a short position in bond 1, say, for 2 units, $(B1=-2)$ produces a cash flow of $-B1 \cdot 189 = -(-2) \cdot 94.5 = 189$ at time zero and of $B1 \cdot 105 = -210$ at time 1. Our convention is that a negative amount of money means payment and a positive amount of money means income. Thus, since a short position is denoted by a negative number, e.g. $B1 = -2$, the expression for the income of 189 at time zero, as a function of the position in the bond is $-B1 \cdot 189$ and the expression for a payment of 210 at time one, is $B1 \cdot 105$. In general, therefore, the cash flow at time zero from taking a position B in a bond with a price of P is, $-B1 \cdot P$ (for a short or a long position) and similarly the consequence cash flow at a future coupon payment time is $B1 \cdot C$, when C is the coupon payment.

A short position in Bond 1 is like taking a loan of $94.5 at time zero, which requires repayment of $105 at time 1, that is a loan at an interest rate of $\dfrac{105}{94.5} - 1 = 11.11\%$. Similarly taking a short position in bond 3 will give rise to a cash flow of $89 at time zero, $-\$8$ at time 1 and time 2, and $-\$108$ at time 3. The cash flow from a short position in bond 3 is the negative of the cash flow of the long position in this bond. Thus, another way of interpreting a short position is to think about the investor acting as the issuer of the bond. In summary, therefore, a short position in a bond is like borrowing and a long position is like loaning.

Consider a portfolio composed of a long position in two units of bond 1, i.e., $B1 = 2$, a short position in two units of bond 2, i.e., $B2 = -2$ and none of bond 3, i.e., $B3 = 0$. Such a portfolio generates proceeds from the position, at time zero, of $-B1 \cdot 94.5 - B2 \cdot 97 = -2 \cdot 94.5 - (-) \cdot 2 \cdot 97 = -189 + 194 = 5$.

```
> -2*94.5-(-2)*97;
```

$$5.0$$

Thus the total (**net**) proceeds of such a portfolio is $5, i.e., a net **income** of $5.

At time 1 the cash flow from the portfolio is

$$105 \cdot B1 + 10 \cdot B2 = 105.2 - 10.2 = 190$$

```
> 105*2+10*(-2);
```

$$190$$

at time 2 the cash flow is

$$110 B2 + 8 B3 = -2 \cdot 110 = -220$$

```
> 110*(-2)+0*8;
```

$$-220$$

and at time 3 the cash flow is

$$B3 \cdot 108 = 0 \cdot 108 = 0$$

Hence this portfolio is equivalent to receiving \$5 now, receiving \$190 at time 1 and paying \$220 at time 2.

In general, the (net) proceeds from the transaction of buying a portfolio of *B1*, *B2*, and *B3* units of each of the three bonds is

$$-94.5B1 - 97B2 - 89B3. \qquad (2.1)$$

If this last quantity is negative, then establishing this position does indeed cost money; if it is zero, then establishing the position costs nothing; and if it is positive, then establishing the position actually produces income. Portfolios for which $0 \leq -94.5B1 - 97B2 - 89B3$ that is, for which the proceeds of the sale is non negative, are referred to as *self-financing portfolios*, or as zero-cost portfolios if $0 = -94.5B1 - 97B2 - 89B3$. Such portfolios require no out-of-pocket cost to establish the position and thus are also called self-financed portfolios.

Holding such a portfolio may however commit the investor to some payments in the future. The portfolio also produces cash flow in the future i.e., $105 \cdot B1 + 10 \cdot B2 + 8 \cdot B3$ at time 1, $110 \cdot B2 + 8 \cdot B3$ at time 2, and $108 \cdot B3$ at time 3 and each of these might be negative, as -220 at time 2 in the above example.

Let us look at another such example. Consider the following portfolio $B3 = -132.6259947$, $B2 = 9.64552688$, $B1 = 9.186216083$.

```
> subs(B3=-132.6259947, B2=9.64552688, B1=9.186216083,
-94.5*B1-97*B2-B3*89);
```

$$10000.00000$$

This is a self-financed portfolio, the proceeds of the sale generate income of

$$-94.5 \cdot B1 - 97 \cdot B2 - 89 \cdot B3 = 10000,$$

and its future cash flow is:

```
> subs(B3=-132.6259947, B2=9.64552688, B1=9.186216083,
105*B1+10*B2+8*B3);
```

$$-5.10^{-7}$$

$$105 \cdot B1 + 10 \cdot B2 + 8 \cdot B3 = 0 \qquad \text{at time 1}$$

```
> subs(B3=-132.6259947, B2=9.64552688, B1=9.186216083,
0*B1+110*B2+8*B3);
```

$$-0.000001$$

$$0 \cdot B1 + 110 \cdot B2 + 8 \cdot B3 = 0 \qquad \text{at time 2, and}$$

```
> subs(B3=-132.6259947, B2=9.64552688, B1=9.186216083,
0*B1+0*B2+108*B3);
```

$$-14323.60743$$

$$0 \cdot B1 + 0 \cdot B2 + 108 \cdot B3 = -14323.60743 \qquad \text{at time 3.}$$

Thus holding this portfolio is like taking a loan of 10000 at time zero to pay back 14323.60743 at time 3. It is easy to see that the interest rate charge for this loan (over the three periods is) $\dfrac{14323.60743}{10000} - 1 = 0.4323607430$.

The equivalent per period rate is the solution to $10000 \cdot (1 + r)^3 = 14323.60743$ which yields $r = 0.1272427997$. It follows therefore, that implicit in the prices of the bonds is the information that the term structure in this market is not flat. We shall come back to discuss this point in the sequel.

Composing the bonds in our market to generate different portfolios allows for the creation of various profiles of cash flows. The cash flows generated from the portfolio $B1 = 1$, $B2 = -1$, $B3 = 1$ is:

```
> subs(B1=1, B2=-1, B3=1,\
> [CashTime0=-94.5*B1-97*B2-89*B3,\
> CashTime1=105*B1+10*B2+8*B3,\
> CashTime2=0*B1+110*B2+8*B3,\
> CashTime3=0*B1+0*B2+108*B3]);
```

$$[CashTime0 = -86.5, \ CashTime1 = 103,$$
$$CashTime2 = -102, \ CashTime3 = 108]$$

The reader is invited to experiment with the different possibilities. (This can be done, for example, by simply changing the values $B1 = 1$, $B2 = -1$,

B3 = 1 to *B1* = 100, *B2* = 119, *B3* = −87 and keeping the cursor anywhere in the red font and pressing return. The results are displayed in a blue font.)

```
> subs(B1=100,B2=119,B3=-87,\
> [CashTime0=-94.5*B1-97*B2-89*B3,\
> CashTime1=105*B1+10*B2+8*B3,\
> CashTime2=0*B1+110*B2+8*B3,\
> CashTime3=0*B1+0*B2+108*B3]);
```

$$[CashTime0 = -13250.0, \ CashTime1 = 10994,$$
$$CashTime2 = 12394, \ CashTime3 = -9396]$$

Consider a portfolio that has short and long positions. The short part of the portfolio produces income at the time the transaction takes place. These proceeds may be enough to finance the long part of the portfolio, or may even produce positive net cash inflow at time zero. Is it possible to find such a self-financed portfolio that generates positive net cash inflow at time zero and imposes no future liability on the investor?

At a coupon payment time, a bond held at a short position requires the investor to pay the coupon while a bond held in a long position pays the coupon to the investor. We are seeking a self financed portfolio such that at each future time period, the long part of the portfolio should be at least enough to cover the commitment resulting from the short part of the portfolio. Hence we are seeking a portfolio such that proceeds, $-94.5 \cdot B1 - 97 \cdot B2 - 89 \cdot B3$, are positive but also that no future liability is imposed by the portfolio. Thus we need to ensure that at each future payment time, the payoff from the portfolio is nonnegative, i.e.,

$$105 \cdot B1 + 10 \cdot B2 + 8 \cdot B3 \geq 0$$
$$0 \cdot B1 + 110 \cdot B2 + 8 \cdot B3 \geq 0$$
$$0 \cdot B1 + 0 \cdot B2 + 108 \cdot B3 \geq 0$$

The portfolio we are looking for seems to be the solution to the optimization problem (2.2) below.

$$\text{Max } -94.5 \cdot B1 - 97 \cdot B2 - 89 \cdot B3$$

such that

$$105 \cdot B1 + 10 \cdot B2 + 8 \cdot B3 \geq 0$$

$$0 \cdot B1 + 110 \cdot B2 + 8 \cdot B3 >= 0$$
$$0 \cdot B1 + 0 \cdot B2 + 108 \cdot B3 >= 0 \qquad (2.2)$$

Actually this is not the best way of identifying an arbitrage portfolio: there are some subtleties involved here that will be uncovered in the forthcoming discussion. We start by solving the maximization problem above that corresponds to our simple bond market specification. (You can put the cursor anywhere on the red fonts and hit return to execute this command. The structure is self explanatory, the first expression is the proceeds and in the curly brackets we have the constraints per each time payment in the future. You can also modify the numbers listed below to investigate a different market.)

```
> simplex[maximize](-94.5*B1-97*B2-89*B3\
> ,{105*B1+10*B2+8*B3>=0, 110*B2+8*B3>=0,108*B3>=0});
```

$$\{B1 = 0, B2 = 0, B3 = 0\}$$

The solution to this optimization is $B1 = 0$, $B2 = 0$, $B3 = 0$. It seems therefore that the only way to satisfy the constraints, about the cash flow in the future being non-negative, is simply to not buy any portfolio. In this way the proceeds are zero and so are the future cash flows.

The reader may already recognize that what we are looking for is "too good to be true". A portfolio that requires no out-of-pocket cost or produces income when it is initiated, never requires a future payment and may even produce cash inflows in the future, is a utopian portfolio. It imposes no risk on the investor, requires no investment and produces income in the future. Such a portfolio is a money machine. An opportunity like the one described above is "a free lunch".

If such a portfolio did exist, every investor would like to purchase it at an unlimited amount, as it could make an unlimited amount of money. This enormous demand for the portfolio would affect prices: bonds that are held long in the portfolio will increase in price while bonds that are held short in the portfolio will decrease in price. This pressure on the prices will stop only when prices adjust such that the opportunity will no longer exist.

Therefore, our assumption throughout this book will be that such a portfolio does not exist in the market. The opportunity of making money with no initial investment and without assuming any risk is called an *arbitrage opportunity*. Arbitrage, or rather the lack of it in financial markets, is one of the key concepts in modern financial theory. The no-arbitrage (NA) condition, frequently referred to as the "law of one price", or by the idiom "no free lunch", is an essential tool in developing estimation procedures and pricing methodologies. Before formally defining it, let us look at a few examples that will help us appreciate its intricacies. It will also show that there is not much sense in continuing our journey into the land of fixed income securities without assuming that the no arbitrage opportunities exist — that is, the no arbitrage condition is satisfied.

Let us start by examining a trivial case where the NA is not satisfied. Consider a market that includes two zero coupon bonds, both maturing at the same time. A zero coupon bond usually has a face value of say $100, and it is being sold at a discount. Assume that our market includes two such bonds but the price of one bond is $95 and the other is $98.

Taking a short position in the more expensive bond will produce a cash inflow of $98 and a commitment to pay $100 at the maturity time. Using $95 of the proceeds to purchase (long position) the other bond will leave $3 for the investor but will also produce $100 at the maturity time that can be used to pay the commitment of the short position. This is a pure arbitrage opportunity that produces $3 of arbitrage profit. However if such an opportunity exists why stop at $3? One can take a position of 100 units of long and short position and make $300. Investors therefore will keep demanding this portfolio at an unlimited amount to generate unlimited arbitrage profits, causing the prices to adjust until this opportunity is wiped out.

Let us see what is the solution of the counter part of the optimization problem **MaxProc** when it is adapted to the current example.

$$\text{Max} -95 \cdot B1 - 98 \cdot B2$$

such that

$$100 \cdot B1 + 100 \cdot B2 >= 0$$

Using the same structure as before we now try to solve:

```
> simplex[maximize](-95*B1-98*B2\
> ,{100*B1+100*B2=0});
```

There is no output returned (no blue font), which means that this problem has no finite solution. We are aware of this as we know that if arbitrage profit is feasible — it is possible for an infinite amount. In order to receive an output so we can identify the arbitrage portfolio, we can impose a constraint on the magnitude of short sales. Since we know that bond *B2* will have to be in a short position to generate arbitrage, we impose the restriction of $B2 \geq -1$. This will make the arbitrage profit finite and generate an output of the arbitrage portfolio.[4] This time the structure of the problem will be:

```
> simplex[maximize](-95*B1-98*B2\
> ,{100*B1+100*B2=0, B2>=-1});
```

$$\{B1 = 1, B2 = -1\}$$

Indeed the solution returned, is the one we anticipated. We can also verify the resultant cash flow from this position as we did before:

```
> subs(B1=1,B2=-1,\
> [CashTime0=-95*B1-98*B2,\
> CashTime1=100*B1+100*B2]);
```

$$[CashTime0 = 3, CashTime1 = 0]$$

This simple example also justifies the name "the law of one price". The two bonds are actually the same asset. Both generate a cash flow of $100 at their mutual maturity time, therefore they should be sold at the same price or else an arbitrage opportunity would exist. There is another lesson we can take from this example. Implicit in the two bonds is a different value for the discount factor of one dollar obtained at the maturity time. According to one bond the value of a dollar obtained at the maturity time is $\frac{95}{100}$ while according to the other bond it is $\frac{98}{100}$. This inconsistency in the discount factors implicit in the prices of the bonds, as we shall soon see, is always an indication of arbitrage opportunities.

---

[4]The strategies which we are investigating are static. Such strategies are often referred to as buy-and-hold strategies. Once a portfolio has been purchased, no change in the portfolio is made in subsequent time periods. This fact allows us to use the one-period equity model to investigate the multiperiod bond market. We will investigate some dynamic strategies in later chapters. Meanwhile, we continue to see what can be said in the current context, assuming that no buy-and-hold strategies exist which generate arbitrage profit.

The example also points to the mechanism of arbitrage generation. Identify two portfolios, one dominating the other such that the price of the dominating portfolio is smaller than or equal to the other. At each future time the cash flow from the dominating portfolio, is at least as much as that of the other. Taking a short position in the dominated portfolio and a long position in the dominating portfolio generates arbitrage profit. To cement this idea let us look at another example that is not as trivial as this example.

Consider a market with two bonds both issued now, they mature in two years and pay an annual coupon. Each has a face value of $100. Bond *B1* is a 5% bond with a price of $95 and bond *B2* is an 8% bond with a price of $97. Clearly if the price of *B2* is less than or equal to that of *B1* an arbitrage opportunity exists. We would like to determine if the prices above prevent arbitrage opportunities from existing. Let us approach this question from a different angle as we did before, and first try to determine if the discount factors implicit in the price of each bond are consistent with each other.

Unlike the first examples, here we are dealing with two periods so we have two discount factors d_1 and d_2 for a dollar obtained in one year and in two years from now, respectively. Furthermore, in this example the discount factors are not as exposed as in the first examples, they are kind of in the shadow.[5] Let us see how we can shed some light on these discount factors and bring them to the open.

Bond 1 pays $5 in a year hence the present value of it is $5 \cdot d_1$. It also pays $105 in two years and its present value is $105 \cdot d_2$. Hence if the bond costs $95 it means that the present value of the cash flow $5 in a year and $105 in two years, is 95. Therefore while we cannot determine from this relation the discount factor uniquely, we can identify a relation that they must satisfy, that is:

$$5 \cdot d_1 + 105 \cdot d_2 = 95$$

Similarly the price of bond 2 implies that

$$8 \cdot d_1 + 108 \cdot d_2 = 97.$$

It might be worth emphasizing here that the discount factors are associ-

---

[5] These discount factors are indeed the shadow prices (Lagrangian multipliers) of an optimization problem in which arbitrage profit is maximized.

ated with time and not with bonds. Hence if bond 1 offers $5 in a year and bond 2 offers $8 in a year, the present value of the $5 and the $8 is obtained by applying the same discount factor to each as they are both obtained at the same future time.[6]

Furthermore, discount factors are numbers between zero and one, as they encompass the time value of money. Thus the information about d_1 and d_2, which is implicit in the prices of the bonds, will be consistent only if the two equations above have a solution such that $0 < d_1 < 1, 0 < d_2 < 1$ and, as we shall soon realize, also such that $d_1 > d_2$. However, solving these two equations with two unknowns produces a unique and unaccept-able solution, namely $d_1 = \dfrac{-1}{4}$ and $d_2 = \dfrac{11}{12}$. (The two equations with two unknowns can be solved using the self explanatory structure below.)

```
> solve({5*d1+105*d2=95,8*d1+108*d2=97});
```

$$\left\{ d1 = \frac{-1}{4}, d2 = \frac{11}{12} \right\}$$

Therefore, based on our above analysis, this suggests (later on we will see that it actually implies) the violation of the NA conditions. With this in mind let us see if we can find an arbitrage portfolio composed of these two bonds. We start again by composing an optimization problem in which we try to maximize the proceeds of the sale, ensuring that the cash flow in the future is nonnegative. The counter part of the optimization problem **MaxProc** modified to reflect the current prices and coupons of the bonds is presented in the structure below:

```
> simplex[maximize](-95*B1-97*B2\
> ,{5*B1+8*B2>=0, 105*B1+108*B2>=0});
```

Having no output as before suggests the existence of arbitrage opportu-nities. Hence we impose a constraint on $B1 \geq -1$ and try again.

```
> simplex[maximize](-95*B1-97*B2\
> ,{5*B1+8*B2>=0, 105*B1+108*B2>=0,B1>=-1});
```

---

[6]We assume here that the cash flows promised by the bonds is risk free e.g. government bonds. However a similar analysis can be conducted as long as the universe of the bonds are all in the same risk category. In such cases the discount factor discounts a future cash flow taking into account time value of money and the risk of default.

$$\left\{ B1 = -1, B2 = \frac{35}{36} \right\}$$

Utilizing the structure as above we determine the cash flow from a portfolio composed of a short position in bond 1 and a long position of $\frac{35}{36}$ units of bond 2.

```
> subs(B1=-1,B2=35/36,\
> [CashTime0=-95*B1-97*B2,\
> CashTime1=5*B1+8*B2,\
> CashTime2=105*B1+108*B2]);
```

$$[CashTime0 = \frac{25}{36}, CashTime1 = \frac{25}{9}, CashTime2 = 0]$$

The portfolio produces income as the proceeds of the sale of $\$\frac{25}{36}$ and also pays $\$\frac{25}{9}$ in the second period. No liability and no risk is assumed. We already know that if an arbitrage portfolio is found, then the arbitrage profit has no limit. One can simply increase the scale of this portfolio by taking a short position in 36 units of bond 1 and a long position in 35 units of bond 2, to generate a cash flow of $\frac{36 \cdot 25}{36} = 25$ at time zero, and $\frac{36 \cdot 25}{9} = 25 \cdot 4 = 100$ in time 1. But why stop here? You can make even more money by further increasing the scale.

Markets which allow such arbitrage opportunities are not realistic. If such an opportunity existed investors would realize this and go for it, affecting prices so that the opportunity will eventually disappear. Hence, our analysis throughout this book is based on the satisfaction of the NA conditions. As we go along we will see that many operational and practical conclusions can be deducted assuming the NA condition. Furthermore, if such opportunities exist, the concept of the time value of money is at best redundant. If an unlimited amount of money can be generated at zero investment and no risk, then money would be worthless and would consequently render the term 'discount factors' meaningless.

Our analysis so far exemplifies that mathematically, if arbitrage opportunities exist, no discount factor exists. We shall make this a rigorous claim very soon, but there are still some aspects of arbitrage portfolios that we need to examine before we are ready for this stage.

Consider a market that includes two bonds: *B1* with a price of $90 and *B2* the price of which is $130 with an annual coupon of 3% and 11% respectively. *B1* matures in two years, *B2* matures in three years and the face value of both is $100. In order to determine if an arbitrage portfolio exists in this market we try to solve the optimization

$$\text{Max} - 90 \cdot B1 - 130 \cdot B2$$

Subject to

$$3B1 + 11B2 >= 0$$
$$103B1 + 11B2 >= 0$$
$$0B1 + 111B2 \geq 0$$

Using our structure below we find out that the answer is $B1 = 0$ and $B2 = 0$.

```
> simplex[maximize](-90*B1-130*B2,\
> {3*B1+11*B2>=0, 103*B1+11*B2>=0, 111*B2>=0});
```

$$\{B1 = 0, B2 = 0\}$$

Seemingly, as we hinted before, such an output suggests that no arbitrage profit is possible. Nevertheless, we check the position $B1 = 119$ and $B2 = -87$:

```
> subs(B1 = 119, B2 =-87,\
> [CashTime0=-90*B1-130*B2,\
> CashTime1=3*B1+11*B2,\
> CashTime2=103*B1+11*B2,\
> CashTime3=111*B2]);
```

$$[CashTime0 = 600, CashTime1 = -600,$$
$$CashTime2 = 11300, CashTime3 = -9657]$$

Voila! You may not realize it but here is an arbitrage portfolio. While at the moment it seems like we pulled these numbers out of thin air there is, of course, a systemic way of identifying an arbitrage portfolio. We will stipulate this method after the formal definition of the NA condition is given.

Let us examine this portfolio. The proceeds are $600 but the portfolio also requires you to pay $600 at time 1 as its cash flow at time 1 is $-\$600$. That explains why this portfolio was not identified by the solution of the optimization problem, as it does not satisfy the constraint about the no negativity of the cash flow at time 1 or at time 3. Yet this can still be an arbitrage portfolio.

Arbitrage portfolios must generate the arbitrage profit with no risk whatsoever. The fact that the cash flow is $-\$9657$ at time 3 however, does not present any risk since at time 2 the produced cash flow is $\$11130$. Hence one can invest the $\$11300$ at time 2 for one period, to time 3, and collect $\$11300(1+r)$ where r is the interest rate that will prevail in the market at time 2 for an investment of one year. The lower bound on the value of $\$11300(1+r)$ is 11300 since $0 \le r$. Thus the commitment of $-\$9657$ will be covered by the portfolio. This is correct even though we do not know at time zero the numerical value of that r, but we do know that $r > 0$ and hence an investment of 11300 at time 2 for one year produces at least 11300 at time 3.

Note however that if the situation would have been reversed, i.e. the cash flow at time 2 would have been -9657 and at time 3, 11300, the strategy of using the 11300 obtained at time 3 to cover the liability of -9657 at time 2 would not have been risk free. The present value of 11300 would be $\frac{11300}{(1+r)}$ and at time zero the value of this r (that would be paid on an investment of one year from year 2 to year 3), is not known. Thus counting on $\frac{11300}{(1+r)}$ to equal 9657 is subject to a risk about the realization of the value of r. While one may assess this risk as being very small — arbitrage is classified as being risk free and our conclusions from the absence of it are based on it being defined as risk free.

By the same argument the commitment of $-\$600$ at time 2 is covered by the portfolio proceeds at time zero. This portfolio therefore does not subject the holder to any risk, requires no payment at initiation and at the minimum will produce a net cash inflow of $11300 - 9657 = 1643$. Thus it is a pure arbitrage portfolio and the reason it was not identified is already spelled out — it is since we have not allowed using a dollar obtained at time t_1 to cover a dollar liability at time t_2 when $t_2 > t_1$.

We are nearly ready to give the formal definition of the NA. However there is another property of the discount factors that we can infer from the absence of arbitrage, using a strategy similar to the one we just described. Hence we will stipulate this property prior to the NA definition.

Consider a market with two zero coupon bonds each with a face value of $100. The bond *B1* matures in 2 months and the bond *B2* matures in 3 months. One immediately realizes that the price of *B2*, *P2*, must be strictly smaller than that of *B1*, *P1*, or else arbitrage opportunities will exist. If *P1* = *P2* one would short *B2* and take a long position in *B1*. The proceeds of the sale will be zero. After a month *B1* would pay $100 which the investor will invest for a month and collect $100(1 + r)$ in two months, where *r* is the monthly rate will be in the market at that time. After two months the investor will have to pay 100 due to the short position in bond *B2* and will have an arbitrage profit of 100*r*.

The same argument will apply if *P1* < *P2*, just that arbitrage profit will be collected also at the initiation time as the proceeds will be positive. It is therefore clear that *P2* must be strictly smaller than *P1*. Thus implicit in the prices of the bonds is that the discount factor for time 1 is $\frac{P1}{100}$ and for time 2 is $\frac{P2}{100}$ and thus that $d_1 > d_2$. These examples can be generalized to conclude that a discount factor for time t_1 must be strictly larger than a discount factor for time t_2, when $t_2 > t_1$. It also reinforces what we just saw that when searching for arbitrage portfolios, the requirement that the cash flow from the portfolio is nonnegative at each payment time is too strong.

2.3 Defining the No-Arbitrage Condition

In an arbitrage portfolio, the arbitrage profit might not be obtained at time zero. It might be obtained at some future time and given the structure of the market it may not be possible to find an arbitrage portfolio for which the profit is obtained at time zero. Our modification of the optimization problem (2.2) should take this into account.

In order to construct the portfolio completely free of risk we have no other alternative but to assume that a dollar in period one can cover at most a dollar liability in period two. If we allow for more than a dollar liability at time two, some risk will be involved in the position. If even an "infinitesimal" risk is involved in the portfolio, it is no longer an arbitrage portfolio. Thus, as in the above example, we can take the excess cash obtained at time j and use it to cover a shortage, if such exists, at time $j+1$.

This is done by introducing the additional variables Z_0, Z_1, and Z_2, etc. which are constrained to be nonnegative. The variable Z_0 represents the cash we move from period zero to period one. Thus it can be used to cover any shortage that might arise in period one. In the same manner, Z_1 is the amount we might want to transfer from period one to period two. Hence we subtract Z_j from the cash flow obtained at time j and add it to the cash flow obtained at time $j+1$. The Zs are constrained to be positive, since negative values mean we allow cash to be moved backward through time. (In other words, negative values of Z mean borrowing at the current period against excess cash which will be obtained in the next time period.) However, as of time zero, if we would like to have a portfolio free of risk, we have no way of knowing for sure what a dollar obtained in some future period $1 < j$ might be worth at time $j-1$.

We bring this final example to motivate our definition of the NA condition. Consider a market with 2 bonds, the price of each is \$95. Bond B_1 has a coupon rate of 10% and matures in one year, B_2 is a zero coupon which matures in two years and its face value is \$110. That is, the market is represented by what we call a payoff matrix A

$$A = \begin{bmatrix} 110 & 0 \\ 0 & 110 \end{bmatrix} \text{ and a price vector } P, \ P = \begin{bmatrix} 95 \\ 95 \end{bmatrix}.$$

The proceeds from the sale are $-B_1 \cdot 95 - B_2 \cdot 95$.
The cash flow in period 1 is $B_1 \cdot 110 + B_2 \cdot 0$.
The cash flow in period 2 is $B_1 \cdot 0 + B_2 \cdot 110$.

Clearly there is an arbitrage opportunity in this market, can you the reader stipulate it? However, our structure would not identify it. Let us verify below that indeed the output of this structure is $B_1 = 0$ and $B_2 = 0$.

```
> simplex[maximize](-95*B1-95*B2,\
> {110*B1+0*B2>=0, 0*B1+110*B2>=0});
```

$$\{B1 = 0, B2 = 0\}$$

Let us introduce the additional variables Z_0 and Z_1 which are constrained to be nonnegative. The variable Z_0 represents the cash we move from period zero to period one. Thus it can be used to cover any shortage that might arise in period one. In the same manner Z_1 is the amount we might want to transfer from period one to period two. Hence we subtract it from the cash flow obtained at time one and add it to the cash flow obtained at time two. We also define variables for the cash flow in each period C_0, C_1 and C_2 (these can be avoided but are added for clarity). Hence we now have

$$C_0 = -B_1 \cdot 95 - B_2 \cdot 95 - Z_0$$
$$C_1 = 110 \cdot B_1 + Z_0 - Z_1$$
$$C_2 = 110 \cdot B_2 + Z_1.$$

In an arbitrage portfolio, C_0, C_1 and C_2 are all nonnegative. Arbitrage will be realized if either; at least one of the Cs is strictly positive, i.e., $C_0 + C_1 + C_2 > 0$, or if $C_0 = C_1 = C_2 = 0$ and at least one of the Zs is strictly positive. That is, arbitrage is realized if and only if $C_0 + C_1 + C_2 + Z_0 + Z_1 > 0$. Hence to identify an arbitrage portfolio we can solve:

$$Max \ C_0 + C_1 + C_2 + Z_0 + Z_1$$

subject to

$$C_0 = -B_1 \cdot 95 - B_2 \cdot 95 - Z_0$$
$$C_1 = 110 \cdot B_1 + 0 \cdot B_2 + Z_0 - Z_1$$
$$C_2 = 0 \cdot B_1 + 110 \cdot B_2 + Z_1$$
$$Z_0 \geq 0, \ Z_1 \geq 0, \ C_0 \geq 0, \ C_1 \geq 0, \ C_2 \geq 0$$

If the optimal solution of this problem is $Z_0 = Z_1 = C_0 = C_1 = C_2 = B_1 = B_2 = 0$, no arbitrage portfolio exists and the no arbitrage condition is satisfied. If this is not the case, the problem has no finite solution, as the arbitrage profit will be unfounded. As before, an arbitrage portfolio can be identified in these cases by imposing constraints on short sales.

Here is the solution of this optimization.

```
> simplex[maximize](C0+C1+C2+Z0+Z1,{C0=-B1*95-B2*95-Z0,\
> C1=B1*110+B2*0+Z0-Z1,C2=B1*0+B2*110+Z1,\
> Z0>=0,Z1>=0, C0>=0,C1>=0,C2>=0});
```

As we see, no output is generated as the problem is unbounded. We thus proceed to impose a constraint on bond 2 short position. (An exercise at the end of the Chapter will ask you to explain why imposing a constraint on the short position of bond 2 will suffice but posting it on bond 1 will not generate an output showing an arbitrage portfolio.)

```
> simplex[maximize](C0+C1+C2+Z0+Z1,\
> {C0=-B1*95-B2*95-Z0, C1=B1*110+B2*0+Z0-Z1,
C2=B1*0+B2*110+Z1,\
> Z0>=0,Z1>=0, C0>=0,C1>=0,C2>=0,B2>=-1});
```

$$\{B1 = 1, \ B2 = -1, \ C0 = 0, \ C1 = 0, \ C2 = 0, \ Z0 = 0, \ Z1 = 110\}$$

We are finally ready to have the general formulation of the No-Arbitrage condition.

Definition: (The No-Arbitrage Condition)

Let a_{ij} be the payoff (coupon payment or face value) from bond i in period j, where $i = 1, \ldots, N$ and $j = 0, \ldots, K$. The No Arbitrage condition is satisfied if the optimal value of the optimization problem below is zero.

$$Max_{x_1,\ldots,x_n,z_0,\ldots,z_k} \left[\sum_{j=0}^{K} C_j + \sum_{j=0}^{K-1} Z_j \right]$$

such that

$$\sum_{i=1}^{N} (-x_i P_i) - z_0 = C_0$$

$$\sum_{i=1}^{N} x_i a_{ij} + z_{j-1} - z_j = C_j, j = 1, \ldots, K-1$$

$$\sum_{i=1}^{N} x_i a_{ij} + z_{k-1} = C_k$$

$$0 \leq z_j, j = 0, \ldots, K-1, 0 \leq C_j, j = 0, \ldots, K \qquad (2.3)$$

We conclude this subsection by introducing the procedure **NarbitB** that determines if the no arbitrage condition in a market is satisfied. The input to the procedure is the prices of the bonds and their payoff. The presumption of this procedure is that the time intervals are equal. That is, the time interval between the current time (on which the price of the bonds are given) and the first coupon payment is equal to the time between the first and second coupon payment etc. The prices of the bonds are represented by an array with its elements being the prices of the bonds. Hence if there are two outstanding bonds the price of the first being 95 and the second being 95 this will be entered as [95,95]. The cash flow from each bond is entered in the same manner. If the first bond's cash flow is $110 followed by $0 it will be entered as [110,0] and if the second bond's cash flow is $0 followed by $110 it will be entered as [0,110]. The above example can represent a case where the first bond matures in a year, the second bond in two years and the prices are observed a year before the first bond matures. Both the second bond and the first bond are zero coupon bonds. The cash flow from the bonds will be entered as the first parameter to the procedure in the form [[110,0], [0,110]] and the understanding is that the first price is the price of the first bond and the second is the price of the second bond. To find if the NA is satisfied in this market you run:

```
> NarbitB([[110,0],[0,110]],[95,95]);
```

The no-arbitrage condition is not satisfied
An arbitrage portfolio is:

$$Buy, \frac{1}{110}, \text{ of Bond, } 1$$

$$Short, \frac{1}{110}, \text{ of Bond, } 2$$

The cost of this portfolio is zero
This portfolio produces income of, 1, at time, 1
This portfolio produces income of, −1, at time, 2

The procedure identifies an arbitrage portfolio if it exists, and reports its composition. If an arbitrage portfolio does not exist the procedure states this, and produces further output that will be discussed shortly. The reader may already anticipate the meaning of this output given the discussions above. Note that the arbitrage amount is not known at the time the positions are taken. The arbitrage is actually generated from investing the $1 cash inflow obtained at time 1, (a year after the initiation of the portfolio) for a year and then using it to pay the cash outflow of $1 at time 2 (a year after the $1 was invested). At time 2, the $1 invested at time 1 for a year will grow to $1 + r$, but the r is not known at time zero. Hence the arbitrage amount is the r obtained at time 2, but the value of r, the one-year spot rate as of time 1, will be known only at time 1.

Let us see what happens if we change the prices of the bonds so that the price of the first bond is 95 and the second is 94:

```
> NarbitB([[110,0],[0,110]],[95,94]);
```

The no-arbitrage condition is satisfied.

The discount factor for time, 1, *is given by,* $\dfrac{19}{22}$

The interest rate spanning the time interval, $[0,1]$, *is given by,* 0.1579

The discount factor for time, 2, *is given by,* $\dfrac{47}{55}$

The interest rate spanning the time interval, $[0,2]$, *is given by,* 0.1702

The function Vdis ([c1,c2,..]), values the cashflow [c1,c2,..]

Let us examine another example of a market with 3 bonds and 3 time periods as stipulated below

```
> simplex[maximize](-94.5*B1-97*B2-89*B3,
{105*B1+10*B2+8*B3>=0, 110*B2+8*B3>=0,108*B3>=0});
```

$$\{B1 = 0,\ B2 = 0,\ B3 = 0\}$$

and then run it again using the **NarbitB** procedure.

```
> NarbitB([[105,0,0],[10,110,0],[8,8,108]],
[94.5,97,89]);
```

The no-arbitrage condition is satisfied.

The discount factor for time, 1, *is given by,* 0.9000000000

The interest rate spanning the time interval, $[0,1]$, *is given by,* 0.111

The discount factor for time, 2, *is given by,* 0.8000000000

The interest rate spanning the time interval, $[0,2]$, *is given by,* 0.250

The discount factor for time, 3, *is given by,* 0.6981481481

The interest rate spanning the time interval, $[0,3]$, *is given by,* 0.432

The function Vdis ([c1,c2,..]), values the cashflow [c1,c2,..]

You, the reader, may wish to explore this procedure further, changing the prices or the payment structure, before reading on. For example, let us examine the effect of making bond 2 mature at time 3, instead of at time 2, while leaving its price unchanged.

```
> NarbitB([[105,0,0],[10,10,110],[8,8,108]],
[94.5,97,89]);
```

The no-arbitrage condition is not satisfied
An arbitrage portfolio is:
Buy, 0.02910762160, *of Bond*, 1
Short, 1.0, *of Bond*, 2
Buy, 1.058981233, *of Bond*, 3
Buying this portfolio produces income of, 2.10^{-8} *at time*, 0
This portfolio produces income of, 1.528150132, *at time*, 1
This portfolio produces income of, -1.528150136, *at time*, 2
This portfolio produces income of, 4.3699732, *at time*, 3

Here is another example: Note that in this market there are two bonds and three time-periods. A market where certain cash flows cannot be generated is referred to as an incomplete market. A market where the number of time periods is larger than the number of bonds must be an incomplete market. We will investigate this concept shortly.

```
> NarbitB([[3,103,0],[11,11,111]],[100,122]);
```

This is an incomplete market.
The no-arbitrage condition is satisfied.
The set of discount factors is,

$$\left\{ d_1 = -\frac{103}{3} d_2 + \frac{100}{3}, \ d_3 = \frac{1100}{333} d_2 - \frac{734}{333}, \ \frac{97}{103} < d_2, \ d_2 < \frac{50}{53} \right\}$$

The reader is encouraged to experiment with other combinations of bond prices and bond payoffs to arrive at an appreciation for the features of the debt market.

The **NarbitB** procedure is also capable of handling a situation when the period between the current time and the next coupon payment is not the same as the time between coupon payments. Assume that the above example reflects a case where the bonds pay annual payments and there is a year between the current time and the next coupon payment. If we now change the assumption that time between the current time and the next coupon payment is only half a year we need to use this as a basic unit of time. Hence the cash flow from the bonds will also be reported based on the time of unit of half a year. Consequently the cash flow from the first bond will be represented as [0,3,0,103,0,0] and from the second bond as [0,11,0,11,0,111], and if the prices of the bonds are now 90 and 130 we have to run:

```
> NarbitB([[0,3,0,103,0,0],[0,11,0,11,0,111]],[90,130]);
```

This is an incomplete market.
The no-arbitrage condition is not satisfied
An arbitrage portfolio is:
Buy, $\dfrac{119}{87}$, of Bond, 1
Short, 1, of Bond, 2
Buying this portfolio produces income of, $\dfrac{200}{29}$, at time, 0
This portfolio produces income of, 0, at time, 1
This portfolio produces income of, $-\dfrac{200}{29}$, at time, 2
This portfolio produces income of, 0, at time, 3
This portfolio produces income of, $\dfrac{11300}{87}$, at time, 4
This portfolio produces income of, 0, at time, 5
This portfolio produces income of, -111, at time, 6

When a bond is purchased between coupon payments, the next coupon is divided between the old owner and the new owner in a prorated fashion. Assume coupon payments are every six months and a bond was purchased two months before a coupon payment. Thus, the first coupon will be divided such that the old owner will receive $\dfrac{4}{6}$ of it and the new owner will receive $\dfrac{2}{6}$ of it. Hence, the new owner, upon purchasing the bond, pays $\dfrac{4}{6}$ of a coupon to the old owner.

Quoted bond prices (in North America) do not include the payment of the fraction of the first coupon to be paid to the old owner. That is, the quoted price of a coupon bond does not include accrued interest, but only the present value of the future cash flow. A bond price that does not include accrued interest is referred to as a clean price, while if the accrued interest is included, it is referred to as a dirty price. The latter, in the main, is quoted in European bond markets. Hence, Dirty Price = Clean Price + Accrued Interest. A price of a bond that is quoted immediately after a coupon payment is clean and dirty, as there is no accrued interest to include. Clean prices change for economic reasons only, while dirty prices change due to the passage of time as well, because the prorated portion changes.

Thus when bond prices are quoted at a time that is not immediately after a coupon payment, clean prices should be used to infer the interest rates that are implicit in bond prices.

Note that in the above representation clean prices should be used. As well, the market becomes an incomplete market as there are more time periods than bonds. If we change the prices of the bonds so that the no arbitrage condition is satisfied, e.g., to [90,110] and re-run NarbitB, we have the following output:

```
> NarbitB([[0,3,0,103,0,0],[0,11,0,11,0,111]],[90,110]);
```

This is an incomplete market.
The no-arbitrage condition is satisfied.

$$\text{The set of discount factors is, } \left\{ d_2 = -\frac{103}{3}d_4 + 30, \right.$$

$$d_6 = \frac{1100}{333}d_4 - \frac{220}{111}, \ \frac{87}{103} < d_4, \ d_1 < 1, \ d_3 < -\frac{103}{3}d_4 + 30,$$

$$d_4 < \frac{45}{53}, \ d_4 < d_3, \ d_5 < d_4, \ -\frac{103}{3}d_4 + 30 < d_1, \ \frac{1100}{333}d_4 - \frac{220}{111} < d_5 \right\}$$

The results regarding the set of discount factors are not so applicable since in an incomplete market there is a set of such factors. While the concept of incomplete market is an important one, in the context of the bond markets it is suppressed due to some features of the bond market. This will become apparent when we deal with the estimation of the discount factors or equivalently of the term structure.

2.4 Pricing by Replication and Discount Factors

In a market where there are no arbitrage opportunities, the following question can be posed: Given the profile of a certain cash flow in the future, what should its price be? Only in markets with no arbitrage opportunities can such a question make sense. As noted above, if arbitrage opportunities exist there may be more than one price assigned to a portfolio, as the law of one price does not hold. Moreover, one would not bother buying any security if one can make infinite amounts of money with no risk and no initial investment.

The question posed, however, may not have a solution. The absence of a solution may occur in markets termed *incomplete markets*. An incomplete market is a market where, given a cash flow profile, there might not be a portfolio that generates this cash flow. A *complete market* is a market where, given a cash flow profile, there exists a portfolio that generates this cash flow.

Our aim in this section is to further introduce the pricing by replication approach. We initialized this approach when we spoke about forward contracts and the cost of carry model. In the current setting of a bond market the pricing by replication approach means that the price of a given cash flow should be the price of the portfolio generating such a cash flow. We shall return to the case of *incomplete markets* in the sequel but for now we assume and exemplify our approach in a complete market. This will also help with our understanding of the concept of incomplete markets.

Assuming a complete market, the price of a cash flow is obtained by minimizing the price of a portfolio generating the given cash flow. Note, that this time the cost of the portfolio is minimized instead of maximizing the proceeds. The same results will be obtained either way but it might be more intuitive to minimize the cost. Hence if we use our example of Chapter 1 (Table 1.1) to price the cash flow of 0 at time 1, \$1 at time 2 and 0 at time 3 we need to solve the following optimization.

```
> simplex[minimize](94.5*B1+97*B2+89*B3,\
> {105*B1+10*B2+8*B3>=0, 110*B2+8*B3>=1,108*B3>=0});
```

$$\left\{ B1 = -\frac{1}{1155}, \; B2 = \frac{1}{110}, \; B3 = 0 \right\}$$

Let us see the cash flow produced by this portfolio. To this end we use our structure as before, namely:

```
> subs(B2=1/110,B1=(-1)/1155,B3 = 0,\
> [CashTime0=-94.5*B1-97*B2-89*B3,\
> CashTime1=105*B1+10*B2+8*B3,\
> CashTime2=0*B1+110*B2+8*B3,\
> CashTime3=0*B1+0*B2+108*B3]);
```

$$[CashTime0 = -0.8000000000, \; CashTime1 = 0,$$
$$CashTime2 = 1, \; CashTime3 = 0]$$

The implication is that a dollar at time 2 can be generated by buying a portfolio, the cost of which is 0.8. Thus if there are no arbitrage opportunities in the market, the cost (the present value) of a dollar at time 2 must be 0.8.

If this were the case and the price of a dollar at time 2 had been more than $0.8, say $0.9, one would act as follows: Borrow a dollar to be returned at time 2, using the price of 0.9. Receive $0.9, invest $0.8 in the above portfolio to generate a dollar at time 2. At time 2 take this dollar and pay off the loan. Arbitrage profit of $0.1 was generated at time 0.

If the price of a dollar at time 2 had been less than $0.8, say $0.7, one would act as follows: Borrow a dollar to be returned at time 2 using the price of 0.8. This can be accomplished by reversing the short position to a long position, and vice versa, in the portfolio that generates a dollar at time 2 as shown below.

```
> subs(B2=-1/110,B1=1/1155,B3 = 0,\
> [CashTime0=-94.5*B1-97*B2-89*B3,\
> CashTime1=105*B1+10*B2+8*B3,\
> CashTime2=0*B1+110*B2+8*B3,\
> CashTime3=0*B1+0*B2+108*B3]);
```

$$[CashTime0 = 0.8000000000,\ CashTime1 = 0,$$
$$CashTime2 = -1,\ CashTime3 = 0]$$

Thus one receives the $0.8 invests $0.7 to get a dollar at time 2. Use this dollar to pay off the loan. Arbitrage profit of $0.1 was generated at time 0.

Now it is also understood why, from a technical point of view, if the NA is not satisfied the question of the price of a dollar at time 2 is meaningless. The minimization problem above would not be bounded, as one can generate infinite arbitrage profit and the cost of the cash flow in question will be negative infinity.

If the NA is satisfied, finding a portfolio that generates the above cash flow does not require solving a minimization problem; it is sufficient to solve a system of equations as below:

```
> solve({105*B1+10*B2+8*B3=0, 110*B2+8*B3=1,108*B3=0});
```

$$\left\{ B1 = -\frac{1}{1155}, \ B2 = \frac{1}{110}, \ B3 = 0 \right\}$$

There are two advantages to solving the optimization problem. If we are given a market and we are not told whether or not the NA is satisfied, the above system of equations could have a solution but it will be meaningless. However the optimization problem in this case is unbounded. Moreover, in an incomplete market the system of equations might have no solution while the optimization problem still produces useful information in this case, as we shall see later.

The market in our example therefore does satisfy the NA as the optimization problem produced a solution. One of the bonds in the market pays only in one period (bond one). Consequently, it is trivial to find the cost of the cash flow of a dollar at time 1 and zero at other times, while for the cost of a dollar at time 3 and zero at other times, an optimization problem should be solved. We present the optimization problems accomplishing these tasks next. Each optimization is followed by the substitutions of the solution to confirm the resultant cash flow of the solved portfolio.

```
> simplex[minimize](94.5*B1+97*B2+89*B3,\
> {105*B1+10*B2+8*B3>=1, 110*B2+8*B3>=0,108*B3>=0});
```

$$\left\{ B1 = \frac{1}{105}, \ B2 = 0, \ B3 = 0 \right\}$$

```
> subs(B3=0,B1=1/105,B2=0,\
> [CashTime0=-94.5*B1-97*B2-89*B3,\
> CashTime1=105*B1+10*B2+8*B3,\
> CashTime2=0*B1+110*B2+8*B3,\
> CashTime3=0*B1+0*B2+108*B3]);
```

$$[CashTime0 = -0.9000000000, \ CashTime1 = 1,$$
$$CashTime2 = 0, \ CashTime3 = 0]$$

```
> simplex[minimize](94.5*B1+97*B2+89*B3,\
> {105*B1+10*B2+8*B3>=0, 110*B2+8*B3>=0,108*B3>=1});
```

$$\left\{ B1 = -\frac{4}{6237}, \ B2 = -\frac{1}{1485}, \ B3 = \frac{1}{108} \right\}$$

```
> subs(B2=-1/1485,B1=-4/6237,B3=1/108,\
> [CashTime0=-94.5*B1-97*B2-89*B3,\
> CashTime1=105*B1+10*B2+8*B3,\
> CashTime2=0*B1+110*B2+8*B3,\
> CashTime3=0*B1+0*B2+108*B3]);
```

$$[CashTime0 = -0.6981481482, \ CashTime1 = 0,$$
$$CashTime2 = 0, CashTime3 = 1]$$

The three cash flows just priced are "special" cash flows in this market, sometimes also referred to as elementary cash flows. The first cash flow is $(1,0,0)$ i.e., receive \$1 at time t_1, \$0 at time t_2 and \$0 at time t_3. Similarly the other two cash flows (interpreted as above) are $(0,1,0)$ and $(0,0,1)$. The table below summarizes the price of each cash flow.

Table 2.2   Three Elementary Cash Flows.

cost	t_1	t_2	t_3
0.9000	\$1	\$0	\$0
0.8000	\$0	\$1	\$0
0.6981	\$0	\$0	\$1

In fact, now that we have the prices of these elementary cash flows, it is possible to value any cash flow in this market in a very simple way. Consider the cash flow (c_1, c_2, c_3) and suppose we can find three portfolios: portfolio j denoted by Por_j with a price of $PPor_j$ that pays \$$c_j$ at time t_j and zero otherwise, for $j = 1, 2, 3$. In this case the price of the cash flow

(c_1, c_2, c_3) must equal (by the replication arguments) $\sum_{j=1}^{3} PPor_j$. However, the cash flow from Por_j is actually c_j times the cash flow from the jth elementary cash flow. Consequently, portfolio Por_j that produces $\$c_j$ at time t_j is equivalent to buying c_j times the portfolio producing $\$1$ at time t_j. Portfolios producing the elementary cash flows will be referred to as elementary portfolios and will be denoted by $EPor_j$, $j = 1, 2, 3$. In our example the compositions of the elementary portfolios are summarized in Table 2.3.

Table 2.3   The Portfolios Generating the Elementary Cash Flows.

"(1,0,0)"	"(0,1,0)"	"(0,0,1)"	*Bond*
$\dfrac{1}{105}$	$\dfrac{1}{110}$	$\dfrac{-4}{6237}$	*B1*
0	$\dfrac{-1}{1155}$	$\dfrac{-1}{1485}$	*B2*
0	0	$\dfrac{1}{108}$	*B3*

Indeed, we already know the prices of the elementary portfolios. In our example the portfolio producing $\$1$ at time t_1 costs $\$0.9$. Thus the portfolio producing $\$c_1$ contingent at time t_1 will cost $\$0.9c_1$ and the cost of the cash flow (c_1, c_2, c_3) is simply

$$0.9\,c_1 + 0.8\,c_2 + 0.6981\,c_3$$

$$(2.3)$$

The above argument also shows that the cash flow (c_1, c_2, c_3) is generated by buying c_1 times the portfolio $EPor_1$, c_2 times the portfolio $EPor_2$, and c_3 times the portfolio $EPor_3$.

The reader may realize that prices of the portfolios producing the elementary cash flows can be interpreted as discount factors. Consequently the cost (value) of a future cash flow is this present value, but the justification is provided using the NA and the replication approach.

We essentially described in this section two methods of finding the value, or price, of a certain cash flow. A direct replication approach in which a portfolio producing the cash flows at hand is solved. The cost of the portfolio must be the cost of the further cash flow or else arbitrage opportunities will exist. Alternatively, each cash flow (c_1, c_2, c_3) in this market can be valued by its present value, i.e., as $0.9\,c_1 + 0.8\,c_2 + 0.6981\,c_3$.

The next section elaborates on the meaning of discount factors and their intimate connection to the NA. This section ends with applying the two valuation techniques to an example showing that the results are the same.

Consider the cash flow $(100, -20, 45)$, its price (present value) should be

```
> 0.9*100-0.8*20+0.6981*45;
```

$$105.4145$$

This result can be confirmed by solving the optimization problem that finds the least-cost portfolio producing this cash flow.

```
> simplex[minimize](94.5*B1+97*B2+89*B3,\
> {105*B1+10*B2+8*B3>=100,110*B2+8*B3>=-20,108*B3>=45});
```

$$\left\{ B1 = \frac{652}{693}, B2 = -\frac{7}{33}, B3 = \frac{5}{12} \right\}$$

The cost of this portfolio is found by using our structure:

```
> subs(B1=652/693,B2=(-7)/33,B3 = 5/12,\
> [CashTime0=94.5*B1+97*B2+89*B3,\
> CashTime1=105*B1+10*B2+8*B3,\
> CashTime2=0*B1+110*B2+8*B3,\
> CashTime3=0*B1+0*B2+108*B3]);
```

$$[CashTime0 = 105.4166667, \; CashTime1 = 100,$$
$$CashTime2 = -20, \; CashTime3 = 45]$$

We see that indeed the two methods produce the same cost (but for round off errors).

Alternatively, confirmation can be carried out without the need to solve an optimization problem. Since we already know the units of bonds 1 and 2 and 3 in each of the elementary portfolios, we can find the portfolio producing this cash flow utilizing the information in the tables. The reader is asked to show this as well as the arbitrage strategies that exist if the price of the cash flow in question is not $105.416. We move next to the interpretation of the discount factors and their relation to the NA.

2.5 Discount Factors and NA

There is another way to calculate prices in markets which do not allow arbitrage opportunities. Consider the structure of bonds from the first example of this Chapter. Take bond 3: it can actually be "stripped" into three zero coupon bonds:[7]

- a bond which pays $8 at time t_1, and $0 at times t_2 and t_3;
- a bond which pays $8 at time t_2, and $0 in either time t_1 or t_3; and
- a bond which pays $108 at time t_3, and $0 in the first two times.

In fact, these three bonds can be further decomposed into even more elementary securities. The security that pays $8 at time t_1 and $0 otherwise can actually be thought of as 8 units of a bond that pays $1 at time t_1 and $0 otherwise, or 8 units of the first "special cash flow" (elementary cash flow), as described above.

---

[7]This terminology is used in the fixed income market where bonds are decomposed ("stripped") into their component parts. A bond promises payment of a coupon (the interest) every half a year (usually) and, at maturity, a payment of the last coupon and return of the principal value. Consider a bond maturing one year from today with a principal value of $1000 and which pays 8% interest. It pays $40 in half a year and $40 plus $1000 in a year. It can be stripped into a bond (zero coupon) which pays $40 and matures in half a year, another zero coupon bond paying $40 and maturing in one year, and a third zero coupon bond paying $1000 when it matures also in one year. The price of the original bond must be the sum of the prices of its component parts, the parts into which it can be stripped. The states of nature in our example play the role of time in the bond example.

In the same manner,[8] the other two securities into which security 1 was stripped, can also be decomposed into the corresponding elementary cash flows. In a market where the no-arbitrage condition is satisfied, the law of one price holds. Thus, if the price of bond 3 is $89, it must equal the sum of the prices of the elementary cash flows which make it up. If the price of $1 obtained at time t_j is d_j, $j = 1, 2, 3$, then the price of bond 1 should be equal to the sum of the prices of the securities from which it is composed, namely,

$$8 d_1 + 8 d_2 + 108 d_3 = 89 \tag{2.4}$$

The other two bonds in the market can be stripped in the same manner. Actually these bonds are all composed of the same elementary cash flows, just in different quantities. It is analogous to different recipes which each use the same ingredients, but in different amounts, resulting in different taste treats. Consequently, an equation like (2.5) can be written for each security in the market. Since the d_j, $j = 1, 2, 3$, are in fact discount factors we already know that each must be positive and that $1 >= d_1 >= d_2 >= d_3 >= 0$. The following system of equations is thus obtained:

$$
\begin{aligned}
105 \, d_1 + 0 \, d_2 + 0 \, d_3 &= 94.5 \\
10 \, d_1 + 110 \, d_2 + 0 \, d_3 &= 97 \\
8 \, d_1 + 8 \, d_2 + 108 \, d_3 &= 89 \\
1 > d_1 > d_2 &> d_3 > 0
\end{aligned}
\tag{2.5}
$$

The reasoning above suggests that if the law of one price holds, there must be a solution to this system.[9] The solution should equal the value calculated for these elementary cash flows by the replication method in the previous section. The solution to the system of equations is

```
> solve({105*d1+0*d2+0*d3=94.5,10*d1+110*d2+0*d3=97,
> 8*d1+8*d2+108*d3=89,d1<1,d2<d1,d3<d2,d3>0});
```

---

[8]The reader who is familiar with linear algebra will realize that this is nothing but representing the vectors of cash flows in terms of the natural basis of R^3 and requiring the prices of the securities to satisfy the same linear relation.

[9]In fact, the no-arbitrage condition is equivalent to this system of equations being consistent. In incomplete markets, there will be no unique solution for the d_j, $j = 1, 2, 3$. See the Appendix for more on this issue.

$$\{d1 = 0.9000000000, \quad d2 = 0.8000000000, \quad d3 = 0.6981481481\}$$

It can now be seen that the solutions above have the same values as the prices for the three elementary cash flows in Table 1.2. The meaning of the d_j is confirmed: each d_j is the present value of \$1 to be obtained at time d_j. The present value of the cash flow (1,0,0) is $d_1 = 0.9$.

Every security, or cash flow, in this market can be "stripped" into its basic building blocks of \$1 to be obtained at time t_j with respective prices of d_j. Thus, the price of every bond in this market can be calculated as the sum of the prices of the elementary cash flows composing the bond.

If however, the no-arbitrage condition is not satisfied, there will exist no solution to this system. To demonstrate, we change the maturity of bond 2 to time t_3 without changing its price.

```
> solve({105*d1+0*d2+0*d3=94.5,10*d1+10*d2+110*d3=97,\
> 8*d1+8*d2+108*d3=89,d1<1,d2<d1,d3<d2,d3>0});
```

Indeed now there is no solution to the system of equations and we make use of the **NarbitB** to show that the NA is not satisfied.

```
> NarbitB([[105,0,0],[10,10,110],[8,8,108]],
[94.5,97,89]);
```

The no-arbitrage condition is not satisfied
An arbitrage portfolio is:
Buy, 0.02910762160, of Bond, 1
Short, 1, of Bond, 2
Buy, 1.058981233, of Bond, 3
Buying this portfolio produces income of, 2.10^{-8}, at time, 0
This portfolio produces income of, 1.528150132, at time, 1
This portfolio produces income of, -1.528150136, at time, 2
This portfolio produces income of, 4.3699732, at time, 3

We demonstrated by an example in a complete market that if the NA is satisfied there is a solution to the system of equations from which the discount factors can be recovered. The discount factors are implicit in the prices of the bonds, however they can be recovered only if the NA is satisfied. If the NA is not satisfied the system of equations will have no solution. The argument below proves that, in a complete market, the

NA is satisfied if and only if the discount factors can be recovered in the above way. That is if the system of equations has a solution. The rigorous argument proving it to be the case for every market is presented in the appendix.

Recall that a market where the number of time periods is larger than the number of bonds is referred to as an incomplete market. In such a market the set of equations solved to determine the discount fact (e.g. equation 2.5) the number of variables (the discount factors) is larger than the number of equations. Hence there are two possibilities. Either the equations are consistent, a case where the NA is satisfied, and there will be multiple solutions for the discount factors or the equations are inconsistent and there will be not even one solution.

Consider the market describe below already seen before:

```
> NarbitB([[3,103,0],[11,11,111]],[100,122]);
```

This is an incomplete market.
The no-arbitrage condition is satisfied.
The set of discount factors is,

$$\left\{ d_1 = -\frac{103}{3},\ d_2 + \frac{100}{3},\ d_3 = \frac{1100}{333}\ d_2 - \frac{734}{333},\ \frac{97}{103} < d_2,\ d_2 < \frac{50}{53} \right\}$$

The discount factors for this market are solved for (like in equation 2.6) by setting the following system:

$$3\ d_1 + 103\ d_2 + 0\ d_3 = 100$$
$$11\ d_1 + 11\ d_2 + 111\ d_3 = 122$$
$$1 > d_1 > d_2 > d_3 > 0$$

Solving it with Maple will confirm that existence of multiple solutions:

```
> solve({3*d1+103*d2+0*d3=100,11*d1+11*d2+111*d3=122,
d1<1,d2<d1,d3<d2,d1>0,d3<1});
```

$$\left\{ d2 = -\frac{3}{103}\ d1 + \frac{100}{103},\ d3 = -\frac{1100}{11433}\ d1 + \frac{3822}{3811},\ \frac{50}{53} < d1,\ d1 < 1 \right\}$$

There could be a situation where the market is incomplete but there does not exist even one solution for the set of discount factors, i.e., the no arbitrage condition is not satisfied. This situation can occur even when there are more time periods than bonds. Let us change the price of the bonds in the above system of equations to be [90,122] instead of [100,122] and re-solve the system:

```
> solve({3*d1+103*d2+0*d3=90,11*d1+11*d2+111*d3=122,
d1<1,d2<d1,d3<d2,d1>0,d3<1});
```

We see that no solution exists, and hence the NA is not satisfied. This is confirmed running the NarbitB:

```
> NarbitB([[3,103,0],[11,11,111]],[90,130]);
```

This is an incomplete market.
The no-arbitrage condition is not satisfied
An arbitrage portfolio is:
$$Buy, \frac{119}{87}, of\ Bond,\ 1$$
Short, 1, *of Bond,* 2
$$Buying\ this\ portfolio\ produces\ income\ of,\ \frac{200}{29},\ at\ time,\ 0$$
$$This\ portfolio\ produces\ income\ of,\ -\frac{200}{29},\ at\ time,\ 1$$
$$This\ portfolio\ produces\ income\ of,\ \frac{11300}{87},\ at\ time,\ 2$$
This portfolio produces income of, -111, *at time,* 3

If the NA is satisfied (and the market is complete) solving for the minimum cost of a portfolio that produces a cash flow of a dollar at time t_j and zero otherwise must have a solution. This solution is the discount factor for time j. These solutions must also satisfy the system of equations stipulating that the price of a bond equals its present value otherwise the NA is not satisfied.

Conversely, assume that there exists discount factors. That is there exists a solution to the optimization problems (as in the previous subsection) of minimizing the cost of a portfolio that produces a cash flow of a dollar at time t_j and zero otherwise. Consequently, the no arbitrage condition must be satisfied, since if it does not the optimizing problems would be unbounded and will not have finite solutions.

2.6 Rates, Discount Factors, and Continuous Compounding

There is, of course, a link between the interest rates and the discount factors. This is a part of the output of **NarbitB** that we have not explicitly addressed. The discounting is a result of the opportunity to invest (the opportunity cost) at the risk-free rate. Hence, if the discount factor from time zero to some time t is d then

$$d_t = \frac{1}{1+r}. \tag{2.6}$$

The (simple) risk-free rate spanning the interval $[0,t]$ is thus recovered from d_t by

$$r = \frac{1}{d_t} - 1 \tag{2.7}$$

and is reported by **NarbitB**. We shall return to the structure of the interest rate and its connection to the discount factors in the next Chapter.

2.6.1 *Continuous Compounding*

Modern finance uses continuous-time models of the term structure as opposed to the discrete-time models which have been discussed thus far. It is therefore customary and convenient to treat the compounding period as continuous, i.e., every instant of time rather than semiannually. As a consequence, the term structure of interest rates and its estimation are also often reported based on the continuous compounding assumption.

There are two possible ways to explain continuous compounding and we will concisely mention both. One applies to the limit concept and the other uses ordinary differential equation. We present the first argument in the text and the second in the Appendix. Assume that the risk-free rate of interest for one year is r and interest is being paid only once at the end of the year. One dollar invested for one year will thus grow to $1 + r$ at the end of the year. If interest is being paid semiannually instead, then after six months $1 + \frac{r}{2}$ can be reinvested and will grow to $\left(1 + \frac{r}{2}\right)^2$ at the end of the year. When interest is paid n times a year, at the end of the year \$1 will become $\left(1 + \frac{r}{n}\right)^n$. In the case of continuous payments of interest rate $\left(1+\dfrac{r}{n}\right)^n$ correspond to the limit of $\left(1+\dfrac{r}{n}\right)^n$ as n approaches infinity. We can calculate this limit. Assuming we invest $\$V_0$ for t years at a continuously compounded interest rate, what will be its value at the end of the year?

```
> limit(V0*(1+r/n)^(t*n),n=infinity);
```

$$e^{rt}V0$$

The discount factor from time zero to time t will be the reciprocal of the future factor generating $\dfrac{1}{e^r t} = e^{(-rt)}$. Thus, if the annual risk-free rate of interest is r and we would like to use continuous compounding, we should use the rate r_f such that $e^{r_f} = 1 + r$; hence

$$r_f = \ln(1+r),$$

as shown below.

```
> solve({exp(rf)=1+r},{rf});
```

$$\{rf = \ln(1+r)\}$$

2.7 Concluding Remarks

We will return to the topic of valuation in the bond market taking advantage of the discount factors implied by the prices of bonds. However, this will be done in a multiperiod setting in the next few chapters where a second look at swaps, forwards, and futures will be taken. The current chapter introduced us to a setting of a bond market, defined the no arbitrage conditions and highlighted the connections between the latter, discount factors and the present value concept.

2.8 Questions and Problems

Problem 1

Show that assuming the interest rate in the market is positive implies that the discount function should be monotonically decreasing.

In the questions below we make use of the term payoff matrix whereby each row corresponds to a bond and a column to a time period. Thus for example the second element in the second row is the cash flow from the second bond at the second time period. Similarly the price vector has the first element as the price of bond 1 etc.

Problem 2

Assume that the payoff matrix of the bonds available in the market is $A = \begin{bmatrix} 110 & 0 \\ 5 & 105 \end{bmatrix}$ and that the price of the 10 percent bond is $100.

(1) Determine all possible prices for the 5 percent bond that would make the market arbitrage free.

(2) What is the set of prices P_1, P_2 that if assigned to the two bonds will keep the market arbitrage free?

Problem 3

Suppose that the bond market is represented by the payoff matrix A and a price vector P, where $A = \begin{bmatrix} 7 & 107 \\ 111 & 0 \end{bmatrix}$ and $P = \begin{bmatrix} 93 \\ 101 \end{bmatrix}$.

(1) Is this market arbitrage free?

(2) Is it complete?

(3) Find the discount factors d's and explain their meaning.

(4) What is an arbitrage free value of a security that pays $150 at time one and $25 at time 2?

(5) Without calculating the price of the cash flow $[100, -98]$ determine whether or not it should have a positive or negative value and explain your answer.

(6) What if the cash flow of interest is $[-98, 100]$. Explain whether or not you can determine its price without calculating it.

Problem 4

Suppose that the bond market is represented by the payoff matrix $A = \begin{bmatrix} 105 & 0 \\ 8 & 108 \end{bmatrix}$ and the price vector $P = \begin{bmatrix} 98 \\ 95 \end{bmatrix}$.

Answer parts 1, 2, and 3 below using the discount factors and replication arguments.

(1) Is this market arbitrage free?

(2) Is it complete?

(3) Consider a cash flow $c = [1, 1]$. What can be said about the present value of this cash flow?

(4) Assume that the term structure is flat at 5% and that the bonds pay annual coupon. What will be the prices of the bonds 6 months before the coupon payment time, i.e., before bond one pays $105 and bond 2 pays $8?

Problem 5

Suppose that the bond market is represented by the payoff matrix $A = \begin{bmatrix} 6 & 106 & 0 \\ 10 & 10 & 110 \end{bmatrix}$ and $P = \begin{bmatrix} 98 \\ 95 \end{bmatrix}$.

(1) Is this market arbitrage free?

(2) Is it complete?

(3) Formulate the optimization problems that determine the lower and upper bound for the price of a cash flow c.

(4) Calculate problems dual to the ones you have formulated above.

(5) Identify the set of all cash flows that can be priced uniquely.

Problem 6

Consider a bond market that is represented by the payoff matrix $A = \begin{bmatrix} 6 & 106 \\ 110 & 0 \end{bmatrix}$ and $P = \begin{bmatrix} ? \\ 100 \end{bmatrix}$. Assume that coupons are paid annually and that there is a year until the next coupon payment and the maturity of the 10% bond. Furthermore assume that the term structure in this market is flat.

a. What should be the price of the 6% coupon bond?
b. Consider the following strategy:

- *buy one unit of the 10 percent bond now*
- *when it matures invest all the proceeds in the second bond and hold until it matures*

Is this a riskless strategy? Explain your answer.

Problem 7

There is no solution to the optimization

$$Max - 95 \cdot B1 - 98 \cdot B2$$

such that

$$100 \cdot B1 + 100 \cdot B2 >= 0$$

since it describes a market where the NA is not satisfied as seen below.

```
> simplex[maximize](-95*B1-98*B2\
> ,100*B1+100*B2=0);
```

The text imposes the restriction of $B2 >= -1$ to make the arbitrage profit finite and generate an output of the arbitrage portfolio. This time the structure of the problem will be:

```
> simplex[maximize](-95*B1-98*B2\
> ,100*B1+100*B2=0, B2>=-1);
```

$$\{B1 = 1, B2 = -1\}$$

(1.7.1)

Can you suggest another restriction on $B2$ that will also generate an output?

Can you explain why imposing a constraint on the short position of bond 1 will not generate an output showing an arbitrage portfolio?

```
> simplex[maximize](C0+C1+C2,\
> C0=-B1*95-B2*95-Z0,C1=B1*10+B2*0+Z0-Z1,
C2=B1*110+B2*110+Z1,\
> Z0>=0,Z1>=0, C0>=0,C1>=0,C2>=0,B1>=-1);
```

Problem 8

Consider a bond market that is represented by the payoff matrix $A = \begin{bmatrix} 3 & 103 & 0 \\ 11 & 11 & 111 \end{bmatrix}$ and $P = \begin{bmatrix} 100 \\ 122 \end{bmatrix}$ Formulate and solve the NA with and without the provision of allowing to transfer cash flow from period i to i+1 Explain your conclusion regarding the satisfaction of the NA condition. Formulate and solve for the portfolio that generate a cash flow of at least $10 in each period such that the proceeds from the transaction is maximized. Note that the portfolio that maximizes the proceeds is also the one that minimizes the cost. Do this with and without the provision of allowing to transfer cash flow from period i to i+1. Explain the results.

2.9   Appendix

2.9.1   *No-Arbitrage Condition in the Bond Market*

The text in the Chapter suggests that the No Arbitrage condition is satisfied if the optimal value of the optimization problem below is zero.

$$Max_{x_1,\ldots,x_n,z_0,\ldots,z_k} \left[\sum_{j=0}^{K} C_j + \sum_{j=0}^{K-1} Z_j \right]$$

such that

$$\sum_{i=1}^{N} (-x_i P_i) - z_0 = C_0$$

$$\sum_{i=1}^{N} x_i a_{ij} + z_{j-1} - z_j = C_j, j = 1,\ldots,K-1$$

$$\sum_{i=1}^{N} x_i a_{ij} + z_{k-1} = C_k$$

$$0 \le z_j, j = 0,\ldots,K-1, 0 \le C_j, j = 0,\ldots,K$$

A rigorous definition can also be given in terms of the system of inequalities below:

$$0 \le \sum_{i=1}^{N} (-x_i P_i - z_0)$$

$$0 \leq \sum_{i=1}^{N} (x_i a_{ij} + z_{j-1} - z_j), j = 1, \ldots, K-1$$

$$0 \leq \sum_{i=1}^{N} (x_i a_{ik} + z_K).$$

Definition of the No-Arbitrage Condition

The no arbitrage condition in the bond market is satisfied if for every solution of the above system all the inequalities are satisfied as equalities.

There are no arbitrage opportunities if and only if there exists a set of these discount factors. This is proven by the application of separation theorems or by applying a set of results known as the theorem of alternatives. Application of a theorem of alternatives known as Farkas' Lemma (actually a slight modification of it), yields that the condition in the definition is satisfied if and only if the system of equations and inequalities below is consistent.

$$a_{i1} \, d_1 + a_{i2} \, d_2 + \ldots + a_{ik} \, d_k = P_i, \; i = 1, \ldots, N$$
$$d_{j+1} < d_j, \; j = 1, \ldots, K-1$$
$$d_1 < 1$$
$$d_k > 0.$$

2.9.2 *Geometric interpretation of the NA*

Consider a market with two bonds both mature in 2 years with coupon rates of 5% and 9%, and prices of 91 and 98, respectively. That in this market the NA is satisfied is demonstrated by applying to it the **NarbitB** procedure.

```
> NarbitB([[5,105],[9,109]],[91,98]);
```

The no-arbitrage condition is satisfied.

The discount factor for time, 1, *is given by,* $\dfrac{371}{400}$

The interest rate spanning the time interval, $[0,1]$, *is given by,* 0.07817

The discount factor for time, 2, *is given by,* $\dfrac{329}{400}$

The interest rate spanning the time interval, $[0,2]$, *is given by,* 0.2158

The function Vdis ([c1,c2,..]), values the cashflow [c1,c2,..]

The set of portfolios $(x1, x2)$ with positive cash flows for each year is the solution to the system of inequalities

$$0 < 5\,x1 + 9\,x2 \text{ and } 0 < 105\,x1 + 109\,x2.$$

Graphically this set is plotted in the Figure below (where the horizontal axis is x_1 and the vertical axis is x_2):

```
> plots[inequal]({5*x1+9*x2>0,105*x1+109*x2>0},
x1=-100..100,x2=-100..100, optionsfeasible=(color=pink),
optionsopen=(color=red,thickness=2),
optionsclosed=(color=red, thickness=2),
optionsexcluded=(color=white),title='Geometric
Exposition of the No-Arbitrage
Condition',titlefont=[TIMES,BOLD,8]);
```

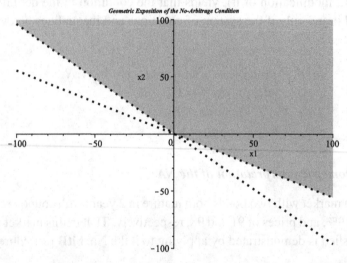

Geometric Exposition of the No-Arbitrage Condition

The dotted lines are the graphs of $5\,x1 + 9\,x2 = 0$ and $105\,x1 + 109\,x2 = 0$. The shaded gray region is the set of portfolios that produce positive cash flows for each state of nature. The shaded gray region is thus the intersection of

$$0 < 5\,x1 + 9\,x2 \text{ and } 0 < 105\,x1 + 109\,x2.$$

The no-arbitrage condition essentially says that every portfolio in the gray region must have a positive price. Since the cost of the portfolio

$(x1, x2)$ is $x1\,p_1 + x2\,p_2$ (where p_1 and p_2 are the prices of the bonds), this last expression must be positive for every $(x1, x2)$ in the shaded (gray) region, i.e., the shaded (gray) region must be completely contained in the region $\{(x1, x2)|0 \leq x1\,p_1 + x2\,p_2\}$. This is the concept of "no-free lunch". A portfolio producing a positive cash flow in at least one year, and non-negative cash flows in every other year, must cost something to purchase today. We can verify whether the vector of prices (p_1, p_2) satisfies the no-arbitrage condition by adding the equality

$$x1\,p_1 + x2p_2 = 0$$

to the set of inequalities plotted above. If the new line intersects the gray set above, the no-arbitrage condition is not satisfied. For example, to determine if $p_1 = 95$ and $p_2 = 92$ satisfy the no-arbitrage condition we add the the graph of the equality for $p_1 = 95$ and $p_2 = 92$ to the figure above to obtain:

```
> plots[inequal]({110*x1+90*x2>0,110*x1+120*x2>0,
91*x1+98*x2=0},x1=-100..100,x2=-100..100,
optionsfeasible=(color=pink),
optionsopen=(color=red,thickness=2),
optionsclosed=(color=blue, thickness=3),
optionsexcluded=(color=white),title='The Price Vector
and the No-Arbitrage
Condition',titlefont=[TIMES,BOLD,8]);
```

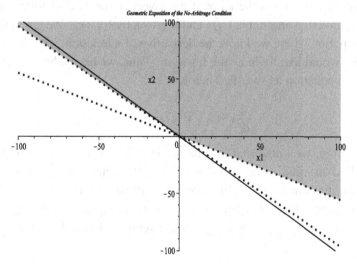

Geometric Exposition of the No-Arbitrage Condition

Since the new line does intersect the gray region, $p_1 = 95$ and $p_2 = 92$ do not satisfy the no-arbitrage condition. The fact that $p_1 = 95$ and $p_2 = 92$ do not satisfy the no arbitrage condition should be obvious as bond 1 dominates bond 2 and thus a trivial arbitrage position will be short bond 1 and long bond 2.

2.9.3 *Continues compounding and ordinary differential equations*

There is another way of producing the explanation of continuous compounding. If interest is being paid every instant of time, then the value of an amount invested at the risk-free rate of interest grows every instant in time. Let us denote the value V of the amount invested as a function of time t, by $V(t)$. Thus, every instant of time adds $V(t)r_f$ to the amount $V(t)$. Or to put it more precisely, for t_1, t_2, and $\Delta t = t_2 - t_1$, the difference between $V(t_1)$ and $V(t_2) = V(t_1 + \Delta t)$, divided by Δt, e.g.,

$$\frac{V(t_1 + \Delta t) - V(t_1)}{\Delta t},$$

is the average growth rate of $V(t_1)$ per unit time. The instantaneous growth rate at time t_1, is the limit of the above expression as Δt approaches zero, or as t_2 approaches t_1. Therefore the instantaneous growth rate is $\frac{\mathrm{d}}{\mathrm{d}t}V(t)$, the derivative (as defined in calculus) of $V(t)$ with respect to t.

Assume that at time t_0 the amount we invested was V_0. At time t the value of the invested amount is $V(t)$ and it grows by $V(t)r_f$. We are therefore in a situation where we know the derivative of a function, with respect to t, and we would like to know the function. Thus, we have what is called a differential equation as specified below:

$$\frac{\mathrm{d}}{\mathrm{d}t}V(t) = V(t)r_f.$$

Furthermore, we know that at time t_0 the value of the function is V_0. This is called an initial condition, since it specifies the value of the function at the initial time. (The initial condition allows determination of the constant of integration.) The following differential equation with the initial condition that at time zero, $V(0) = V_0$, is submitted, and the solution is displayed below:

```
> dsolve({diff(V(t),t)=V(t)*rf,V(0)=V0},V(t));
```

$$V(t) = V0\,e^{rf\,t}$$

We see that V_0 invested for the period 0 to t grows to $V_0 e^{r_f t}$. The future value coefficient is $e^{r_f t}$, and consequently the discount factor is its reciprocal $e^{-r_f t}$. If the risk-free rate is not the same for each time period, but rather a function of time, say, $r_f(t)$, this can also be solved to generate our discount factor:

```
> dsolve({diff(V(t),t)=V(t)*rf(t),V(0)=V0},V(t));
```

$$V(t) = V0\,e^{\int_0^t rf(\_z1)\,\mathrm{d}\_z1}$$

Hence the discount factor in such a case is: $e^{\left(-\int_0^t -r_f(u)\,\mathrm{d}u\right)}$.

Chapter 3

The Term Structure, its Estimation, and Smoothing

In the last chapter we investigated the meaning of the discount factors and their relation to the NA condition, and valuing future cash flows utilizing the present value concept. Some financial instruments, that also fall into the class of derivative securities, are valued based on risk-free discount factors. The valuation concept of these instruments is induced by the no-arbitrage condition. These securities are valued either by replication or by applying to their cash flow the discount factors.

The risk-free discount factors are implicit in bond prices, as we saw in Chapter 2. They are consequences of the no-arbitrage condition. However before we dwell on the valuation issue, we introduce the reader to some estimation matters, terminology such as yield, yield curve, spot curve, and zero-coupon curve, and their interrelation.

3.1 The Term Structure of Interest Rates

The discount factors (ds) reflect the discounting due to the time value of money. Thus, they have implicit in them the interest rate that prevails in the market. For example, if $d_1 = 0.9$ it means that in this market a dollar at time one is worth 0.9 of a dollar today. The difference in value between a dollar today and a dollar received in the future results from the opportunity cost of investing that dollar at the risk-free rate of interest. A dollar today can be invested in a risk-free asset from time zero to time one and will earn a rate of interest which we denote by r_1. Hence a dollar today will be equal to $1 + r_1$ dollars at time one. Consequently, $\frac{1}{1+r}$, if invested at the risk-free rate from time zero to time one, will grow to be one dollar. It thus follows that

$$d_1 = \frac{1}{1+r} \qquad (3.1)$$

and we can solve for r_1 in terms of d_1.

```
> solve(d1=1/(1+r1),r1);
```

$$-\frac{d_1 - 1}{d_1}$$

The rate r_1 is called the *spot rate* spanning the time interval zero to one. It is the rate applied to loans which commence now (at time zero) and which mature at some time in the future — time one in this example. In the same manner we can calculate the rate r_2, spanning the time interval zero to two, i.e.,

```
> solve(d2=1/(1+r2),r2);
```

$$-\frac{d_2 - 1}{d_2}$$

With complete precision of notation, the rates r_1 and r_2 should have a second index. After all, these rates are payable from time zero to times one and two, respectively. For simplicity, however, we omit the index reference to time zero, and thus instead of using r_{01}, we use r_1, with the understanding that if only one index is mentioned, it is the second one, and the first is (implicitly) zero. These rates, as mentioned, are applicable to a loan which commences now (on the spot) and lasts until some future time. Hence they are termed *spot rates*.

Equivalently, we can solve for r_1 by utilizing the function **Vdis** defined by **NarbitB**. Consider, for simplicity, a bond market with three bonds in which coupons are paid annually, the payment dates of the bonds coincide, and the longest maturity is three years. The structure of the market is described in **NarbitB** below, where time is measured in years, and the current time is a year before the first coupon payment:

```
> NarbitB([[105,0,0],[8,108,0],[3,3,103]],[96,97,89]);
```

The no-arbitrage condition is satisfied.

The discount factor for time, 1, is given by, $\frac{32}{35}$

The interest rate spanning the time interval, $[0,1]$, is given by, 0.09375
The discount factor for time, 2, is given by, $\dfrac{3139}{3780}$
The interest rate spanning the time interval, $[0,2]$, is given by, 0.2042
The discount factor for time, 3, is given by, $\dfrac{21109}{25956}$
The interest rate spanning the time interval, $[0,3]$, is given by, 0.2296
The function Vdis ($[c1,c2,..]$), values the cashflow $[c1,c2,..]$

The rate r_1, for example, applicable to money invested for one year, can be found by solving $Vdis([1+r_1,0,0]) = 1$. The reader may wish to try and solve for some of the rs and compare them to the values reported by **NarbitB**.

```
> solve(Vdis([1+r1, 0, 0]) = 1.0);
```

$$0.09375000000$$

It is customary to report interest rates for different terms in such a way that they can be compared. Obviously, r_2 is a larger number than r_1, since the former represents the rate earned over the longer period of time $[0,2]$ for which the first period $[0,1]$ is a subperiod. If this were not the case, arbitrage opportunities would exist as stipulated in the former chapter.

In order to report the rates in a comparable manner, the rates are reported (usually) on a per annum basis. It is therefore natural to measure the time in units of a year. The spot rate for time n (n years from now) is reported as the annual rate which, if compounded semiannually, will produce the rate applicable to the period $[0,n]$. Hence, the spot rate applicable to time n is the solution r_n to equation (3.2),

$$d_n = \frac{1}{\left(1+\frac{r_n}{2}\right)^{(2n)}}$$

$$(3.2)$$

The use of the annual rate (and semiannual compounding) gives rise to the term $\dfrac{r_n}{2}$, and since time is measured in units of a year, the relevant exponent is $2n$. This is where special care should be given to the assumption regarding the length of the time intervals $[0,1]$, $[1,2]$, and $[2,3]$ that are used in the input to **NarbitB**.[1] Thus, for example, the spot rate for time

---

[1] The procedure **NarbitB** assumes that time 1 is the time of the first payment and that the

one (a year in our example), r_1, is given by the solution to $d_1 = \dfrac{1}{\left(1+\frac{r_1}{2}\right)^2}$.

```
> solve({d1=1/(1+r1/2)^2},{r1});
```

$$\left\{ r1 = -\frac{2(\sqrt{d1}-1)}{\sqrt{d1}} \right\}, \quad \left\{ r1 = -\frac{2(\sqrt{d1}+1)}{\sqrt{d1}} \right\}$$

As we see, there are two solutions to this equation and we choose the positive one, $\dfrac{2\sqrt{d_1}}{d_1} - 2$. In our example the value of the spot rate is obtained by substituting $d_1 = 0.9$ in the chosen solution.

```
> subs(d1=0.9,-2+2/sqrt(d1));
```

$$0.108185106$$

In the same manner r_2 will be given by

```
> solve(d2=1/(1+r2/2)^4,r2);
```

$$\frac{2}{d2^{1/4}} - 2, \ \frac{2I}{d2^{1/4}} - 2, \ -\frac{2}{d2^{1/4}} - 2, \ -\frac{2I}{d2^{1/4}} - 2$$

We choose again the positive real solution $2\,d_2^{\left(-\frac{1}{4}\right)} - 2$ and substitute $d_2 = 0.8$ in it to get the value of r_2 in our example.

```
> subs(d2=0.8,-2+2*d2^(-1/4));
```

$$0.114742526$$

payments are equally spaced between time 0 and the largest maturity. Thus time 2 is the time of the second payment, and time k is the time of the kth payment. Consequently, the output of **NarbitB**, when reporting a rate spanning the time interval $[0,k]$, pertains to the time interval from the current time to that time of the kth payment, and the reported rate is the simple rate spanning the time interval. It is therefore important to notice the time period entered into **NarbitB** and the way in which the spot rates are reported. Similarly, when **NarbitB** defines a discount factor function for time t, it uses the same units as entered by the user.

If the length of the time intervals $[0,1]$, $[1,2]$, etc., used in **NarbitB** is half a year, the spot rate, rs_n, applicable to the time interval $[0,n]$, i.e., n half years, will be reported by **NarbitB** as a simple rate. Thus, when the rate is reported as an annual rate semiannually compounded, the spot rate for n half years, will be the solution $r_{\frac{n}{2}}$ (i.e., $\frac{n}{2}years$) to the

equation $1 + rs_n = \left(1 + \dfrac{\left(r_{\frac{n}{2}}\right)}{2}\right)^n$ or $r_{\frac{n}{2}} = 2\left(\dfrac{\ln(1+rs_n)}{n} - 1\right).$

The discount factor for time t is the present value (price) of one dollar obtainable at time t. Hence, the discount factor for time three, for example, will be given by

```
> evalf(Vdis([0,0,1]));
```

$$0.8132609031$$

We can therefore solve numerically for r_3 by combining the **solve** (or **fsolve** command with the feasible range for r_3) with the value of d_3 given in terms of **Vdis** as below.

```
> fsolve((Vdis([0,0,1]))=1/(1+r3/2)^(6),r3=0..1);
```

$$0.07010169009$$

```
> solve({evalf(Vdis([0,0,1]))=1/(1+r3/2)^(6),r3>=0,
r3<=1});
```

$$\{r3 = 0.07010169007\}$$

Continuing in this manner, we obtain a schedule, a structure of spot rates for each payment date in the future. This structure is referred to as the *term structure of interest rates* or, in short, the *term structure*. In general, the spot rate r_n spanning the time interval $[0, n]$ based on compounding m times per unit of time, will be the solution to

$$d_n = \frac{1}{\left(1 + \frac{r_n}{m}\right)^{(nm)}}.$$

Thus, if the unit of time is half a year and the rates are reported per annum based on semiannual compounding, a dollar invested from time zero to time three is invested for 1.5 years and will grow to $\left(1 + \frac{r_3}{2}\right)^{2\cdot1.5} = \left(1 + \frac{r_3}{2}\right)^{3}$.

3.1.1 *Zero-Coupon, Spot, and Yield Curves*

The Term Structure, Zero-Coupon, and Spot Curves

The term structure is actually a function, which we will denote by $r(t)$, that relates time to the interest rate prevailing in the market. For each t,

$r(t)$ is the interest rate per period (a year) paid for a dollar invested for t years, from time zero to time t. **We keep our units of time measured in years and report the interest rate based on semiannual compounding**. Hence, $r(t)$ is the rate such that a dollar invested from time zero to time t will grow to be

$$\left(1 + \frac{r(t)}{2}\right)^{(2t)}$$

at time t. This function is referred to as the *term structure of interest rates*, and for each t the rate $r(t)$ is called a *spot rate*.

These are the rates paid on an investment over a period that starts now (on the spot) and ends at some future time t. The graph of this function is sometimes referred to as the *spot curve* or the *zero-coupon curve*. In what follows, we justify this name followed by a graphical representation of the term structure which will be explored shortly afterward.

Certain bonds pay only one payment at the maturity time of the bond. These bonds are referred to as zero-coupon bonds, since they make no coupon payments. Furthermore, zero-coupon bonds are sold at a discount. The interest rate offered by such bonds is implicit in the difference between the face value of the bond and its market price. Namely, if the price of a zero-coupon bond maturing at time t, t years from now, is P and its face value is \$100, the interest it pays is the solution r to the equation

$$P = 100 \left(1 + \frac{r}{2}\right)^{(-2t)}. \qquad (3.3)$$

Hence r will be given by

```
> solve({P=100*(1+r/2)^(-2*t)},{r});
```

$$\left\{ r = 2e^{-\frac{1}{2}\frac{\ln\left(\frac{1}{100}P\right)}{t}} - 2 \right\}$$

where we assume again that t is measured in years and compounding is done semiannually.

The zero-coupon bonds are bonds which repay the principal at some time t and pay nothing at any other time. The zero-coupon bonds, therefore, are the elementary building blocks of coupon bonds as the latter can be interpreted as a portfolio of zero-coupon bonds.

Consider a bond that pays a coupon of $\frac{c}{2}$ at times $t_1, t_2, \ldots, t_{n-1}$ and matures at time t_n where it pays $100 + \frac{c}{2}$. This bond may be replicated by a portfolio of zero-coupon bonds, each with a face value of \$1. A portfolio composed of $\frac{c}{2}$ units of zero-coupon bonds maturing at times $t_1, t_2, \ldots, t_{n-1}$, and $100 + \frac{c}{2}$ of a zero-coupon bond which matures at time t_n, has the same cash flow as the coupon-paying bond. Zero-coupon bonds each with a face value of \$1 is equivalent to $\frac{1}{100}$ of a zero coupon bond with a face value of \$100. Hence, the above argument can be done utilizing zero coupon bonds with \$100 of face value.

If the principal (face value) of a zero-coupon bond maturing at time t is \$1, the price of the bond is the discount factor for time t. Hence, the spot rates extracted from coupon-paying bonds or those extracted from zero-coupon bonds which are the building blocks of the coupon bonds, will be the same. Thus, the term structure of interest rates is sometimes referred to as the *zero-coupon curve*.

Let us consider an example in order to demonstrate this idea. We will start with a market of coupon bonds and estimate the discount factors. Then we will replace the bonds in this market by zero-coupon bonds with face values of \$1. The prices we will assign to these zero-coupon bonds will be the discount factors obtained in the first market. We then re-estimate the discount factors. Of course, the discount factors in these two markets should be the same.

Consider the market specified in **NarbitB** below, where executing **NarbitB** confirms that the no-arbitrage condition is satisfied, and the discount factors and the function **Vdis** are solved for.

```
> NarbitB([[105,0,0],[5,105,0],[4,4,104]],[94,97,89]);
```

The no-arbitrage condition is satisfied.
The discount factor for time, 1, *is given by,* $\frac{94}{105}$
The interest rate spanning the time interval, $[0,1]$, *is given by,* 0.1170
The discount factor for time, 2, *is given by,* $\frac{1943}{2205}$
The interest rate spanning the time interval, $[0,2]$, *is given by,* 0.1348

The discount factor for time, 3, is given by, $\dfrac{180577}{229320}$
The interest rate spanning the time interval, $[0,3]$, *is given by,* 0.2699
The function Vdis ([c1,c2,..]), values the cashflow [c1,c2,..]

The discount factors are specified above, but of course, the discount factor for time one will be the value of a zero-coupon bond maturing at time one and paying $1. Hence the discount factors for times one, two, and three are given by $Vdis([1,0,0])$, $Vdis([0,1,0])$ *and* $Vdis([0,0,1])$, respectively.

```
> Vdis([1,0,0]),Vdis([0,1,0]),Vdis([0,0,1]);
```

$$\frac{94}{105}, \frac{1943}{2205}, \frac{180577}{229320}$$

Let us now re-run **NarbitB** on a market composed of only these three zero-coupon bonds. The prices are specified above and applied to the corresponding zero-coupon bond.

```
> NarbitB([[1,0,0],[0,1,0],[0,0,1]],[94/105, 1943/2205,
180577/229320]);
```

The no-arbitrage condition is satisfied.
The discount factor for time, 1, is given by, $\dfrac{94}{105}$
The interest rate spanning the time interval, $[0,1]$, *is given by,* 0.1170
The discount factor for time, 2, is given by, $\dfrac{1943}{2205}$
The interest rate spanning the time interval, $[0,2]$, *is given by,* 0.1348
The discount factor for time, 3, is given by, $\dfrac{180577}{229320}$
The interest rate spanning the time interval, $[0,3]$, *is given by,* 0.2699
The function Vdis ([c1,c2,..]), values the cashflow [c1,c2,..]

We indeed confirm that the resultant market and discount factors are the same as those in the first market. This should come as no surprise to the reader. The bond market specified by the coupon bonds and the one specified by the zero coupon bonds are in fact the same markets. Two markets are the same if every (risk free) cash flow in these two markets has exactly the same price. That this is the case in our two markets, is evidenced from the fact that the discount factors in these two markets are the same. The price of every (risk free) cash flow in each of these markets, c_1, c_2 and c_3 is the value of the linear function

$$f(c_1,c_2,c_3) = d_1 \cdot c_1 + d_2 \cdot c_2 + d_3 \cdot c_3.$$

Consequently these two markets are equivalent. Hence, the zero-coupon curve, or the discount factor function, is like the DNA of the market.

There is another way of viewing equivalent markets. The initial securities defining a market are called primary securities. Consider the market where the primary securities were the coupon bonds. If a primary security is removed from the market (the market is assumed to be complete and not including redundant bonds) and another security (replicated by the primary securities) is added in its place, an equivalent market is obtained. Let us demonstrate this below.

The following structure calculates a portfolio of the three primary bonds that replicate the cash flow 0,1,0. It also calculates the price of this portfolio.

```
> solve({105*B1+5*B2+4*B3=0,0*B1+105*B2+4*B3=1,
0*B1+0*B2+104*B3=0,Price=B1*94+B2*97+B3*89});
```

$$\left\{ B1 = -\frac{1}{2205}, B2 = \frac{1}{105}, B3 = 0, Price = \frac{1943}{2205} \right\}$$

Notice that the cash flow 0,1,0 can be generated by a combination of bond 1 and bond 2, specifically a short position in bond 1 and a long position in bond 2. Not surprisingly the price of this portfolio is exactly the value of the second discount factor. If we now replace one of the primary bonds, bond 1 or bond 2, with this new portfolio we will again obtain an equivalent market to our original market. This is demonstrated below by solving, utilizing **NarbitB**, for the discount factors in this market and noticing that they are the same as the original discount factors.

```
> NarbitB([[0,1,0],[5,105,0],[4,4,104]],
[1943/2205,97,89]);
```

The no-arbitrage condition is satisfied.

The discount factor for time, 1, *is given by*, $\frac{94}{105}$

The interest rate spanning the time interval, $[0,1]$, *is given by*, 0.1170

The discount factor for time, 2, is given by, $\dfrac{1943}{2205}$
The interest rate spanning the time interval, $[0,2]$, *is given by,* 0.1348
The discount factor for time, 3, is given by, $\dfrac{180577}{229320}$
The interest rate spanning the time interval, $[0,3]$, *is given by,* 0.2699
The function Vdis ($[c1,c2,..]$), values the cashflow $[c1,c2,..]$

Yield and Spot Curves

The financial press reports a measure of a bond's return, which is called a yield. The yield of a bond maturing in n years that pays coupons semiannually, is defined as the rate y that solves the equation

$$\left(\sum_{i=1}^{2n}\left(\frac{c}{2}\right)\left(1+\frac{y}{2}\right)^{(-i)}\right)+FC\left(1+\frac{y}{2}\right)^{(-2n)}=P, \tag{3.4}$$

where c is the coupon of the bond, FC is its face value, and P is its price. Therefore the yield of a bond is a rate such that if payments from the bond obtained in i years are discounted to its present value by $\dfrac{1}{\left(1+\frac{y}{2}\right)^{(2i)}}$, the price of the bond equals its present value. Readers who are already familiar with the concept of *internal rate of return* will immediately recognize that the yield is the same. From equation (3.3) it follows that the yield of a zero-coupon bond, maturing at time t and having a face value of \$1, is the spot rate for time t. Hence, if the market is populated only with such zero-coupon bonds, the concept of a yield would be equivalent to that of a spot rate. Let us calculate the yield for some zero-coupon bonds using the examples above.

Consider the bond with the semiannual cash flow of $(0,0,1)$. Since, for this bond, $c=0$ and $FC=1$, equation (3.4) reduces to equation (3.3). Hence we can solve for the yield of this bond by solving the equation:

$$Vdis\left([0,0,1]\right)=\frac{1}{\left(1+\frac{y}{2}\right)^{3}}$$

There might be multiple solutions to this equation, and not all solutions must be positive numbers or even real numbers. Let us solve for y

numerically (note we use 'fsolve' instead of 'solve')

```
> fsolve(Vdis([0,0,1])=(1+y/2)^(-3));
```

$$0.1658240012$$

Our structure below can solve the equation symbolically and chooses those solutions which are both real and positive.

```
> #evalf(map(proc (x) if type(x,'realcons') and evalf(0
<= x) then x else NULL fi end,\
> [solve(Vdis([0,0,1])=(1+y/2)^(-3))]));
```

$$[0.165824001]$$

If no positive solution exists, a NULL will be returned.

To compare and to confirm that this is the same result as that obtained from **NarbitB**, we can calculate the interest rate which spans the time interval $[0, 1.5]$. This is done below.

```
> (1+%/2)^3-1;(1/Vdis([0,0,1.0]))-1;
```

$$0.269929173$$
$$0.269929172$$

We confirm that the results are those reported by **NarbitB**, albeit 1.5 years is three units of half a year and thus reported as time three in **NarbitB**. The yield of a zero-coupon bond coincides with the spot rate for the length of time corresponding to the maturity of the bond.

A different result is obtained for the case of yields of coupon-paying bonds. We examine now the yield of the bond maturing in a year with a cash flow of $(5, 105, 0)$ and a current price of \$97. To solve for the yield of this bond, equation (3.4) is solved, using values of $\frac{c}{2} = 5$ and $FC = 100$, i.e.,

$$\frac{5}{1+\frac{y}{2}} + \frac{105}{\left(1+\frac{y}{2}\right)^2} = 97$$

```
> fsolve(5/(1+y/2)+105/(1+y/2)^2=97);
```

$$0.1330251780$$

```
> #evalf(map(proc (x) if type(x,'realcons') and evalf(0
<= x) then x else NULL fi end,\
> [solve(5/(1+y/2)+105/(1+y/2)^2=97)])));
```

$$[0.133025178]$$

This time if we solve for the one year spot interest rate, based on this yield, we obtain

```
> (1+%/2)^2-1;(1/Vdis([0,1.0,0]))-1;
```

$$0.137449102$$
$$0.134843026$$

while, on the other hand, the result from **NarbitB** is 0.1348. This is not due to a roundoff error.

This example serves to demonstrate a few key points. The yields of two bonds which mature at the same time may be different even though their maturity dates coincide. It also highlights that the yield measure suffers from some deficiencies. The price of a bond is the discounted value of its future cash flow. This is a consequence of the no-arbitrage condition. Hence, the contribution of each future payment to the price of the bond is the present value of that payment.

The price of a sure dollar to be obtained in a future time period is independent of the bond from which it is to be obtained. The bonds, as explained above, can all be constructed from the same basic building blocks: one dollar obtained at time i. These building blocks must therefore also have the same value in the current time period, regardless of the bonds they are used in. The yield concept, however, is a result of using different discount factors for payments obtained from different bonds at the same time.

As was demonstrated by the example, a dollar obtained from the coupon bond with a maturity of one year (obtaining in one year) was discounted using the yield of the bond, which was different from the one year spot rate. There is no economic rationale for using different discount factors for a dollar which has the same risk characteristics just because it is obtained from a different financial instrument, i.e., a zero-coupon versus a coupon-paying bond. Hence, the calculation of present values using yields (unless it is a zero-coupon bond) is an incorrect procedure.

One should think about the yield to maturity of a bond as some sort of "average" or mixture of returns on the bond. We know that instead of $\dfrac{1}{\left(1+\frac{y}{2}\right)^{(2i)}}$ in equation (3.4) we should have used $\dfrac{1}{\left(1+\frac{r_i}{2}\right)^{(2i)}}$, where r_i is the spot rate for i years. Solving for the yield as is done in equation (3.4), we are actually constraining the spot rate to be the same for all time periods (referred to as a *flat term structure* of interest rates). The y is really some sort of a "mixture" of the different spot rates r_i.

We demonstrate this below by solving for y, in terms of r_{05} and r_1. Given a bond which matures in one year, pays a coupon of $\dfrac{c}{2}$, and has a face value of FC, we display the first of the solutions produced (this is the meaning of the "[1]" below).

```
> assume (r05>0,r1>0,c>0,FC>0);

> simplify(solve((c/2)/(1+r05/2)+(FC+(c/2))/(1+r1/2)^2=
(c/2)/(1+y/2) +(FC+(c/2))/(1+y/2)^2,y)[1]);
```

$$
-\frac{1}{2}\Big(-c\sim r05\sim r1\sim^2 -4c\sim r05\sim r1\sim +2c\sim r1^2 +16FC\sim r05\sim
$$
$$
-\sqrt{2+r05\sim}\,\big(c\sim^2 r05\sim r1\sim^2 +16FC\sim c\sim r1\sim^2 +4c\sim^2 r05\sim
$$
$$
r1\sim +10c\sim^2 r1\sim^2 +64FC\sim^2 r05\sim +64FC\sim c\sim r05\sim
$$
$$
+64FC\sim c\sim r1\sim +20c\sim^2 r05\sim +40c\sim^2 r1\sim +128FC\sim^2
$$
$$
+192FC\sim c\sim +72c\sim^2\big)^{1/2} r1\sim +4c\sim r05\sim +8c\sim r1\sim
$$
$$
+32FC\sim -2\sqrt{2+r05\sim}\,\big(c\sim^2 r05\sim r1\sim^2 +16FC\sim c\sim
$$
$$
r1\sim^2 +4c\sim^2 r05\sim r1\sim +10c\sim^2 r1\sim^2 +64FC\sim^2 r05\sim
$$
$$
+64FC\sim c\sim r05\sim +64FC\sim c\sim r1\sim +20c\sim^2 r05\sim +40c\sim^2 r1\sim
$$
$$
+128FC\sim^2 +192FC\sim c\sim +72c\sim^2\big)^{1/2} +24c\sim\Big)/
$$
$$
\big(c\sim r1\sim^2 +4FC\sim r05\sim +2c\sim r05\sim +4c\sim r1\sim +8FC\sim +8c\sim\big)
$$

The next section elaborates on the term structure of interest rates and on its estimation.

3.2 Smoothing of the Term Structure

The term structure is a function $r(t)$ from the time domain to the interest rate domain i.e., the argument of the function is a time and the value of the function is the spot interest rate at that time. A realistic market requires the knowledge of the discount factors and of the spot rates, not only for times one, two, and three, as in our examples, but for every possible t in some interval $[0, T]$. Sometimes the value of $r(t)$ is required even for a time period which extends beyond the maximum maturity, time three in our example. The common practice in the marketplace is to use the knowledge of the spot rate of interest for the discrete points (1, 2, and 3 in our examples) and generate from these an estimation of a discount factor or a spot rate for each t in a certain time interval. This process is referred to as *smoothing*.

In the scope of this book, we will give only an overview of these techniques. The Appendix will explore these ideas further. Since spot rates are recovered from discount factors, and vice versa, the smoothing can be done in terms of either spot rates or discount factors. Our discussion of smoothing will be with respect to discount factors. Equation (3.2) showed how one determines the discount factor from the spot rate and vice versa.

The general form of smoothing techniques is based on the assumption that the discount factor for time t, $d(t)$, is a function which can be approximated by some structure. Usually, the estimation of the discount factor, denoted below by d_{es}, is of the form

$$d_{es}(t) = \sum_{i=0}^{K} \alpha_i f_i(t), \qquad (3.5)$$

where the f_i are certain functions and the α_i, for $i = 0, \ldots, K$ are numerical coefficients. Hence utilizing (3.5) implicitly assumes that the discount factor function can be written in such a form. The different smoothing techniques are based on choices of the approximating functions f_i, $i = 0, \ldots, K$.

The first step is to choose the set of $K + 1$ functions $f_0, \ldots, f_K$. Next, an optimization problem is solved in order to uncover the values of the α_i, for $i = 0, \ldots, K$, such that the present value of the cash flow from bond i, $\left(\sum_{t=1}^{T_i} d_{es}(t) \right) a_{it}$ where a_{it} is the payment from bond i at time t, is as close as possible to P_i, the market price of bond i.

To this end, one must choose how to measure the distance between the present value, calculated based on d_{es}, and the market price of the bond. Here again, methods differ from one another. Some selection criteria are based on the sum of squared differences and some on the sum of the absolute value of the differences.

The procedure **NarbitB** is also capable of producing the smoothing. It uses the criteria of absolute values for measuring the distance. It is possible to think of, and display, the smoothing process as being done in two phases. In the first phase the discount factors for the discrete payment dates of the bonds are identified. In the second phase an optimization problem is solved. It uncovers the values of the α_i, for $i = 0, \ldots, K$, such that the value of the continuous curve $d_{es}(t)$ is as close as possible to the value of the discount factors at the payment dates. Whenever this is possible, **NarbitB** will demonstrate it with a graph. The reader will find more information about these techniques and the specification of the functions $f_i(t)$ in the Appendix.

Let us now examine an example of smoothing the discount factors. *For simplicity we assume a market in which coupons are paid annually. Hence in* **NarbitB** *and its output, the time unit is a year.* In order to accomplish this, we need to run the procedure **NarbitB** as before, but with the addition of two parameters. We need to specify the number of approximating functions and the name which will be assigned to our new (smooth) discount factors function. This function is termed the *continuous approximation of the discount factors.*

Suppose we would like to have six approximating functions (i.e., $K = 5$), and we would like to call the continuous approximation **ConApp**. We thus need to run **NarbitB** as demonstrated below. The output of the procedure also generates a graph. This is illustrated in the Figure which appears directly following the output. (You can add a zero as a parameter at the end to suppress the graph of the discount factor, i.e., execute 'NarbitB([[105,0,0], [10,110,0], [8,8,108]], [94,97,85], 6,ConApp,0);' instead of the below)

```
> NarbitB([[105,0,0],[10,110,0],[8,8,108]],[94,97,85],6,
ConApp);
```

The no-arbitrage condition is satisfied.

The discount factor for time, 1, is given by, $\dfrac{94}{105}$

The interest rate spanning the time interval, $[0,1]$, *is given by,* 0.1170

The discount factor for time, 2, is given by, $\dfrac{1849}{2310}$
The interest rate spanning the time interval, $[0,2]$, *is given by,* 0.2493
The discount factor for time, 3, is given by, $\dfrac{82507}{124740}$
The interest rate spanning the time interval, $[0,3]$, *is given by,* 0.5119
The function Vdis ([c1,c2,..]), values the cashflow [c1,c2,..]
The continuous discount factor is given by the function, 'ConApp', (.)

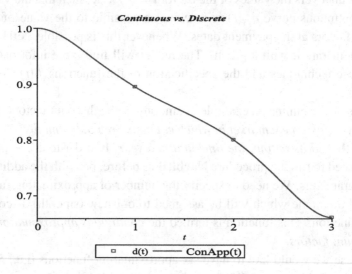

The figure demonstrates the smoothing process. The boxes are the values of the discrete discount factors for the times at which the bonds are making coupon payments, or are repaying the face value. The continuous graph is the result of our approximation. The function **ConApp** estimates the discount factor associated with every t in the interval $[0,3]$ and is being used[2] to value the cash flows payable at times other than 1, 2, or 3. Hence,

---

[2]By interpolation, it is possible to obtain an estimation for discount factors beyond $t = 3$ as well. To this end, one needs to specify the range to which the function should be extrapolated. This is done when a fifth parameter is added to the input. This added parameter can be either 'zero' for surpassing the graph or 'one' to produce the graph. The default value of this parameter is one. To produce the extrapolation, a sixth parameter must be added specifying the right end point of the range. However, in this case, the fifth parameter must be specified. Hence to extrapolate the example in the text for 6.5 years with the graph, one should run:

```
> NarbitB([[105,0,0],[10,110,0],[8,8,108]],[94,97,89],6,
```

```
ConApp,1,6.5);
```

The no-arbitrage condition is satisfied.
The discount factor for time, 1, *is given by,* $\dfrac{94}{105}$
The interest rate spanning the time interval, $[0,1]$, *is given by,* 0.1170
The discount factor for time, 2, *is given by,* $\dfrac{1849}{2310}$
The interest rate spanning the time interval, $[0,2]$, *is given by,* 0.2493
The discount factor for time, 3, *is given by,* $\dfrac{87127}{124740}$
The interest rate spanning the time interval, $[0,3]$, *is given by,* 0.4317
The function Vdis ([c1,c2,..]), values the cashflow [c1,c2,..]
The continuous discount factor is given by the function, 'ConApp', (.)

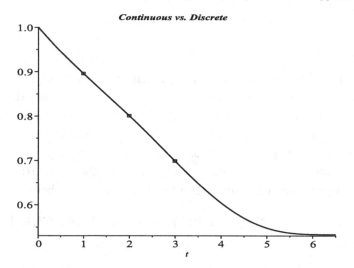

Continuous vs. Discrete

To produce the extrapolation without a graph one should run:

```
> NarbitB([[105,0,0],[10,110,0],[8,8,108]],[94.5,97,89],6,
ConApp,0,6.5);
```

The no-arbitrage condition is satisfied.
The discount factor for time, 1, *is given by,* 0.9000000000
The interest rate spanning the time interval, $[0,1]$, *is given by,* 0.111
The discount factor for time, 2, *is given by,* 0.8000000000
The interest rate spanning the time interval, $[0,2]$, *is given by,* 0.250
The discount factor for time, 3, *is given by,* 0.6981481481
The interest rate spanning the time interval, $[0,3]$, *is given by,* 0.432
The function Vdis ([c1,c2,..]), values the cashflow [c1,c2,..]
The continuous discount factor is given by the function, 'ConApp', (.)

to calculate the present value of $4 obtainable at time 1.75, we perform the following calculation:

```
> ConApp(1.75)*4;
```

$$3.311229336$$

Similarly, to value the cash flow $4 at time 1.75, $4 at time 2.25, and $100 at time 2.75, we calculate

```
> ConApp(1.75)*4+ConApp(2.25)*4+ConApp(2.75)*100;
```

$$74.55914878$$

In this last example, we see that the graph passes through the value of the discrete discount factors obtained directly from the market. In this case above, we manage to fit the estimated discount factor function defined by equation (3.5) to coincide with the discrete factors obtained from the market. This, of course, is not always possible and will depend on the type and number of approximating functions chosen for the approximation. Suppose we attempt to do the same fitting with only three approximation functions. The resultant discount factor function is displayed below:

```
> NarbitB([[105,0,0],[10,110,0],[8,8,108]],[94,97,85],3,
ConApp1);
```

The no-arbitrage condition is satisfied.
The discount factor for time, 1, is given by, $\dfrac{94}{105}$
The interest rate spanning the time interval, $[0,1]$, *is given by,* 0.1170
The discount factor for time, 2, is given by, $\dfrac{1849}{2310}$
The interest rate spanning the time interval, $[0,2]$, *is given by,* 0.2493
The discount factor for time, 3, is given by, $\dfrac{82507}{124740}$
The interest rate spanning the time interval, $[0,3]$, *is given by,* 0.5119
The function Vdis ([c1,c2,..]), values the cashflow [c1,c2,..]
The continuous discount factor is given by the function, 'ConApp1', (.)

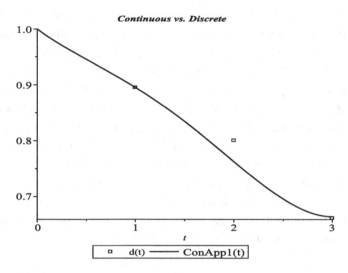

It is now apparent from the figure that we do not have a perfect fit. The procedure **NarbitB** also defines a variable **SumAbsDiv**. It measures the "goodness-of-fit" in terms of the sum of the absolute deviations of the approximation from the actual observations. Thus, if the value of this variable is zero, the fit is perfect. The Appendix elaborates on this point. Each time **NarbitB** is run and a continuous approximation of the term structure is solved for, the variable **SumAbsDiv** is redefined. To check its value, issue the following command:

```
> SumAbsDiv;
```

$$\frac{464839}{111363}$$

Sometimes a perfect fit is not possible and we have to make do with the best approximation possible. In fact, the situation in real world markets is somewhat more complicated. Realistic markets are incomplete. That is, in realistic markets the number of bonds is smaller than the dates on which there are payments from at least one outstanding bond. Therefore if the NA condition is satisfied, there will be multiple solutions for the set of discount factors. However, unlike the equity market, trading in the bond market is done via a set of dealers and not in a central market place. Consequently, the quotes of bond prices are with errors. These errors are due to the structure of the market as well as non synchronization. Not all the bonds are

Fixed Income Fundamentals

traded at all times. Hence the observed prices of the bonds are prices of the last transactions and they may include prices of different times for different bonds. Consequently, even though theoretically there are no arbitrage opportunities, the NA is not satisfied by the observed prices. This however means that the set of equations solved in order to determine the discount factors or the term structure, is inconsistent. This is in spite of the fact that there are more equations than variables. Thus the term structure and or the discount factor function is estimated based on a second-best solution concept (see the explanation in the Appendix). The **NarbitB** procedure is capable of handling such a situation. It will report that the NA is not satisfied and an arbitrage portfolio. However, when graphing the discount factor, it will not show the discrete solution of the discount factor, as it does not exist. This is demonstrated in the example below.

```
> NarbitB([[105,0,0],[10,110,0],[8,8,108]],[94,10,787],
5,ConNNA);
```

The no-arbitrage condition is not satisfied
An arbitrage portfolio is:
Short, 1, of Bond, 1
$$Buy, \frac{881}{10}, of Bond, 2$$
Short, 1, of Bond, 3
The cost of this portfolio is zero
This portfolio produces income of, 768, at time, 1
This portfolio produces income of, 9683, at time, 2
This portfolio produces income of, −108, at time, 3
The continuous discount factor is given by the function, 'ConNNA', (.)

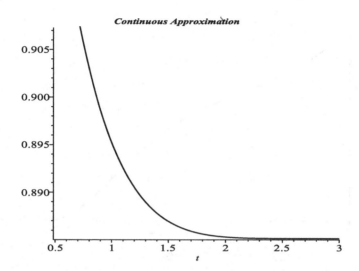

As mentioned before, once we have the continuous approximation of the discount factors, we can generate the continuous approximation of the term structure of interest rates. Let us try an example using only five approximating functions.

```
> NarbitB([[105,0,0],[10,110,0],[8,8,108]],[94,97,85],
5,ConApp2);
```

The no-arbitrage condition is satisfied.

The discount factor for time, 1, is given by, $\dfrac{94}{105}$

The interest rate spanning the time interval, $[0,1]$*, is given by,* 0.1170

The discount factor for time, 2, is given by, $\dfrac{1849}{2310}$

The interest rate spanning the time interval, $[0,2]$*, is given by,* 0.2493

The discount factor for time, 3, is given by, $\dfrac{82507}{124740}$

The interest rate spanning the time interval, $[0,3]$*, is given by,* 0.5119

The function Vdis ([c1,c2,..]), values the cashflow [c1,c2,..]

The continuous discount factor is given by the function, 'ConApp2', (.)

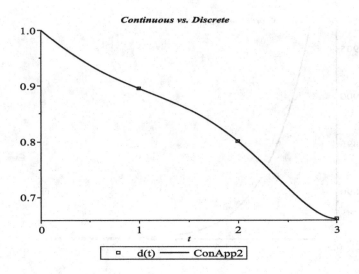

Continuous vs. Discrete

> SumAbsDiv;

$$0$$

As we see in this example, the value of **SumAbsDiv** is zero which means that a perfect fit was possible.[3] The relation between the discount factors, $d(t)$ and the zero coupon curve, $r(t)$, when the letters reported based on semi annual compounding is given by

$$d(t) = \left(\frac{1}{1 + \frac{r(t)}{2}} \right)^{2 \cdot t}.$$

Thus given the value of $d(t)$, denoted in our calculations by **ConApp2(t)**, it is possible to solve for $r(t)$. The command below solves for $r(t)$ as a function of **ConApp2(t)** and defines the term structure function $r(t)$. Specifically, the spot rate for time t, will be given by the function $r(t)$ defined below:

```
> solve(d(t) = (1/(1+(1/2)*r(t)))^(2*t),r(t));
```

$$-\frac{2 \left(e^{\frac{1}{2} \frac{\ln(d(t))}{t}} - 1 \right)}{e^{\frac{1}{2} \frac{\ln(d(t))}{t}}}$$

---

[3]In certain cases multiple solutions exist for the approximation. Hence running the same procedure with the same parameters may result in a different answer.

```
> subs(d(t)=ConApp2(t),%):
> r:=unapply(%,t):
> simplify(r(t));
```

$$\left[-2 + 2\,e^{-\frac{1}{2}}\; \frac{-4\ln(2)-7\ln(3)-\ln(5)-\ln(7)-\ln(11)-\ln(23)+\ln\left(370656\,t^6-569096\,t^5-4900521\,t^4+7474916\,t^3+10467567 \right)}{t} \right.$$

$$\textit{undefined} + \textit{undefined}\,I$$

$$\textit{undefined} + \textit{undefined}\,I$$

```
> r(1);
```

$$-\frac{1}{47}\left(\frac{1}{105}\sqrt{9870}-1\right)\sqrt{9870}$$

```
> r(2):
```

We can now plot this function and see how the spot rate in this market behaves.

```
> plot(r(t),t=0..3,labels=[Time,'Rate'],thickness=2,
title='A Continuous Approximation of a Term
Structure',titlefont=[TIMES,BOLD,10]);
```

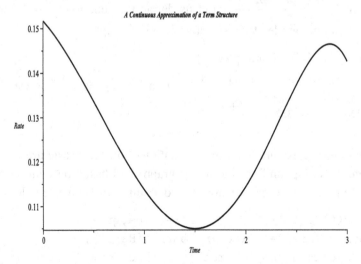

The fact that the rates are reported on an annual basis allows us to compare the rates for different maturities. We see that the rates are decreasing as time increases and then, at about 1.5 years, the rates increase. Different shapes of the term structure are possible. There are a few theories which explain the shape of the term structure of interest rates. These theories are summarized in the Appendix.

3.2.1 Smoothing and Continuous Compounding

Given the discount factor for time t, $d(t)$, (we will measure time in years henceforth), the continuously compounded rate $r(t)$ is the solution to equation (3.7),

$$d(t) = e^{(-r(t)t)}. \tag{3.6}$$

Hence $r(t)$ is given by

$$r(t) = -\frac{\ln(d(t))}{t}. \tag{3.7}$$

Previously we calculated the discount factor function, **ConApp2**, when the units of time were measured in years. Therefore, the continuous approximation of the term structure based on continuous compounding will be given by $-\dfrac{\ln(ConApp2(t))}{t}$. Let us define the function Ts to be the continuously compounded term structure in our example.

```
> Ts:=unapply(-ln(ConApp2(t))/t,t);
```

$$Ts := t \rightarrow -\frac{1}{t}\left(\ln\left(piecewise\left(0 \le t \text{ and } t \le 3, 1 - \frac{193}{1320}t + \frac{105733}{3129840}t^2 + \frac{1868729}{77463540}t^3 \right.\right.\right.$$
$$\left.\left.\left. -\frac{1633507}{103284720}t^4 - \frac{6467}{3521070}t^5 + \frac{26}{21735}t^6, undefined\right)\right)\right)$$

The graphs of the continuous approximation of the term structure based on semiannual compounding (the upper graph) and based on continuous compounding (the lower graph), are plotted together in the figure below.

```
> plot([r(t),Ts(t)],t=0..3,color=[blue,green],
thickness=2,labels=['Time in Years','Rate'],
title='Continuous Approximation of the Term Structure:
Semiannual Compounding vs.  Continuous
Compounding',titlefont=[TIMES,BOLD,8]);
```

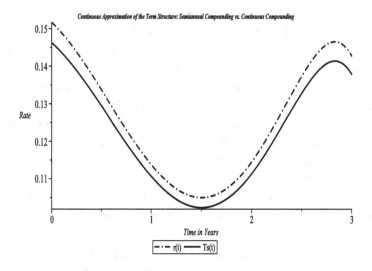

The discount for time *t* in terms of **Ts** is given by the expression $e^{(-Ts(t)t)}$ and is plotted in the following figure. Note that indeed the discount factor is a decreasing function for which the range is between zero and one — as it should be.

```
> plot(exp(-Ts(t)*t),t=0..3,color=[blue],thickness=2,
labels=['Time in Years',' Rate'],title='The discount
factor function implied by the term structure
Ts.',titlefont=[TIMES,BOLD,10]);
```

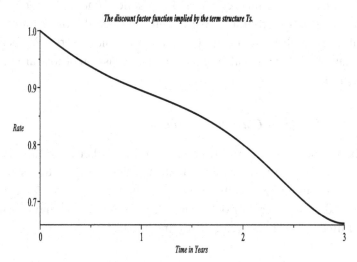

Note that we have not discussed or specified the evolution of the term structure across time. Rather, our discussion has been devoted to the term structure or set of discount factors that prevail in the market at a certain point. It is as if we take a "snapshot" of bond prices in the market at a certain moment, and extract the term structure prevailing in the market at that time. As time passes, the term structure may, and usually does, change. Many valuation methods, as we will see later, require some specification of a model governing the evolution of the term structure.

Yet, there are many instruments and types of cash flows that could be valued given only the current discount factor $d(t)$. The rest of this chapter is devoted to two such examples. Some other instruments of these types are valued in the next chapters. Not surprisingly, most of the cash flows we are able to value in this manner (and their replicating strategies) are static. They do not require (optimal) actions in the future and the valued cash flows are fixed and known (not stochastic) as of the the current time. These cash flows do not include any random or stochastic components that depend on a realization of some future interest rates that are not known at the present time. There is, however, an exception to this rule and this is the cash flow valued in our second example in this chapter.

3.3   Forward Rate

We offer two explanations for the concept of forward rates: a classical explanation that is more theoretical, and a practical one. The former is related to valuation by arbitrage. We therefore utilize the opportunity to review valuation both by replication and via discount factors. We begin our examination of the classical approach to the discussion of forward rates with an example.

3.3.1   *Forward Rate: A Classical Approach*

Let $r(t)$ be the interest rate which prevails in the market from time zero to time t. For simplicity, we assume that the rates are quoted based on continuous compounding and that time is measured in years. Hence, a dollar invested at time zero for one year will grow into $e^{r(1)\cdot 1}$ and a dollar invested at time zero for two years will grow into $e^{r(2)\cdot 2}$.

There is another way to invest money from time zero to time two. The dollar could be invested from time zero to time one, and then invested from time one to time two at the rate that will prevail in the market at that time. At the current time this rate is unknown, as it is a random variable. Under this investment strategy, a dollar invested from time zero to time one will be worth $e^{r(1)}$ at time one. This amount is then invested for one further time period at the rate prevailing in the market at that time. If the dollar had been invested for two time periods at the prevailing rate of interest covering the interval from time zero to time two, it would have grown to a value of $e^{r(2)\cdot2}$.

Let us denote by $x_1(1,2)$ the (as yet unknown) interest rate from time one to time two. The subindex 1 of x means that this is the interest rate that will prevail at time one and the $(1,2)$ means that this rate is spanning the time interval $[1,2]$. Hence, the dollar at time zero amounts to $e^{r(1)}$ at time one, which grows to $e^{r(1)}e^{x_1(1,2)}$ at the end of two time periods. The value of $x_1(1,2)$ which solves

$$e^{r(1)}e^{x(1,2)} = e^{r(2)\cdot2} \tag{3.8}$$

is the *forward rate* from time one to time two, as of time zero. As has been our custom before, we omit the index for zero and use two indexes in order to denote the span of time for which this forward rate is applicable. That is, we use $r(1,2)$ instead of $r_0(1,2)$ in the same manner we use $r(t)$ instead of $r_0(t)$ when the span is $[0,t]$.

The intuitive meaning of the forward rate is that it is a rate implicit in the spot rate which will prevail in the market from time one to time two. If an investor perceives that $r(2)$ is not high enough to induce the investor to pursue a two-period investment horizon, then that investor will prefer to use a rollover strategy. The investor invests for one period, from time zero to time one, and then "rolls over" the investment for another period, from time one to time two. From the definition of a forward rate it is apparent that $r(1,2)$ is the rate that makes our "rollover" strategy equivalent to the "buy and hold" one. The rates prevailing in the market are those which induce an equilibrium: $r(1,2)$ is the value which makes these two strategies equivalent. Hence, these rates convey information about the market's anticipation of future rates which will prevail from time one to time two.

This discussion was based on an example. One can extract the forward rate as of time zero for any future time period t_1 to t_2 ($t_1 < t_2$). A dollar invested from time zero to time t_1 will grow to be $e^{r(t_1)t_1}$ dollars. If the dollar is invested from time zero to time t_2, it will grow to $e^{r(t_2)t_2}$ and $r(t_1,t_2)$ will be the solution to

$$e^{r(t_1)t_1}e^{r(t_1,t_2)(t_2-t_1)} = e^{r(t_2)t_2}. \tag{3.9}$$

Thus $r(t_1,t_2)$ denoted by r12 below will be given by:

```
> solve({exp(rt1*t1)*exp(r12*(t2-t1))=exp(rt)*t2},
{r12});
```

$$\left\{ r12 = -\frac{\ln(t2)+rt-rt1\,t1}{-t2+t1} \right\}$$

In our example we defined the continuously compounded term structure of interest rates as the function **Ts**(t). It is redefined here again in the steps below:

```
> NarbitB([[105,0,0],[10,110,0],[8,8,108]],[94,97,85],
5,ConApp2):
```

> *The no-arbitrage condition is satisfied.*
> *The discount factor for time, 1, is given by,* $\dfrac{94}{105}$
> *The interest rate spanning the time interval,* $[0,1]$, *is given by,* 0.1170
> *The discount factor for time, 2, is given by,* $\dfrac{1849}{2310}$
> *The interest rate spanning the time interval,* $[0,2]$, *is given by,* 0.2493
> *The discount factor for time, 3, is given by,* $\dfrac{82507}{124740}$
> *The interest rate spanning the time interval,* $[0,3]$, *is given by,* 0.5119
> *The function Vdis ([c1,c2,..]), values the cashflow [c1,c2,..]*
> *The continuous discount factor is given by the function,* 'ConApp2', (.)

In our example we defined the continuously compounded term structure of interest rates as the function **Ts**(t).

```
> Ts:=unapply(-ln(ConApp2(t))/t,t);
```

$$Ts := t \to -\frac{1}{t}\left(\ln\left(piecewise\left(0 \le t \text{ and } t \le 3, 1-\frac{193}{1320}t+\frac{105733}{3129840}t^2+\frac{1868729}{77463540}t^3\right.\right.\right.$$
$$\left.\left.\left. -\frac{1633507}{103284720}t^4-\frac{6467}{3521070}t^5+\frac{26}{21735}t^6, undefined\right)\right)\right)$$

We can also now define the function $\mathbf{Fr}(t_1, t_2)$, based on equation (3.10), as the forward rate from time t_1 to time t_2.

```
> Fr:=(t1,t2)->(Ts(t2)*t2-Ts(t1)*t1)/(t2-t1);
```

$$Fr := (t1, t2) \rightarrow \frac{Ts(t2)\,t2 - Ts(t1)\,t1}{t2 - t1}$$

The function $\mathbf{Fr}$ should always have the second argument t_2 greater than the first argument t_1.

Armed with the function so defined, we can plot it together with the term structure and see how the term structure is related to the forward rate. In the following figure, the forward rate (the graph with the lower y-intercept) is graphed together with the term structure (the graph with the higher y-intercept), where the time domain is 0.5 to 3 and the forward rate is graphed from time 0.5 to any time t in the interval $[0.5, 3]$.

```
> plot([Ts(t),Fr(.5,t)],t=0.5..3,color=[green,red],
thickness=2,labels=[Time,Rate],title='The Forward Rate
and the Term Structure',titlefont=[TIMES,BOLD,10]);
```

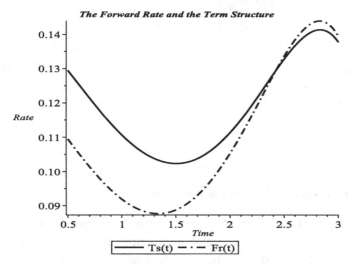

We can also display the forward rate from time t_1 to t_2 where we let t_1 range from 0 to 3 and t_2 from t_1 to 3. This is displayed in the following figure. Note that the graph of the forward rate in the preceding figure is a slice of the graph in the following one, for $t_1 = 0.5$.

```
> plot3d(Fr(t1,t2),t1=0..3,t2=t1..3,axes=normal,
labels=['Initial Time','End
Time',Rate],orientation=[-162,56], title='The Forward
Rate from Time t1 to t2:    0<t1<3,
t1<t2<3',axes=framed,titlefont=[TIMES,BOLD,10]);
```

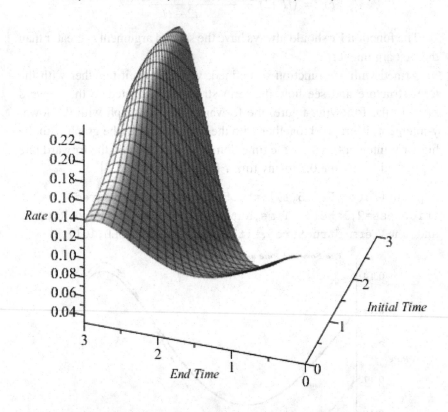

3.3.2 *Forward Rate: A Practical Approach*

A forward rate (not to be confused with a forward agreement or with a forward price) is not only a theoretical concept but an implied rate to prevail in the future. It is actually possible to borrow at this rate. It is the rate at which an investor can secure, or commit to, a loan now (at time zero) which will be taken at some future time t_1 and be repaid at a later time t_2. Hence, in a sense, the forward rate resembles a forward contract and perhaps its name originates from the similarity.

Coincide an agreement made now for delivery of a certain amount of money, x at time t_1 and repayment of x plus interest at time t_2. The interest rate $r_0(t_1, t_2)$, is agreed upon now at time 0. Thus the amount paid back at time t_2 will be $x(1 + r_0(t_1, t_2))$ where we denote by $r_0(t_1, t_2)$ the interest rate paid over the time interval $[t_1, t_2]$. (For simplicity we suppress the 0 subindex and use the notion $r(t_1, t_2)$ instead of $r_0(t_1, t_2)$). Let us demonstrate the above with an example.

Consider a bond market with three periods and three bonds as specified in **NarbitB**:

```
> NarbitB([[105,0,0],[10,110,0],[8,8,108]],[94,97,85]);
```

The no-arbitrage condition is satisfied.
The discount factor for time, 1, is given by, $\dfrac{94}{105}$
The interest rate spanning the time interval, $[0,1]$, *is given by,* 0.1170
The discount factor for time, 2, is given by, $\dfrac{1849}{2310}$
The interest rate spanning the time interval, $[0,2]$, *is given by,* 0.2493
The discount factor for time, 3, is given by, $\dfrac{82507}{124740}$
The interest rate spanning the time interval, $[0,3]$, *is given by,* 0.5119
The function Vdis ([c1,c2,..]), values the cashflow [c1,c2,..]

First we would like to check if it is possible to have a certain self-financing portfolio in this market. The reader will recall that a self-financing portfolio is one with a zero cash flow at time zero. We are interested in a self-financed portfolio with a cash inflow of $1 at time two followed by a cash outflow at time three. If such a portfolio exists in this market, we would like to know what the cash outflow will be at time three.

Since there are no arbitrage opportunities in this market, as was just confirmed, every self-financing portfolio which has a zero cash flow at time one and a cash inflow of $1 at time two, should have a cash outflow at time three. To this end, we solve the system of equations (3.10) where B_1, B_2, and B_3 stand for the holdings of bonds one, two, and three in the portfolio, respectively. The cash outflow at time three is denoted by RF and is also one of the variables for which we seek a solution.

$$94B_1 + 97B_2 + 85B_3 = 0$$

$$105B_1 + 10B_2 + 8B_3 = 0$$
$$110B_2 + 8B_3 = 1$$
$$108B_3 = RF.$$

(3.10)

This system of equations in (3.10) is solved below.

```
> solve({B1*94+B2*97+B3*85=0,B1*105+B2*10+B3*8=0,
B1*0+B2*110+B3*8=1,B1*0+B2*0+B3*108=RF},{B1,B2,B3,RF});
```

$$\left\{ B1 = -\frac{37}{412535}, B2 = \frac{8173}{825070}, B3 = -\frac{1849}{165014}, RF = -\frac{99846}{82507} \right\}$$

Hence, we see that if we hold a long position in bond two of $\frac{8173}{825070}$ units, a short position in bond one of $-\frac{37}{412535}$ units, and a short position in bond three of $-\frac{1849}{165014}$ units, the cost of this portfolio is zero. It produces a cash inflow of \$1 at time two and a cash outflow of $-\frac{99846}{82507}$ dollars at time three. The portfolio is purchased at time zero, at which time no cash changes hands. At time two, the buyer receives \$1 and then repays the loan with $\frac{99846}{82507}$ dollars at time three. The buyer is essentially "buying" this portfolio at time zero to secure a loan which will be in effect from time two to time three. Let us see what interest rate the borrower who purchases this portfolio is paying.

We refer to the transaction above as a synthetic loan since it is the same sort of cash flow as a loan, but it is not a loan in the conventional sense. The cash flows are those of a loan which is agreed upon today but which will be transacted at time two. The interest rate implicit in this loan is the value of r which solves the equation

$$1 + r = \frac{99846}{82507}.$$

(3.11)

Hence, the implicit rate is

```
> solve((1+r)=99846/82507);
```

$$\frac{17339}{82507}$$

Thus, given the current market conditions, the investor can secure, at time zero, a loan which will be transacted at time two and repaid at time three with an interest rate of $\dfrac{17339}{82507}$. This rate is referred to as the *forward rate* from time two to time three. In the same manner, the forward rate from time one to time two can be calculated. This is left as an exercise for the reader.

The above argument demonstrates the concept of a forward rate by the replication argument. Let us see how the same concept will be explained utilizing the discount factor valuation approach. Consider the cash flow generated above. It costs zero to generate, produces \$1 at time two, and $-\$(1+r)$ at time three. We would, thus, like to find the numerical value of r such that the value of the cash flow $[0, 1, -1-r]$ will be zero at time zero. That is, valuing from the point of view of time zero, what should a person return at time three for a dollar he or she receives at time two. This can be calculated easily by the **Vdis** function. We want to solve for the value of r such that $Vdis([0,1,-1-r]) = 0$. This is submitted to Maple.

```
> solve(Vdis([0,1,-1-r])=0);
```

$$\frac{17339}{82507}$$

Indeed, the same value for the forward rate is obtained. The concept of a forward rate is thus the rate, $r(t_1,t_2)$, at which one can secure at time zero a loan from time $0 < t_1$ to some time t_2, $t_1 < t_2$. If the market is not complete, we cannot be sure that these types of loans can actually be executed by purchasing certain portfolio combinations. Nevertheless, the concept of a forward rate has been extended for every t_1 and t_2 making use of the continuous approximation of the discount factors.

We can then offer yet another explanation for forward rates to justify equation (3.9). Given an approximation of the continuously compounded interest rate $r(t)$ spanning the time interval $[0,t]$, proceed in the following manner. Consider an investor who borrows a dollar at time zero which will be returned at time t_2. In other words the investor receives $e^{(-r(t_2)t_2)}$ dollars at time zero. This amount is immediately invested until time t_1, where $t_1 < t_2$. Hence, at time t_1 the investor will have $e^{(r(t_1)t_1)}e^{(-r(t_2)t_2)}$ dollars and will have to give back one dollar at time t_1. The interest rate implicit in such a loan, reported as a continuously compounded rate, is the $r(t_1,t_2)$

that solves

$$e^{(r(t_1)t_1)}e^{(-r(t_2)t_2)}e^{(r(t_1,t_2)(t_2-t_1))} = 1. \tag{3.12}$$

Multiplying (3.12) by $e^{(r(t_2)t_2)}$ results in equation (3.10), and hence the same solution for the forward rate $r(t_1, t_2)$ is obtained.

3.4 A Variable Rate Bond

A *variable rate bond*, occasionally referred to as a *floater*, is a bond that has no fixed rate of interest. Instead, it pays the interest rate prevailing in the market at the relevant time. Hence, as opposed to the bonds we dealt with until now, we cannot specify at the current time the future cash flow of this bond. Instead, the future cash flow will vary with the interest rate that prevails in the market.

Consider a variable rate bond with a face value of FC that pays a coupon periodically, e.g., semiannually. At the beginning of each time period the interest rate spanning the period is known. The bond will thus pay, at the end of each period, the interest rate spanning that period i.e., a certain percentage of FC. If, for example, the bond was issued now, at time t_0, and pays at times $t_1, t_2, \ldots, t_n$ then at time t_0 the interest rate spanning the time interval (t_0, t_1), the spot rate would be known. Let us denote it by $r_{t0}(t_0, t_1)$. The interest rate that will prevail in the market at time t_1 spanning the time interval $[t_1, t_2]$ is not known at time t_0. Let us denote it by $r_{t1}(t_1, t_2)$, not to be confused with the forward rate $r(t_1, t_2)$, which in this notation will be $r_{t0}(t_1, t_2)$. The bond will therefore pay $FCr_{t0}(t_0, t_1)$ at time t_1, at time t_2 it will pay $FCr_{t1}(t_1, t_2)$, and so on. Hence, we do not know with certainty the complete payment schedule from the bond in the future. We only know with certainty, the next payment of the bond. The last coupon payment at time t_n will be $FCr_{t_{n-1}}(t_{n-1}, t_n)$.

While we only know with certainty the payoff at the end of period one, it is still possible to value such a bond. Perhaps the simplest way to value such a bond is to show that one needs FC at t_0 to replicate the cash flow of a floater. At time t_0, invest FC to time t_1 at the spot rate $r(t_0, t_1)$. Collect $FC(1 + r_{t_0}(t_0, t_1))$ at time t_1, and invest FC to time t_2 at the spot rate $r_{t_1}(t_1, t_2)$. The net cash flow at t_1 is $FC(r_{t_0}(t_0, t_1))$. At time t_2 collect $FC(1 + r_{t_1}(t_1, t_2))$ and invest FC at the spot rate $r_{t_2}(t_2, t_3)$. The net cash flow at t_2 is $FC(r_{t_1}(t_1,t_2))$. Continue in this manner up to the maturity of the bond. At maturity time, the face value FC plus the last coupon is returned to the buyer, thus the floater's cash flow is replicated. Hence the price of the floater is its face value FC. We demonstrate below two additional arguments for valuing such a bond. The first argument is built upon the replication and discount factor valuation. It exemplifies the type of nondeterministic (random) cash flows we can value without specifying a model for the behavior of the term structure. The second argument is based on logic.

Recall the discussion of an equity swap in Section 1.3. There, we discussed methods of replicating the return on a certain index. The problem we face here is quite similar. This issue is also related to our explanation of the forward rate. Let us see how we can replicate now at time zero, the return on FC dollars invested at the risk-free rate that will prevail in the market from time t_1 to time t_2, (where $0 < t_1 < t_2$). That is, we want to generate now at time 0 a cash flow of $FC \cdot r_{t_1}(t_1,t_2)$ to be received at time t_2. Note that we do not know what the actual cash flow will be since the value of $r_{t_1}(t_1,t_2)$ is a random variable that is currently unknown. We nevertheless can find a replicating strategy that requires actions only at the current time and whose cost is known with certainty at the current time. Such a strategy is referred to as 'static' or 'buy and hold'.

Not only are we able to replicate at FC dollars invested at the risk-free rate from time t_1 to time t_2 and payable at time t_2, but we already derived the cost of such a strategy. This is explained in the discussion of Section 1.3. We repeat this explanation here in terms of the risk-free rate.

Consider the following investment strategy. At time t_0 borrow the amount $\$FC \cdot d(t_2)$ to be repaid at time t_2 and immediately invest an amount of $\$FCd(t_1)$ until time t_1. Since $d(t_2) < d(t_1)$ the amount invested, $\$FC \cdot d(t_1)$, is larger then the amount borrowed, $\$FC \cdot d(t_2)$. The out-of-pocket cost of this strategy is thus $FC \cdot d(t_1) - FC \cdot d(t_2)$. At time t_1 the amount invested at t_0, $FC \cdot d(t_1)$, will be worth FC.

At time t_1 the $\$FC$ will be invested until time t_2 at the rate prevailing in the market at that time, $r_{t_1}(t_1,t_2)$. Thus at time t_2 it will be worth $FC(1 + r_{t_1}(t_1,t_2))$. At t_2 the loan that was initiated at time t_0 should be paid back. Since the loan principal was $\$FCd(t_2)$, the amount to be paid back is FC.

Note that the borrowing and lending discussed here do not necessarily require borrowing from a bank. Instead, one may interpret "lending" or "borrowing" as the purchase of a portfolio of bonds that produces the required cash flow. Thus "borrowing" is a short position in a certain bond portfolio and "lending" is a long position. Of course it may be the case that in order to generate a borrowing-like cash flow, we may require a portfolio that is composed of both short and long positions. One of the exercises in this chapter elaborates on this point.

Let us consider the cost and payoff from the above described strategy. The cost of this strategy is the amount in excess of the loan that we had to invest at t_0, namely, $FC \cdot d(t_1) - FC \cdot d(t_2)$. The payoff from the strategy is the payoff at the end of time t_2, $FC(1 + r_{t_1}(t_1, t_2))$, minus the cost of paying back the loan, FC. The net payoff is therefore $FC - FC(1 + r_{t_1}(t_1, t_2))$, which is equal to $FC \cdot r_{t_1}(t_1, t_2)$. The payoff at t_2 is the return on FC invested from time t_1 to time t_2, i.e., $FC \cdot r_{t_1}(t_1, t_2)$. In terms of $d(t)$ the cost at t_0 of replicating this return is

$$FC \cdot d(t_1) - FC \cdot d(t_2). \tag{3.13}$$

By the same argument, the cost of replicating the return on $\$FC$ invested at the risk-free rate from time t_2 to time t_3, i.e., replicating $FC \cdot r_{t_2}(t_2, t_3)$ payable at time t_3, will be

$$FC \cdot d(t_2) - FC \cdot d(t_3). \tag{3.14}$$

Assume that the bond matures at time t_3. Hence at time t_3 the buyer of such a bond (playing the same role as the lender in the strategy described above) will also get back $\$FC$ whose cost at t_0 is

$$FC\,d(t_3). \tag{3.15}$$

In addition, at time t_1 the buyer will get the return on FC invested from time t_0 to time t_1 whose cost, based on the same argument as above, will be

$$FC - FC \cdot d(t_1). \tag{3.16}$$

Hence the cost of producing this cash flow at times t_1, t_2, and t_3 is the sum of equations (3.13), (3.14), (3.15) and equation (3.16). The total is therefore:

```
> (FC*d(t1)-FC*d(t2))+(FC*d(t2)-FC*d(t3))+(FC*d(t3))
+(FC-FC*d(t1));
```

$$FC$$

The initial cost of the variable-rate bond is thus its face value. The assumption of the bond maturing at time t_3 does not affect the end result. One can easily see that this will be the case for a bond maturing after n payment periods as well. Note, however, that we assumed that the bond was issued at t_0. A slight modification is needed to calculate the value of the bond as of some time between payment times after the issuing time. For example, if the value of the bond is calculated at some midpoint v, between t_0 and t_1, its value will be calculated based on the discount factor function estimated at time v. If we denote this discount function by $d_v(t)$ the bond value will be

$$FC \cdot d_v(t_1) + FC \cdot r_{t_0}(t_0, t_1) d_v(t_1). \tag{3.17}$$

We leave the derivation of this result as an exercise.

There is another approach for calculating the value of a variable rate bond. This approach applies a simple logical argument. Recall that the bond is paying at times $(t_1, \ldots, t_n)$. At time t_{n-1} (immediately after the coupon payment) the value of that bond must be its face value, FC. An investor holding that bond at time t_{n-1} will receive, at time t_n, the face value back and the interest rate prevailing at that time in the market.

Thus, when we discount the future value of the bond at time t_{n-1}, we are discounting $FC(1+r)$ (where r is the interest rate from time t_{n-1} to time t_n) by the discount factor, $\dfrac{1}{1+r}$. Hence, the value of the bond at time t_{n-1} is FC. Now, at time t_{n-2} (immediately after the coupon payment) the value of the bond must again be FC. This is because the value of the bond at time t_{n-1} is FC and the investor holding the bond at time t_{n-2} will receive an interest payment at time t_{n-1}.

At time t_{n-1} the interest payment is according to the rate prevailing in the market from time t_{n-2} to t_{n-1} and the investor will also have the bond, the value of which, at that time is FC. Thus, by the same argument as above, the value of the bond at time t_{n-2} is FC. Proceeding in the same manner we can show that the value of the bond at time zero is again FC.

3.5   Concluding Remarks

In this chapter the no-arbitrage condition was shown to be the source of the existence of the discount factors and thus of the term structure of interest rates. This chapter also explained how the term structure is estimated from bond prices and how a continuous approximation is generated. The concept of a forward rate was introduced and was linked to a valuation by arbitrage.

The discount factor function $d(t)$ or equivalently the term structure of interest rates $r(t)$ is used to value cash flows across time. The discount factor implied in the prices of government bonds can be used to discount only the time value of money. The convention is to perceive government bonds as free from default risk. In contrast, certain bonds, like corporate bonds, are subject to default risk. Thus their market prices reflect the possibility of default. There are, of course, different categories of risk and most markets in the world have rating agencies that classify the default risk of bonds.

The existence of a market populated with enough bonds in a certain grade allows us to estimate the discount factor for the grade of bonds. This is performed in exactly the same manner as we have demonstrated in the "risk-free" government bond market. The discount factor of a grade of bonds is the price of a dollar at time t but subject to the risk of default. Therefore, if $d(t)$ is the discount factor obtained from the government bonds and $d_f(t)$ is the discount factor one obtains from a certain group of risky bonds, the latter should be smaller than the former, otherwise arbitrage opportunities will arise.

Can you delineate an arbitrage portfolio if the relation would have been reversed, i.e., if $d(t) < d_f(t)$? Note, that in this case the arbitrage portfolio produces a sure profit (with no initial investment) at the initiation time, and a positive probability of making further profit in the future. We leave this as an exercise for the reader. Hence, if we need to value certain cash flows across time that are not of the risk-free category, we can do so provided we have the term structure for this type of risk. We shall see an example of such an application in the case of a forward rate agreement discussed in the next chapter.

3.6   Questions and Problems

Problem 1

Consider the following bond market:

	Time 1	Time 2	Time 3	Prices
Bond 1	105	0	0	96
Bond 2	8	108	0	97
Bond 3	3	3	103	89

(1) Check whether this is an arbitrage-free market by using the **NarbitB** procedure.
(2) Explain why the rate *R1* spanning the time interval $[0,1]$ is determined by solving $Vdis([1+R1,0,0]) = 1$.
(3) What are the interest rates spanning the time intervals $[0,1]$, $[0,2]$ and $[0,3]$?
(4) What are the interest rates, as of the current time, spanning the time intervals $[1,2]$, $[2,3]$, $[1,3]$? (You may solve it utilizing the function **Vdis** and setting an equation that each rate must satisfy.)
(5) Identify a portfolio that costs zero, pays zero at time 1, pays a certain amount at time 2, and requires a payment of $1 at time 3. What must the payment of the portfolio be at time 2? Is it necessary for such a portfolio to include a short position?
(6) What is the relation between your answer to the above and the rate spanning the time interval $[2,3]$?
(7) Generate a continuous approximation of the discount factor function that perfectly fits the discrete discount factors. You may use the procedure **NarbitB**.
(8) What is your estimation for the forward rate from time 0.5 to time 2.5?

Problem 2

Assume that $R1$ and $R2$ are the spot rates corresponding to times t_1 and t_2, $t_1 < t_2$, respectively, where the units of time are measured in years.

(1) Show that $R1 < R2$.
(2) Identify an arbitrage strategy in a market where $R2 < R1$.
(3) Determine the corresponding annual interest rates assuming semi-annual compounding.
(4) Let $r1$ and $r2$ be the rates solved for in part 3 of this question. Does the no-arbitrage condition imply that $r1 < r2$ (prove or provide a counterexample)?

Problem 3

Show that if r_n is the annual rate corresponding to time n (measured in years) and is compounded m times per year, the spot rate can be determined as $R_n = \left(1 + \dfrac{r_n}{m}\right)^{nm} - 1.$

Problem 4

Assume the following structure for the bond market.

Time 1	*Time 2*	*Time 3*	*Prices*
107	0	0	94
9	109	0	100
5	5	105	93

(1) Verify in two different ways that the market is arbitrage-free.
(2) Consider the three zero coupon bonds stipulated in the table below:

The Term Structure, its Estimation, and Smoothing

	Maturity Time	Face Value	Price
Bond 1	1	1000	940
Bond 2	2	1090	1000
Bond 3	3	1000	854

Are these prices the "no-arbitrage" prices of the bonds? Justify your answer by pricing these cash flows utilizing the replication method. Identify an arbitrage position if the price(s) admits arbitrage.

(3) Construct a new market consisting of only zero coupon bonds with face values of $100, maturing at times 1, 2, and 3 such that the cash flows of the primary bonds have the same prices as in the original market.

(4) Prove that the new market, constructed in part 3 of this question, actually implies that every cash flow has the same price in both markets.

Problem 5

Consider the following bond market where the time is measured in years and bonds are paying semiannually:

	Time 1	Time 2	Prices
Bond 1	108	0	102.6
Bond 2	2	102	93.7

(1) Give an example of two coupon bonds maturing at time 2 that have different yields.

(2) What would be a yield on a zero-coupon bond maturing at time 2?

(3) Can you give an example of a coupon-paying bond that has a yield the same as the one from a zero coupon bond?

(4) In general, is it possible that a zero coupon bond and a coupon bond having the same face value, both maturing at time 2, will have the same yield? Justify your answer.

Problem 6

Let r_n and r_m be two annual interest rates, in the same market, corresponding to the same maturity but being compounded n and m times per year,
respectively.

  (1) Show that $r_m < r_n$ if and only if $n < m$.
  (2) Show that, for all $n < m$, the term structure of interest rates plotted
       in terms of compounding n times per year is always above the one
       plotted in terms of compounding m times per year.
  (3) Show that a term structure of interest rates plotted in terms of con-
       tinuous compounding is always below the one plotted for any finite
       compounding.

Problem 7

Use the data of Problem 1 to find the value at $t = 0.5$ of a \$100 face value
variable rate bond that pays coupons at times 1, 2, and 3.

Problem 8

Provide an example of a bond market with three bonds and three discrete
payoff periods such that:

- the no-arbitrage condition is satisfied;
- the market is complete; and
- the term structure is flat, i.e., the spot rate (based on annual compounding) is the same for every time t.

  Confirm your results by plotting the term structure in this market.

Problem 9

Consider the market in Problem 1 but where the prices of the bonds are 93,
96, and 90 for bond 1, 2, and 3, respectively. How would you answer parts
3, 4, 5, 6, and 8 of Problem 1, given the new prices?

Problem 10

Delineate an arbitrage strategy if the relation between the discount function estimated from the government bonds, $d()$, and the discount factor obtained from a certain group of risky bonds, $d^f(t)$ would be $d(t) < d^f(t)$. Note that in this case the arbitrage portfolio produces a sure profit at the initiation time, with no initial investment, and a positive probability of making further profit in the future.

Problem 11

Consider the bond market introduced in Problem 4. Devise a portfolio that would replicate a loan of $1 commencing at time 1 to be repaid at time 2. What is the price of this portfolio now? What is the interpretation of the price of such a portfolio?

Problem 12

Consider the bond market introduced in Problem 1.

(1) Devise a portfolio that would have a cash flow of $(c, c, 100+c)$ for some positive number c.
(2) Find such c that would make the value of this cash flow $100 today.
(3) What is an interpretation of c found in 2?
(4) Based on your answer to 3, what will be the yield in this market of a 7.300285163% bond maturing at time 3
(5) Construct a portfolio that would constitutes a loan of $200 commencing at time 1 to be repaid at time 3 with an intermediate interest payment at time 2 of $10.
(6) Identify the short and the long positions of the portfolio in 4.

Problem 13

Suppose you have a bond market and at every point in time in the future a continuous approximation of the discount function is available. Consider a variable rate bond with the face value FC that pays a coupon at some prespecified times $t_1 < t_2 < \ldots < t_n$. Assume it is now time v such that

$t_i < v < t_{i+1}$, for some $i = 1, 2, \ldots, n-1$. Prove that the value of this bond now is

$$FCd_v(t_{i+1}) + FCr_{t_i}(t_i, t_{i+1})d_v(t_{i+1})$$

where d_v is the discount function as of time v and $r_{t_i}(t_i, t_{i+1})$ is the interest rate spanning the time $[t_i, t_{i+1}]$.

Problem 14

Go to http://www.financialpost.com/markets/data/money-yields-can_us.html.

Find the latest yield for 1-month, 3-month and 6-month and the 3-month Forward Rate Agreement for 3-month, 6-month and 9-month.

Use the above yields to estimate the 3-month Forward Rate Agreement for 3-month and the 6-month Forward Rate Agreement for 6-month.

Use the NarbitB procedure to estimate a continuous discount factor function (with 2 approximating functions) based on the latest yield for 3-month, 6-month and 1-year.

Extract the 3-month Forward Rate Agreement for 2-month 1-month and 3-month, and compare the last two rates you estimated to the reported forward rates.

Note: please see http://www.fin.gc.ca/invest/bondprice-eng.asp for the convention in Canada to quote Treasury bills in yield terms.

Hint: The NarbitB procedure implicitly assumes equal time periods between the dates on which bonds prices are sampled and consecutive payment times. Use three months as the length of the time period. Therefore, the payoff array will have some zeros to keep the length of time in the correct way. That is, a payment of $1000 three months from the sampling time of the prices will be represented as [1000,0,0,0,], a payment of $1000 in 6 months will be represented as [0,1000,0,0] and a payment of $1000 in one year as [0,0,0,1000]. The prices of the T-Bills can be calculated based on the yields as per the explanation in http://www.fin.gc.ca/invest/bondprice-eng.asp.

Problem 15

Go to http://www.bankofcanada.ca/rates/interest-rates/bond-yield-curves/ and read the explanation on this page. Note the method by which the Bank of Canada generate the zero coupon curve is slightly different than the on used by the NarbitB. As well Bank of Canada zero-coupon yield curve is defined using the continuously compounded rate of interest see http://www.bankofcanada.ca/publications/glossaries/glossary/#term-287.

Download the .csv file for the zero coupon bond on November 2 2007, use Retrieve data for the following periods, from Start (or single date) 2007-11-02 to 2007-11-02. Open the file with Excel and save it as a .xls (NOT .xlsx) file with the name Nove07.xls.

Retrieved the same data for 2009-9-30 and save it as Nove09.xls.

(1) Deduct the price of a zero coupon bond maturing within 0.25 of a year to one year as of the dates 2007-11-02 and 2009-9-30.
(2) Use the procedure NarbitB to solve for the discount factor function over the same periods.
(3) Solve and graph the term structure based on the continuously compounded rate of return.

Can you relate the shape of the graphs to economic events at that time?

3.7 Appendix

3.7.1 *Theories of the Shape of the Term Structure*

There are several theories which help describe the shape of the term structure of interest rates. Some compete with one another. Others can be viewed more reasonably as complementary. Taken all together, they provide a sensible description of the underlying determinants of the shape of the yield curve.

The Unbiased Expectations Theory

The unbiased expectations theory posits that investors are risk-neutral. Investors, regardless of their investment time horizon, will choose the instruments with the highest return. They require no additional compensation for any perceived risk associated with the time frame involved. There is a direct relationship between the spot rates in the market place and the forward rates of interest. Let r_1 be the one-period spot interest rate (that is, the rate of interest which prevails from time period zero to time period one), and let r_2 be the two-period spot interest rate (prevailing from time zero to time two). The corresponding forward rate, f_{12}, is the one-period rate of interest which prevails from time one to time two which is implicit in these two spot rates. It can be calculated from the two spot rates as follows: $\dfrac{(1+r_2)^2}{1+r_1} - 1$. More generally, any forward rate can be calculated according to the following formula:

$$\frac{(1+r_n)^n}{(1+r_{n-1})^{n-1}} - 1.$$

The expectations theory is based on the idea that these risk-neutral investors set interest rates in a manner so that the forward rate is equal to the spot rate expected in the market one year from now. The theory is expressed in terms of expected one-period spot rates. In terms of bonds, the yield on a two-year bond is set in such a way that the return on that two-year bond is equal to the return on a one-year bond plus the expected return on another one-year bond purchased in one year. This notion is not unique to one- and two-year bonds. If all investors in the marketplace operate this way, then prices will adjust until the expected return from holding a two-year bond is the same as the expected return from holding two one-year bonds.

According to the expectations theory of the term structure, the yield curve can be derived from a series of expected one-year spot rates. Consider, for example, that the one-year spot rate is 5 percent from year zero to year one, the expected spot rate from year one to year two is 6 percent, and the expected spot rate from year two to year three is 7 percent. A two-year bond would earn the spot rate over the period from time zero to time two, which, according to this theory, is the same as investing in a one-year bond from time zero to time one, and then investing in another bond for one year from time one to time two.

Thus, the two-year spot rate from time zero to time two is calculated as $\left(1+\dfrac{r_2}{2}\right)^2 = \left(1+\dfrac{0.05}{2}\right)\left(1+\dfrac{0.06}{2}\right)$. The two-year spot rate is 5.5 percent. The three-year spot rate from time zero to time three can be calculated as $\left(1+\dfrac{r_3}{2}\right)^3 = \left(1+\dfrac{0.05}{2}\right)\left(1+\dfrac{0.06}{2}\right)\left(1+\dfrac{0.07}{2}\right)$. The three-year spot rate is 6 percent. Furthermore, the market's belief about the future of one-year spot rates can be read easily from an observed yield curve. Note that this theory assumes that the expected future spot rate is equal to the corresponding forward rate. This assumption does not hold for some of the other theories of the term structure.

The Liquidity Preference Theory

Under the liquidity preference theory of the term structure, investors again examine the returns from holding bonds of differing maturities. This theory does not assume that investors are risk-neutral. Investors are assumed to demand extra compensation to be induced to hold a bond of a relatively long maturity over a bond of relatively short maturity. Furthermore, the market is populated with relatively more short-term investors, which requires that investors receive additional inducement to hold long-term bonds.

In the example of the section which described the expectations theory of the term structure, we calculated that if the one-period rate from time zero to time one were 5 percent and the one-period rate from time one to time two were 6 percent, then the two-period rate prevailing from time zero to time two would be expected to be 5.5 percent. Under the liquidity preference theory, the two-period rate would have to be higher than 5.5 percent to induce investors to hold relatively longer-term instruments. For an investor with a one-year investment horizon, there is risk associated with the two-year investment.

The liquidity preference theory leads us to different conclusions about the shape of the term structure. Even if expectations are such that there will be no change in one-period rates, it would still be the case that the yield curve would be upward sloping in the presence of a liquidity premium. Even if one-period spot rates were expected to decline, if the liquidity premium were sufficiently large, there could still be an upward sloping term structure. A flat or downward sloping yield curve, under the liquidity preference theory, can only be possible in an environment of decreasing one-period spot rates.

The Market Segmentation Theory

The origin of the market segmentation theory stems from the observation that some investors apparently prefer debt of a particular maturity. This preference is so pronounced that these investors are insensitive to the yield differential of their preferred debt maturity over the debt of another maturity. The theory posits that investors are so risk-averse that they remain in their desired maturity spectrum and cannot be induced by yield differentials to change maturities. In this way, long-term rates are determined by the supply of and demand for long-term debt instruments, and similarly for short-term interest rates. Proponents of this theory closely watch the flow of funds into different segments of the bond market to determine changes in the yield curve.

Consider examples of investors who can reasonably be expected to have strong preference for debt of a particular maturity. An insurance company facing liabilities which are in the distant future will choose to invest for a long time horizon. There may be considerable risk to the insurance company in investing in a series of short-term instruments, compared to the known return and the predictability of available long-term debt. Similarly, corporations may have strong preference for issuing debt of a particular maturity depending on the use to which the funds will be put. Corporations will generally prefer to pay for long-term investment projects over a long period of time and so the corresponding debt issued for those projects is likely to be of long maturity.

The market segmentation theory of the term structure is popular with practitioners. Academics maintain that the market is more likely composed of both investors with definite maturity preferences and those who invest on the basis of relative yields. The predictions of the shape of the term structure based on the market segmentation theory will be offset if there are in fact enough investors who fall into the second category.

3.7.2 Approximating Functions

The text states that the discount factor for time t, $d(t)$, is approximated by the structure

$$d(t) = \sum_{j=0}^{K} \alpha_j f_j(t),$$

where the $f_j(t)$ are certain functions and the α_j are numerical coefficients. In this Appendix we provide more detailed insight into the nature of $f_j(t)$ and the corresponding function $d(t)$.

The approximation technique described in the text, uses a set of polynomials resembling <u>Bernstein polynomials</u>. The use of these polynomials is advantageous as they result in an approximation that is always a decreasing function on the interval $[0,1]$, see Phillips, G. M. and P. J. Taylor, 1970, "Approximation of Convex Data", BIT, 10, 324-332. For this reason we always scale the time interval to $[0,1]$. This is done by dividing the time by the largest maturity. Hence, the longest maturity is always one. We undo this scaling when reporting the discount factors. We know that the montonicity property should be satisfied by the discount factors or else arbitrage opportunities would exist.

The functions $f_j(t)$, for $j = 1, \ldots, K$, are defined as

$$f_j(t) = \sum_{l=0}^{K-j} \frac{(-1)^{(l+1)} \operatorname{binomial}(K-j,l) t^{(j+l)}}{i+l},$$

where binomial (n,k) is $\dfrac{n!}{k!(n-k)!}$ while for $j = 0$, $f_0(t) = 1$ and $\alpha_0 = 1$.

The discount function **dis**(t) in terms of the approximating function, is given by

$$dis(t) = \sum_{j=0}^{K} \alpha_j f_j\left(\frac{t}{nst}\right),$$

where nst is the longest maturity and $\dfrac{t}{nst}$ is the scaling mentioned earlier.

To solve for the value of coeffcients α_j, we solve an optimization problem. We minimize, with respect to the α_i, the sum of absolute deviations of the bond price p_i from its discounted cash flow, where $a_i(t)$ is the cash flow from bond i at time t. Thus, we solve the optimization problem below with respect to $\alpha_1, \ldots, \alpha_K$ and $\varepsilon_1, \ldots, \varepsilon_n$:

$$\min \sum_{i=1}^{n} |\varepsilon_i|$$

subject to

$$\sum_{t=1}^{nst} a_i(t) \left(\sum_{j=0}^{K} \alpha_j f_j \left(\frac{t}{nst} \right) \right) = p_i + \varepsilon_i, \quad \text{for } i = 1, \ldots, n.$$

Since the above problem can be transformed into an equivalent linear programming problem, the procedure **NarbitB** solves it using the simplex method.

Indeed, the situation in a real market is more complicated. Due to both the nonsynchronization of markets and the fact that not every bond is traded on every day, the prices of the bonds include some statistical noise. Hence, in almost all cases the data will allow for arbitrage opportunities. Moreover, most bond markets are incomplete. In a typical bond market the number of bonds is about a third of the number of payment dates. Consequently, even when the discount factors are not approximated by $dis(t)$, there does not exist a set of discount factors according to which the present value of the bonds equals the prices. Therefore, the constraints of the optimization problem above are not feasible. Hence, the term structure is estimated as a second-best solution by the optimization problem above. The ε are thus a combination of statistical noises and misspecification of the approximating function.

Chapter 4

Duration and Immunization

This lecture is dedicated to the study of the sensitivity of the price of bonds and portfolios of bonds to the changes in the interest rates. A measure of the sensitivity of bond prices to changes in interest rates, called Duration, was first suggested by **Macaulay** in 1938. The field of fixed income securities has evolved tremendously since that time and the academic literature now criticizes this measure. As we proceed with the development and understanding of this measure we will also gain an insight into this critique.

Despite the criticisms, we have decided to dedicate few lectures to this issue because Duration is intimately related to risk management of bond portfolios. And while risk management methods that are based on durations are also subject to the same critique, empirical observations prove these methods to be quite successful. The literature mentions that pension funds and insurance companies that have used such methods over a few decades rarely missed their goals. Furthermore, we believe that this chapter will significantly help in developing the readers' intuitions about interest rate risk, volatility of bond prices and thereby will pave the road to more advanced models that are beyond the scope of this book.

4.1 Duration: a sensitivity measure of bonds' prices to changes in interest rates

Our starting point is the definition of Duration and its intuitive motivation. We start by assuming that the term structure is flat but soon we will see that this assumption can be easily relaxed.That is, the rate spanning one period, the time interval $(0,1)$, is r, hence a dollar invested for t periods of time will grow to $(1+r)^t$. For simplicity we assume in this section that interest rate are reported based on annual compounding and think about a period as a year.

Let $c(t)$ be the cash flow (coupon or coupon plus principal at maturity) from a bond at time t, $t = 1, \ldots, n$, where n is the maturity time of the bond. The no-arbitrage condition implies that the price of the bond P is given by

$$P = \sum_{t=1}^{n} \frac{c(t)}{(1+r)^t}. \tag{4.1}$$

where interest rates are reported as explained above. Denoting $1+r$ by R and substituting it in the above equation yields:

$$\sum_{t=1}^{n} \frac{c(t)}{R^t} \tag{4.2}$$

In this simplistic model the effect of the change in the interest rate (in r) on the price of the bond can be measured by the derivative of $P = \sum_{t=1}^{n} \frac{c(t)}{R^t}$ with respect to R, i.e., by $\dfrac{dP}{dR}$.

Note that since $\dfrac{\partial R}{\partial r} = 1$ then $\dfrac{\partial}{\partial R}\left(\sum_{t=1}^{n} \frac{c(t)}{R^t}\right) = \dfrac{\partial}{\partial r}\left(\sum_{t=1}^{n} \frac{c(t)}{R^t}\right)$, and it is given by:

$$\frac{dP}{dR} = -\sum_{t=1}^{n}\left(\frac{c(t)t}{R^t R}\right) \tag{4.3}$$

Before we continue further we would like to make our first observation. Since the bond payments are all positive i.e., $c(t) > 0, t = 1, \ldots n$ and so is R, one can easily verify that the expression above is negative. Hence our first conclusion is that since $\dfrac{dP}{dr} < 0$, P is a decreasing function of r, *i.e.,* ***bond prices increase when interest rates decrease and vice versa***. This is of course a direct consequence of the first derivative being negative. A further look confirms that indeed the present value of a positive cash flow decreases as the interest rate increases. The present value of a (positive) future amount is calculated by multiplying it by the discount factor $\dfrac{1}{1+r}$ so as r increases, the discount factor decreases and hence the result.

Traditionally the sensitivity of bond prices to changes in the interest rate is measured in percentage terms. However before presenting it in the classical way we would like to highlight the concept behind this traditional presentation. Thinking about the price of the bond as a function of the interest rate (since the present value is a function of r), it is possible to approximate the change in a bond price due to a change in the interest rate. The approximation is based on a first order Taylor series that uses only the first derivative of the approximated function. We will use it again with higher order derivatives when we look at generalized durations. However for the current derivation we only need the fact that if the price of the bond P, is represented as a function of r, *i.e.*, as $P(r)$ where $\dfrac{dP(r)}{dr}$ is its first derivative and if there is a change in r represented by Δr, then $P(r+\Delta r)$ can be linearly approximated by

$$P(r+\Delta r) \approx P(r) + \frac{dP(r)}{dr}\Delta r \qquad (4.4)$$

This approximation can be visualized graphically but first let us look at a numerical example. To this end we defined a function that calculates the price of a bond, with semi-annual payments, a face value of \$100, a coupon rate of c (i.e., each coupon payment is $\dfrac{c}{2}\cdot 100$) maturing in n years from now (that is the next coupon is paid in 6 months). Thus the parameter of this function are c, r and n. That is, for $n=2$ coupon rate of c and interest rate of r the price is;

```
> BondPrice(c,r,2);
```

$$\frac{50c}{\sqrt{1+r}} + \frac{50c}{1+r} + \frac{50c}{(1+r)^{3/2}} + \frac{50c}{(1+r)^2} + \frac{100}{(1+r)^2}$$

The generic formula is

```
> BondPrice(c,r,n);
```

$$-\frac{50c\left(\frac{1}{\sqrt{1+r}}\right)^{2n+1}\sqrt{1+r}}{-1+\sqrt{1+r}} + \frac{50c}{-1+\sqrt{1+r}} + \frac{100}{(1+r)^n}$$

Note that Maple presented the expression $\sum\limits_{t=1}^{n}\dfrac{c(t)}{(1+r)^t}$, where $c(n) = 100$, in a compact form based on it being a geometric series. For $n=5$ the result will be:

```
> BondPrice(c,r,5);
```

$$\frac{50c}{\sqrt{1+r}}+\frac{50c}{1+r}+\frac{50c}{(1+r)^{3/2}}+\frac{50c}{(1+r)^2}+\frac{50c}{(1+r)^{5/2}}+\frac{50c}{(1+r)^3}$$

$$+\frac{50c}{(1+r)^{7/2}}+\frac{50c}{(1+r)^4}+\frac{50c}{(1+r)^{9/2}}+\frac{50c}{(1+r)^5}+\frac{100}{(1+r)^5}$$

Hence the price of a bond with a coupon payment of 5% when the interest rate is 7% maturing in 5 years can be calculated as:

```
> BondPrice(.05,.07,5);
```

$$92.15230453$$

Changes in interest rates are traditionally measured in basis points **(bps)**. One basis point is defined to be 1/100th of 1%. Hence 1% change equals change of 100 bps. If the interest rate changes from 7% to 8%, a change of 100 bps, the price of the bond will be

```
> BondPrice(.05,.08,5);
```

$$88.41345975$$

In this case $\Delta r = 0.08 - 0.07$ is 0.01 in order to use first order Taylor linear approximation there is a need to know $\left(\frac{dP(r)}{dr}\right)_{r=0.07}$. This is done below; note that '*diff* $(BondPrice(0.05,r,5,r))$' calculates the derivative with respect to r and the 'subs' command calculates its value at the point $r=0.07$.

```
> diff(BondPrice(.05,r,5),r);
```

$$-\frac{1.250000000}{(1.+r)^{3/2}}-\frac{2.500000000}{(1.+r)^2}-\frac{3.750000000}{(1.+r)^{5/2}}-\frac{5.000000000}{(1.+r)^3}$$

$$-\frac{6.250000000}{(1.+r)^{7/2}}-\frac{7.500000000}{(1.+r)^4}-\frac{8.750000000}{(1.+r)^{9/2}}-\frac{10.00000000}{(1.+r)^5}$$

$$-\frac{11.25000000}{(1.+r)^{11/2}}-\frac{12.50000000}{(1.+r)^6}-\frac{500}{(1+r)^6}$$

```
> subs(r=.07,diff(BondPrice(.05,r,5),r));
```

$$-384.0525897$$

Thus the approximation to the change in the price is the product of $\left(\dfrac{dP(r)}{dr}\right)_{r=0.07} = -384.0525897$ **and** $\Delta r = 0.01$

```
> -384.0525897*0.01;
```

$$-3.840525897$$

Putting it all together utilizing (4.4) the approximation of the bond's price after the change in the interest rate is:

$$P(0.07) + \left(\frac{dP(r)}{dr}\right)_{r=0.07} \cdot \Delta r \qquad (4.5)$$

```
> BondPrice(.05,.07,5)+subs(r=.07,
diff(BondPrice(.05,r,5),r))*.01;
```

$$88.31177863$$

We see that the approximated value of 88.311 is not that far from the true value of 88.413. The reader can recalculate the example above for different values of the parameters, i.e., r, c, n and Δr.

This approximation can be visualized as a function of r, the rate after the change, when the current interest rate is r_0 and $\Delta r = (r - r_0)$, by the graph of the linear function

$$P(r_0) + \left(\frac{dP(r)}{dr}\right)_{r=r_0} \cdot (r_0 - r). \qquad (4.6)$$

A large value of r_0 is chosen to make it more pronounced, the chosen parameters are $r_0 = 0.14$, $c = 0.05$ and $n = 5$. For these values the price of the bond is

```
> BondPrice(.05,0.14,5);
```

$$100.2672919$$

and the figure that visualizes this approximation as in (4.6) is presented:

```
> plot([BondPrice(.05,r,5),BondPrice(.05,.14,5)+(r-0.14)
*subs(r=.14,diff(BondPrice(.05,r,5),r))],[[0.14,0],
```

```
[0.14,BondPrice(.05,.14,5)]]],r=0.04...0.30,y=0..180,
color=[green,red,blue],labels=['Interest rate','Bond
Price'],title='Approximation of the Bond's value
',thickness=2,titlefont=[TIMES,BOLD,10]);
```

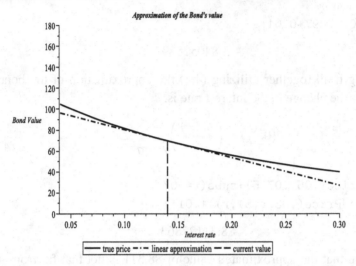

The solid graph is the true value of the bond as a function of the interest rate. The dash-dot graph is the approximation of the value of the bond after the change in the interest rate. It is the line tangent to the dash-dot graph at $r = 0.14$ at the intersection of the perpendicular line with the dash-dot and the solid lines. Hence, the slope of the dash-dot graph is the derivative of the solid graph at the point $r = 0.14$. If the interest rate does not change ($r = 0.14$) we see that the approximation and the true value coincide.

Note that the smaller that change in the rate the better the linear approximation is. However, as the change gets bigger, a gap is opening between the true value (the solid graph) and the approximation (the dash-dot graph). This gap is due to the true value not being a linear function of the interest rate. In this setting, the true value is in fact a convex function of the interest rate. For this reason, as we will see henceforth, the expression that is added to make the approximation more precise is termed 'convexity'.

Let us see how this result can be presented in terms of percentage changes. To this end we denote $P(r + \Delta r) - P(r)$ by ΔP in equation (4.4), repeated below,

$$P(r+\Delta r) \approx P(r) + \left(\frac{d}{dr}P(r)\right)\Delta r.$$

and write it as

$$\Delta P \approx \left(\frac{dP(r)}{dr}\right)\Delta r.$$

$$(4.7)$$

Recall that for $R = (1+r)$, $\Delta r = \Delta R$ and $\dfrac{dP(r)}{dr} = \dfrac{dP}{dR} = -\sum_{t=1}^{n}\left(\dfrac{c(t)\,t}{R^t\,R}\right)$.

Thus

$$\frac{\Delta P}{\Delta R} \approx -\sum_{t=1}^{n}\left(\frac{c(t)\,t}{R^t\,R}\right).$$

$$(4.8)$$

Dividing (4.8) by $P = \sum\limits_{t=1}^{n}\dfrac{c(t)}{R^t}$ and multiplying it by R we obtain

$$\frac{\frac{\Delta P}{\Delta R}R}{P} \approx \frac{-\sum_{t=1}^{n}\left(\frac{c(t)\,t}{R^t}\right)}{\sum_{t=1}^{n}\left(\frac{c(t)}{R^t}\right)} = -\sum_{t=1}^{n}\left(\frac{c(t)R^{-t}}{\sum_{t=1}^{n}c(t)R^{-t}}\right)t$$

$$(4.9)$$

Defining $w(t) = \dfrac{c(t)R^{-t}}{\sum\limits_{t=1}^{n}c(t)R^{-t}} = \dfrac{c(t)R^{-t}}{P}$ equation (4.9) can be written as

:

$$\frac{\Delta P}{\Delta R}\cdot\frac{R}{P} \approx -\sum_{t=1}^{n}w(t)t$$

$$(4.10)$$

Notice that $0 \le w(t)$, $w(t) \le 1$ and that $\sum\limits_{t=1}^{n}w(t) = 1$, hence, $\sum\limits_{t=1}^{n}w(t)t$ can be interpreted as the weighted average of the time of the payment dates of the bond. The weight of time t is the present value of the payment at t, divided by the present value of all the payments — the price. Note also that in our convention the current time is time zero so time t is actually the length of the time period from now to t. Consequently, $\sum\limits_{t=1}^{n}w(t)t$, is the weighted average of the length of times to the payment dates.

One may think of a coupon paying bond as maturing gradually, after all, it pays coupons along its life so it is not really maturing at one point in time — the time of the last coupon (and the face value) payment. Hence, $\sum_{t=1}^{n} w(t)t$ is the average 'duration' of the bond and

$$Du = \sum_{t=1}^{n} w(t)t \tag{4.11}$$

is defined to be the duration of a bond. Consequently the approximation can be written in terms of the bond's duration as

$$\frac{\Delta P}{P} \approx -Du\left[\frac{\Delta R}{R}\right] \tag{4.12}$$

In words, *the percentage change in the price of the bond* $\frac{\Delta P}{P}$*, is minus its duration* $\sum_{t=1}^{n} w(t)t$*, multiplied by the percentage change in R,* $\left[\frac{\Delta R}{R} = \frac{\Delta r}{1+r}\right]$.

Thus the effect of the change in the interest rate is measured, in this simplistic model, by the duration of the bond. The minus sign indicates that an increase in the interest rate causes a decrease in the price of the bond. Since the change in R is a consequence of the change in r and $\Delta r = \Delta R$ we can rewrite (4.12) as

$$\frac{\Delta P}{P} \approx -Du\cdot\left[\frac{\Delta r}{1+r}\right], \text{ or } \Delta P \approx -PDu\cdot\left[\frac{\Delta r}{1+r}\right]. \tag{4.13}$$

In words we can restate it as **the percentage change in the price of a bond is inversely related to the percentage change in the interest rate in the following way**: *an increase (decrease) of one percent in 1+r causes a decrease (increase) of −Du percent in the price of the bond.* The interpretation of duration as the weighted average of the time of the payment dates of the bond implies that the duration of a portfolio of bonds is the weighted average of the durations of the bonds in the portfolio. The weight of the duration of each bond is the price of the bond divided by the price of the portfolio. One of the exercises at the end of the chapter asks the reader to prove this property.

If we define a modified duration

$$MDu = \frac{Du}{1+r} \qquad (4.14)$$

then

$$\frac{\Delta P}{P} = -MDu \cdot \Delta r, \qquad (4.15)$$

which verbally can be conveyed by saying that an increase (decrease) of Δr in the flat term structure causes a decrease (increase) of $MDu \cdot \Delta r$ percent in the bond price. Similarly the change in the bond's price can be written as

$$\Delta P = -P \cdot MDu \cdot \Delta r, \qquad (4.16)$$

and the price after the change is

$$P + \Delta P = P(1 - MDu \cdot \Delta r). \qquad (4.17)$$

Let us look at a few numerical examples. To help us in the calculation we have a function **Dur(c,r,n,F)**, that calculates the duration of a bond where c is the coupon rate (paid semiannually), r is the term structure of the interest rate (assumed to be flat for now), n is the number of years until maturity where the time to the next coupon is 6 months. For simplicity the function **Dur(c,r,n,F)** calculates the duration assuming that the interest rate is reported as the simple annual rate, coupons are paid semiannually and F is the face value of the bond, i.e. it calculates[1]

---

[1] A conventional bond in most countries pays coupons semi-annually, and if its coupon rate is c it pays $\frac{c}{2}$ every 6 months. As well the interest rate is usually reported as an annual rate, compounded semi-annually which means that \$100 invested for 6 months at annual rate of r percent will grow to $100\left(1 + \frac{r}{2}\right)$ and when it is invested for one year it will grow to $100\left(1 + \frac{r}{2}\right)^2$. Hence under this convention the price of a bond with parameters **c,r,n,F** where the time to the next coupon payment is 6 months is:

$$P = \sum_{i=1}^{2n} \frac{c}{2}\left(1 + \frac{r}{2}\right)^{-\frac{i}{2}} + F\left(1 + \frac{r}{2}\right)^{-n}$$

$$\frac{\sum_{t=1}^{2n}\left(F\frac{c}{2}(1+r)^{-\frac{t}{2}}\left(\frac{t}{2}\right)\right)+F(1+r)^{-n}n}{\sum_{t=1}^{n}F\frac{c}{2}(1+r)^{-\frac{t}{2}}+F(1+r)^{-n}} \tag{4.18}$$

Thus the equation for the duration of a bond with a coupon rate of c where the interest rate is r, the time to maturity is 1 year and the face value is F, is given by:

```
> Dur(c,r,1,F);
```

$$\frac{F(1+r)+\frac{1}{4}\frac{Fc}{\sqrt{1+r}}+\frac{1}{2}\frac{Fc}{1+r}}{F(1+r)+\frac{1}{2}\frac{Fc}{\sqrt{1+r}}+\frac{1}{2}\frac{Fc}{1+r}}$$

and if the time to maturity is n years it is

```
> Dur(c,r,n,F);
```

$$\left(F(1+r)^{-n}n-\frac{1}{4}\frac{Fc\left(\frac{1}{\sqrt{1+r}}\right)^{2n+1}\sqrt{1+r}\left((2n+1)\sqrt{1+r}-2n\right)}{\left(-1+\sqrt{1+r}\right)^2}\right.$$

$$\left.+\frac{1}{4}\frac{Fc\sqrt{1+r}}{\left(-1+\sqrt{1+r}\right)^2}\right)\bigg/\left(F(1+r)^{-n}-\frac{1}{2}\frac{\left(\frac{1}{\sqrt{1+r}}\right)^{2n+1}Fc\sqrt{1+r}}{-1+\sqrt{1+r}}\right.$$

$$\left.+\frac{1}{2}\frac{Fc}{-1+\sqrt{1+r}}\right)$$

Note again that Maple uses the geometric series formula to simplify the expression in (4.18).

The duration of a zero coupon bond that matures in three years with a face value of \$100 in a market with a flat term structure of 7% will be calculated by executing

```
> Dur(0,.07,3,100);
```

and the duration of the bond, (in units of 6 months) will be

$$\left(\frac{\sum_{t=1}^{2n}\frac{c}{2}\left(1+\frac{r}{2}\right)^{-\frac{t}{2}}i+F\left(1+\frac{r}{2}\right)^{-n}n}{P}\right).$$

$$3.000000000$$

Keeping in mind the duration definition and its interpretation, as a weighted average of the time to payment of the bond, it should be clear that the duration of such a bond is 3. The weighted average of one number is the number itself. Since the bond pays only once, the weighted average of the time to the payment of the bond is exactly the time to maturity of the bond.

Let us look at another example. The duration of a 5% coupon bond that matures in $n = 10$, paying semi-annual coupons $r = 7\%$ with a face value of $F = 100$, and the time to the next coupon is 6 months can be calculated by executing :

```
> Dur(.05,.07,10,100);
```

$$9.184216684$$

Consider yet another example. A 6% coupon bond, maturing in 5 years in a market in which the interest rate is 7% where the time to the payment of the next coupon is 6 months.

```
> Dur(.06,.07,5,100);
```

$$4.379273110$$

The result of these calculations should not be that surprising. After all, if the bonds mature in 5 years and the highest weight is given to the maturity time, its duration should be close to 5. The weight of each time is the present value of the payment at that time divided by the present value of the future cash flow (the price of the bond). Hence, the face value of the bond will always tilt the duration measure to be close to the maturity time.

The duration of a bond is of course affected by the value of the interest rate. Let us look at the same bond as above but assume now that the interest rate in the market is 2%. The duration of the bond will now be calculated as below.

```
> Dur(.06,0.02,5,100);
```

$$4.531015444$$

The lower the interest rate the higher the present value of each payment. However we see again that the face value of the bond being the largest payment affects the duration calculation the most and hence the duration increases. This however will not be the case for a zero coupon bond. A zero coupon bond will have the same duration regardless of the value of the interest rate.

How does an increase in the coupon rate affect the duration? Let us calculate the duration of the last bond but when the coupon rate is 15%.

```
> Dur(.15,0.02,5,100);
```

$$4.102993923$$

By increasing the coupon rate we essentially increase the weights of the time payment of each coupon **relative** to the payment of the face value at maturity. Hence more weight is given to the coupon payment and we thus decrease the average. Thus the duration, being the weighted average, should decrease as indeed we show above.

What is the effect of increasing the time to maturity on the duration of the bond? Increasing the time to maturity in essence makes the time with the heaviest weight (the maturity of the bond) longer. Thus we expect an increase in the duration. We demonstrate it below when the maturity of the bond is increased to 10 years.

```
> Dur(.15,0.02,10,100);
```

$$7.413734070$$

We can therefore summarize and visualize the following, keeping in mind that duration measures the sensitivity (percentage change in the price of a bond) to changes (a percentage change in $1 + r$) in the interest rate.

(1) The higher the interest rate, the lower the sensitivity of the bond to changes in the interest rate. This can be visualized by graphing the duration of a bond as a function of the interest rate.

```
> plot(Dur(.05,r,10,100),r=0.01..0.15);
```

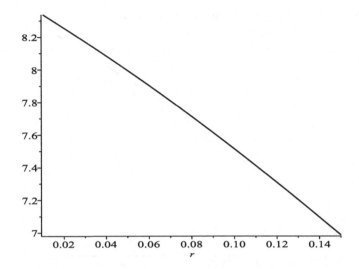

(2) The higher the coupon rate, the lower the sensitivity of the bond to changes in the interest rate. This can be visualized by graphing the duration of a bond as a function of the coupon rate.

```
> plot(Dur(c,.07,10,100),c=.01...0.10);
```

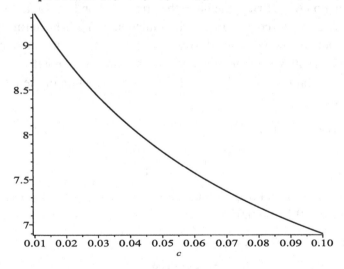

(3) The longer the time to maturity, the higher the sensitivity of the bond to changes in the interest rate. This can be visualized by graphing the duration of a bond as a function of the maturity time.

```
> plot(Dur(.04,.05,n,100),n=1..10);
```

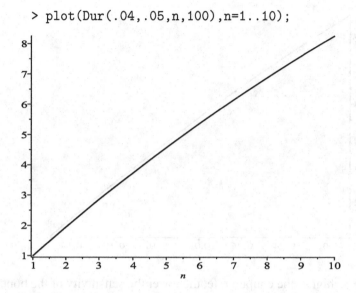

We conclude this section by using the duration approximation in order to calculate the percentage change in the value of a bond due to a change in the interest rate.

The function **BondPrice** calculates the price of a bond with a face value of $100 where c is the coupon rate (paid semiannually), r is the term structure of the interest rate (assumed to be flat for now), n is the number of years until maturity where the time to the next coupon is 6 months. That is for $n = 1$, coupon rate of c when r is the flat term structure of the interest rate we have

```
> BondPrice(c,r,1);
```

$$\frac{50c}{\sqrt{1+r}} + \frac{50c}{1+r} + \frac{100}{1+r}$$

Thus, the price of a bond with a face value of $100 that matures in 10 years where $c = 0.1$, $r = 0.05$ is

```
> BondPrice(.10,0.05,10);
```

$$139.5621188$$

Assume now that the interest rate in the market increased by 50 bbps that is, the new rate is 5.5%, then the price of the bond will be:

```
> BondPrice(.10,0.055,10);
```

$$134.9418679$$

The percentage change in the price of the bond was thus

```
> (134.9418679-139.5621188)/139.5621188;
```

$$-0.03310533646$$

Let us see how the duration will approximate this change. Our approximation says that the percentage change in the price is minus the duration multiplied by the percentage change in $1 + r$. The Duration of the bond is

```
> Dur(.10,.05,10,100);
```

$$7.113188905$$

The percentage change in $1 + r$ is

```
> (1+0.055-(1+0.05))/1.05;
```

$$0.004761904762$$

Hence the duration will approximate the percentage change as

```
> -Dur(.10,.05,10,100)*(1+0.055-(1+0.05))/1.05;
```

$$-0.03387232812$$

The above can be presented in terms of modified duration as

```
> -(Dur(.10,.05,10,100)/1.05)*0.005;
```

$$-0.03966036818$$

where Dur(.10,.05,10,100)/1.05) is the modified duration and 0.005 is the change in interest rates.

That is the modified duration times the change in interest rates is the percentage change in the bond's price. Thus as a result of 50 bps (0.005) increase in interest rate the price of the bond is approximated as

```
> BondPrice(.10,0.05,10,100)*(1-0.03966036818);
```

$$134.0270338$$

Duration therefore measures the sensitivity of bonds, or portfolio of bonds as we shall soon see, to changes in interest rates. Hence duration is used to manage interest rate risk. Interest rate risk is the terminology used to capture the risk one faces as a result of a change in the interest rates.

To better capture the sensitivity of bond prices to interest rate changes, a second order Taylor approximation is used. The first order approximation is a linear approximation to the change while the second order allows quadratic such approximation, based on a second order Taylor approximation, i.e., based on

$$P(r+\Delta r) \approx P(r) + \left(\frac{d}{dr}P(r) \right) \Delta r + \frac{1}{2} \left(\frac{d^2}{dr^2}P(r) \right) \Delta r^2 \tag{4.19}$$

since $\frac{d^2}{dr^2}P(r) = \sum\limits_{t=1}^{n} \left(\frac{c(t)(t+1)t}{R^t R^2} \right)$ following the same steps as in the deviation of (4.13) yields

$$\frac{\Delta P}{P} \approx - \left(\sum_{t=1}^{n} w(t)t \right) \left(\frac{\Delta r}{R} \right) + \frac{1}{2} \left(\sum_{t=1}^{n} w(t)t(t+1) \right) \frac{\Delta r^2}{R^2}.$$

and thus a more accurate measure of the change to the bond prices, as a result of a change in interest rates is obtained. The expression

$$Con = \left(\sum_{t=1}^{n} w(t)t(t+1) \right) \tag{4.20}$$

is termed, for the reason explained earlier, 'convexity'.

Note that this expression is positive, hence omitting it underestimates the true change. The approximation of a bond price without convexity is based on equation (4.6), and with convexity is based on equation (4.21) where r is the rate after the change and the current rate is r_0;

$$P(r) \approx P(r_0) + \left(\frac{dP}{dr} \right)_{r=r_0} (r - r_0) + \frac{1}{2} \left(\frac{d^2P}{dr^2} \right)_{r=r_0} (r - r_0)^2 \tag{4.21}$$

The figure below visualizes the first and second order Taylor approximation, equations (4.6) and (4.21), respectively.

```
> plot([BondPrice(.05,r,5),BondPrice(.05,.14,5)+(r-0.14)
*subs(r=.14,diff(BondPrice(.05,r,5),r)),
BondPrice(.05,.14,5)+(r-0.14)*subs(r=.14,
diff(BondPrice(.05,r,5),r))+0.5*(r-0.14)^2
*subs(r=.14,diff(BondPrice(.05,r,5),r,r)),[[0.14,0],
[0.14, BondPrice(.05,.14,5)]]],r=0.01..0.35,y=30..110,
color=[green,red,black,blue],labels=['Interest
rate','Bond Value'],title='Approximation of the Bond's
value ',thickness=2,titlefont=[TIMES,BOLD,10]);
```

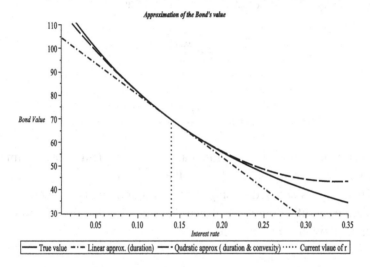

The solid line is the true value. The dash-dot line is the linear approximation, i.e., where the price is approximated by $P - Du \cdot \Delta r$. The long dash line is the quadratic approximation, i.e. where the price is approximated by both duration and convexity as $-Du \cdot \Delta r + \dfrac{Con \cdot \Delta r^2}{2}$. It can be seen that with the convexity term, the approximation nearly coincide with the true price, while the linear approximation is always smaller than the true price.

The definition of duration and convexity, as well as that of a generalized concept of duration are easier to work with if continuous compounding is used to represent the term structure and the discount factor. If the price of a bond, the preset value of its cash flow $c(t)$ at time t, is represented as

$P = \sum_{t=1}^{n} c(t) e^{-rt}$ instead of $P = \sum_{t=1}^{n} \dfrac{c(t)}{(1+r)^t}$ we have that $\dfrac{dP}{dr} =$

$-\sum_{t=1}^{n} tc(t) e^{-rt}$ and $\dfrac{d^2P}{dr^2} = \sum_{t=1}^{n} t^2 c(t) e^{-rt}$, therefore following the steps in the derivation of the duration equation (4.11) it will be defined as

$$Du = \sum_{t=1}^{n} w(t)t$$

and the convexity equation (4.20) will be defined as

$$Con = \sum_{t=1}^{n} w(t)t^2$$

where

$$w(t) = \frac{(c(t) e^{-rt})}{P}.$$

That is the duration is the weighted average of the length of the times until the payments from the bonds, and the convexity is the weighed average of these times squared. Using continuous compounding there is no need to define modified duration. Since the second order Taylor approximation divided by the current price is

$$\frac{(P(r+\Delta r) - P(r))}{P(r)} \approx -\frac{\left(\frac{d}{dr}P(r)\right)}{P(r)} \Delta r + \frac{1}{2} \frac{\left(\frac{d^2}{dr^2}P(r)\right) \Delta r^2}{P(r)} \tag{4.22}$$

and thus

$$\frac{(P(r+\Delta r) - P(r))}{P(r)} = \frac{\Delta P}{P(r)} \approx -Du \cdot \Delta r + \frac{1}{2} Con \cdot \Delta r^2 \tag{4.23}$$

In words, the percentage change in the bond price is minus the duration multiplied by the change in r plus half the convexity multiplied by the squared change in r.

Our next section explores the use of duration in bond portfolio management.

4.2   Immunization, A First look

Immunization (in financial terminology) is the process of eliminating (or reducing) interest rate risks from a bond portfolio. Consider an investor who holds a portfolio of bonds in order to meet a certain liability in the future. If the portfolio is not composed of a zero coupon bond that matures at the time of the liability (with a value equal to the liability value), a risk is assumed. This risk is included by the uncertainty about the reinvestment rate of the coupon paid by the portfolio prior to the liability time. Perhaps the best way to explain immunization is by using a case as described below.

Assume that the current term structure is flat at 11% and that you have a liability of 165.94 to be paid in 4 years from now. Furthermore, assume for simplicity, that in this market the term structure is always flat. Hence, changes in the term structure are always such that the new term structure is flat at another level. The current term structure is flat at 11% and you have 109.3136605 currently. You make a quick calculation and find out that

```
> 109.3136605*(1+0.11)^4;
```

$$165.9458334$$

Thus you actually have a present value of 165.945, your liability. In order to ensure your ability to fulfill your obligation, you are looking into an investment strategy that could guarantee that you will be able to pay your liability. Being conservative, you do not want to assume any risk and hence you are only looking in the government bond market.

You take a look at the bond market and find out that there is a bond that pays an **annual** coupon of 13.52 and matures in 5 years. A coupon was just paid by the bond so the next coupon payment is in a year. As it should be in a market where the no-arbitrage condition is satisfied, such a bond should have the following price (as a function of r):

```
> sum(13.52*(1+r)^(-i),i=1..5)+100*(1+r)^(-5);
```

$$\frac{13.52000000}{1.+r} + \frac{13.52000000}{(1.+r)^{-2}} + \frac{13.52000000}{(1.+r)^3} + \frac{13.52000000}{(1.+r)^4}$$
$$+ \frac{13.52000000}{(1.+r)^5} + \frac{100}{(1+r)^5}$$

and thus if the interest rate is 11% the price of the bond is

```
> subs(r=0.11,sum(13.52*(1+r)^(-i),i=1..5)
+100*(1+r)^(-5));
```

$$109.3136605$$

You are considering buying this bond now and selling it in 4 years to pay your liability. You are just about to buy it when your broker hears that you are going to buy it in order to be able to pay your liability in 4 years. In this case the broker says perhaps you should reconsider, since by buying this bond you may assume a risk you do not want. After all, firstly you are not sure what price you will be able to get for the bond in 4 years. Furthermore, you assume a risk of re-investing, since when the coupons are paid, you are not sure what the interest rate in the market will be at that time.

You thus perform the following analysis: First you calculate the value of the bond at time 4 as a function of the interest rate. That is, the future value of every payment obtained before time 4 is calculated as of time 4, and the present value of every payment obtained after time 4, is also calculated as of time 4. This generates the following expression for the value of the cash flow from the bond at time 4.

```
> sum(13.52*(1+r)^(i),i=-1..3)+100*(1+r)^(-1);
```

$$27.04000000 + \frac{13.52000000}{1.+r} + 13.52000000\,r + 13.52000000\,(1.+r)^2$$
$$+13.52000000\,(1.+r)^3 + \frac{100}{1+r}$$

Then you calculate the value of the cash flow as of time 4 for different scenarios of interest rates. Specifically, the value of the cash flow is calculated for values of r of $0.05, 0.06, \ldots, 0.15$. This is done by defining the above expression as a function of r and substituting the different values of r in the function:

```
> ValueAt4:=unapply(%,r);
```

$$ValueAt4 := r \rightarrow 27.04000000 + \frac{13.52000000}{1.+r} + 13.52000000\,r +$$
$$13.52000000\,(1.+r)^2 + 13.52000000\,(1.+r)^3 + \frac{100}{1+r}$$

```
> seq(ValueAt4(r/100),r=5..15);
```

166.3871757, 166.2391479, 166.1214873, 166.0337454, 165.9754931,
165.9463200, 165.9458334, 165.9736574, 166.0294324, 166.1128142,
166.2234735

Observing the sequence of values you see that you will be able to meet the liability in all of these scenarios. In fact, the minimal value of the bond at time 4 across these scenarios is the value of the liability, so even in the worst case the liability will be met. To be fully convinced, the function **ValueAt4** is graphed and indeed it is verified that the minimal value of the bond is the value of the liability.

```
> plot(ValueAt4(r),r=0.05..0.15);
```

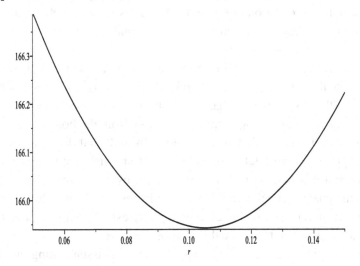

You are puzzled by the result and since duration is a measure of interest rate risks, you try to calculate the duration of this bond. The function defined below called DurA (assumes an annual coupon payment), calculates the duration of a bond with a coupon rate of c, face value of 100, that matures in n years when the interest rate is assumed to be flat at a rate of r.

```
> DurA:=(c,r,n)->(100*(1+r)^(-n)*n+sum(100*(c)
*(1+r)^(-i)*i,i=1..n))/(100*(1+r)^(-n)+sum(100*(c)
*(1+r)^(-i),i = 1 ..  n));
```

$$DurA := (c,r,n) \rightarrow \frac{100(1+r)^{-n}n + \sum\limits_{t=1}^{n} 100c(1+r)^{-1}i}{100(1+r)^{-n}n + \sum\limits_{t=1}^{n} 100c(1+r)^{-1}}$$

Taking advantage of the function you calculate the duration of the suggested bond

```
> DurA(0.1352,0.11,5);
```

$$3.990816117$$

You are now wondering if there is any connection between the duration concept and the fact that you have had to pay the liability in 4 years, which virtually equals the duration of the bond. We investigate this phenomenon using two approaches — an intuitive approach and a more analytical approach.

The fact that the liability in the above case has a duration of 4 (as it is a cash flow like that of a zero coupon bond) which equals the duration of the cash inflow (the asset), means that they both have the same sensitivity to changes in interest rates. However, the cash flow from the bond is positive (cash inflow) and the cash flow (cash outflow) from the liability is negative. Thus changes in interest rates affect the asset and liability in about the same way and this results in them being offset by each other. This also results in the phenomena that the liability is always met. Hence the general conclusion from this case is that eliminating interest rate risks requires the duration of the liability to be equal to that of the asset.

Let us now take a more rigorous approach to this issue stating our assumptions and try to formulate the investment problem.

For the time being we keep the assumption that the term structure is flat. To capture the uncertainty in a simple way, we assume that immediately after we purchase a portfolio the term structure changes. Hence if when we purchase the portfolio the term structure was at a level of say r_0, it will be at a new level of $r_0 + r$, where r is unknown (a random variable). Such a change is referred to as a parallel shift in the term structure. While we cannot control the change in the interest rate we can decide about the composition of our portfolio. Let us denote by x the composition of the portfolio and by V the portfolio's value as a function of its composition and the change in the term structure r at the time the liability is due. Thus, $V(r,x)$ denotes the value of the portfolio at the liability time as a function of the change in the term structure and the portfolio composition. (It will be easier to use continuous compounding in this formulation.)

In our case above we are contemplating the purchase of a certain bond — that is the portfolio was chosen to be one bond and the value of the bond at the liability time as a function of r was given by:

$$\sum_{j=-1}^{3} 13.52\,(1+r)^j + 100\,(1+r)^{(-1)}$$

Note that when the interest rate increases, the future value of coupons obtained before the liability time and re-invested to the liability time, increases. On the other hand, the present value of the coupons obtained after the liability time, decreases. If the interest rate decreases then the reverse is correct. However in both cases it seems that this fact may reduce the risk and allow us to compose the portfolio in such a way that its minimum value (as a function of the interest rate) is the liability value. Mathematically speaking we are trying to solve the problem

$$Max_x Min_r V(x,r)$$

and find a portfolio x such that the worst case scenario for the value of the portfolio is at the current level of the interest rate, r_0, and in this case the minimal value is the liability value. Utilizing the first order condition for the optimal solution

$$\frac{d}{dx}V(x,r) = 0 \qquad \frac{d}{dr}V(x,r) = 0$$

and choosing a portfolio x such that these conditions are satisfied for $r = r_0$ shows that indeed this is the case. The first order condition implies that in order to compose such a portfolio, the duration of the portfolio must equal the time until the liability's due date (i.e., 4 years in the case above).

Under this model the liability is not only met under any scenario, but in fact it is met under the worst case scenario. In any other scenario the value of the asset exceeds the value of the liability. This is the reason these types of models are objected to in the academic literature, as they are not consistent with the no arbitrage condition, even though in practice they have proven to be effective. However, the investigation of this inconsistency and its remedy is beyond the scope of this book.

To fully appreciate this investment strategy the reader is advised to practice by utilizing the exercises at the end of the chapter. In doing so one must remember that this strategy is not passive. As time passes some bonds mature, the duration of the portfolio changes and the length of time to the liability's due date decreases. Hence the portfolio must be revised in order to keep its duration equal to the length of time to the liability time. A property that helps in such a revision is the fact that the duration of a portfolio is the weighted average of the duration of the bonds in the portfolio. The reader is asked to prove this in an exercise at the end of the chapter. Finally, if short positions are allowed, these can be utilized to tailor the correct duration. The duration of a bond held in a short position is minus its duration (when held in a long position).

Our analysis here assumed that the term structure uncertainty is governed by a parallel shift. This is a restrictive assumption. The next section relaxes this assumption.

4.3 Generalized duration and Immunization

Let us generalize our model so that we can assume that the term structure uncertainty is governed by a more generalized process, not only by a parallel shift. Consider the following market, where we estimate the discount function and try to extrapolate it to 6 years.

Note the '3' inNarbitB([[105,0,0], [10,110,0], [8,8,108]], [94,97,85], 3, Dis, 1,6), stands for the number of approximating functions used to estimate the discount factor. 'Dis' is chosen by the user as a name for the discount factor function. '1' is for producing the graph of the discount factor function and if a 0 is entered for this parameter no graph will be produced. Finally '6' is the upper bound of the domain along which the discount factor function is estimated. The presumption of this procedure is that the time intervals are equal. That is the time interval between the current time (on which the price of the bonds are given) and the first coupon payment is equal to the time between the first and second coupon payment, etc.

```
> NarbitB([[105,0,0],[10,110,0],[8,8,108]],[94,97,85],
```

```
3,Dis,1,6);
```

The no-arbitrage condition is satisfied.

The discount factor for time, 1, is given by, $\dfrac{94}{105}$

The interest rate spanning the time interval, $[0,1]$, is given by, 0.1170

The discount factor for time, 2, is given by, $\dfrac{1849}{2310}$

The interest rate spanning the time interval, $[0,2]$, is given by, 0.2493

The discount factor for time, 3, is given by, $\dfrac{82507}{124740}$

The interest rate spanning the time interval, $[0,3]$, is given by, 0.5119

The function Vdis ($[c1,c2,..]$), values the cashflow $[c1,c2,..]$

The continuous discount factor is given by the function, 'Dis', (.)

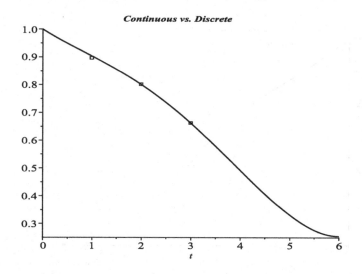

Let us first determine if the discount factor function is a perfect fit, as it does not seem so from the graph:

```
> SumAbsDiv;
```

$$\frac{135043}{171680}$$

Since the value is not zero we try to increase the number of the approximating functions from 3 to 7.

```
> NarbitB([[105,0,0],[10,110,0],[8,8,108]],[94,97,85],
7,Dis,1,6);
```

The no-arbitrage condition is satisfied.
The discount factor for time, 1, is given by, $\dfrac{94}{105}$
The interest rate spanning the time interval, $[0,1]$, *is given by,* 0.1170
The discount factor for time, 2, is given by, $\dfrac{1849}{2310}$
The interest rate spanning the time interval, $[0,2]$, *is given by,* 0.2493
The discount factor for time, 3, is given by, $\dfrac{82507}{124740}$
The interest rate spanning the time interval, $[0,3]$, *is given by,* 0.5119
The function Vdis ([c1,c2,..]), values the cashflow [c1,c2,..]
The continuous discount factor is given by the function, 'Dis', (.)

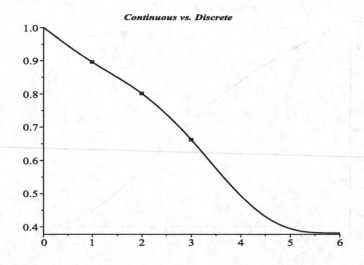

Continuous vs. Discrete

```
> SumAbsDiv;
```

0

Having obtained a good discount function $Dis(t)$, we can define a function for the term structure, i.e., for $R(t)$. Assuming continuous compounding means that $Dis(t) = e^{-R(t)t}$ and consequently that the term structure is the function R such that $-\dfrac{\ln(Dis(t))}{t} = R(t)$. Hence R is defined below :

```
> R:=unapply(evalf(-ln(Dis(t))/t),t);
```

$$R := t \to -\frac{1}{t} \left(1. \ln \left(piecewise \left(0. \le t \textbf{ and } t \le 6., \right. \right. \right.$$
$$-0.1058861591\,t - 0.02051130324\,t^2 + 0.03426317753\,t^3$$
$$-0.01285192791\,t^4 - 0.0006447858262\,t^5 + 0.001030316421\,t^6$$
$$\left. \left. \left. -0.0001698574536\,t^7 + 0.000008634794668\,t^8,\ Float(undefined) \right) \right) \right)$$

It is obvious that the function is not a line parallel to the x-axis, hence we are not dealing with a market in which the term structure is flat. For example the term structure for time 2 is

```
> R(2);
```

$$0.1113012862$$

While for time 5 it is

```
> R(5);
```

$$0.1858648871$$

To see a plot of the term structure we can issue the following command:

```
> plot(R(t),t=0..6,y=0..0.22);
```

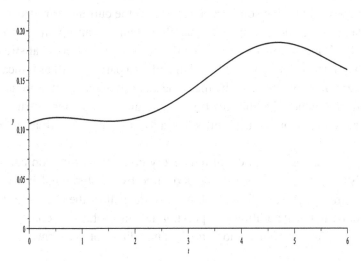

Nevertheless, it is easy to show that if we continue to work with a measure of duration, then as before, it will immunize us against changes in the term structure of a parallel nature. These changes are of the type exemplified as follows — they cause a shift in the term structure curve, up or down, by the same amount.

```
> plot([R(t)+0.05,R(t),R(t)-0.05],t=0..6,
color=[red,green,blue]);
```

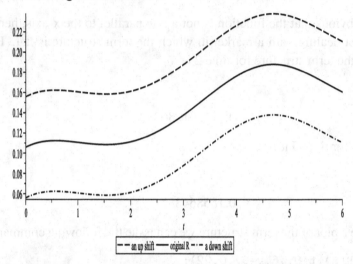

In the above figure the solid graph represents the current term structure of interest rate, R, and two possible parallel changes; an up shift of the curve by 0.05 and a down shift by -0.05. It is however not realistic to assume that the term structure will be changed by a parallel shift as it means that long term rates are changed by the same amount of the short term rates. We thus further generalize the situation and assume that the term structure can change not only by parallel shifts, but allows forms that will affect its curvature.

Recall that under certain conditions every continuous function can be (uniformly) approximated as closely as desired by a polynomial function (the Weierstrass approximation theorem). We thus allow the change to the term structure to be an addition of a polynomial, and not only a constant as in the case of a parallel shift, and consider an addition of the form

$$\sum_{i=1}^{n} \alpha_i t^{(i-1)},$$

$$(4.26)$$

where the alphas are random coefficients. Note that when $i = 1$ the change is of a parallel shift and the duration we defined can be used to immunize the portfolio for such a case. In general, however, we assume that if the current term structure is $R(t)$ it will be changed to

$$R(t) + \sum_{i=1}^{n} \alpha_i t^{(i-1)}.$$

(4.27)

We first define, below, the discount factor function *DisGC* as a function of the array $\alpha = [\alpha_1, \ldots, \alpha_n]$ **and** t, that is induced by such a change i.e,

$$DisGC([\alpha_1, \ldots, \alpha_n], t) = e^{-\left(R(t) + \sum_{i=1}^{n} \alpha_i t^{(i-1)}\right)}$$

(4.28)

```
> DisGC:=(t,alpha)->exp(-(R(t)+sum(alpha[i]*t^(i-1),
i=1..nops(alpha)))*t);
```

$$DisGC := (t, \alpha) \to e^{-\left(R(t) + \sum_{i=1}^{nops(\alpha)} \alpha_i t^{i-1}\right)t}$$

There are two arguments to this function, t the time variable and an array of alpha. Hence if one would like to consider a change to the term structure that is of the form $\sum_{i=1}^{3} \alpha_i t^{(i-1)}$ where the alphas are [0.05,0.0,0.005] the new term structure will be

```
> DisGC(t,[0.05,0.0,0.005]);
```

$$e^{-\left(R(t) + 0.05 + 0.005 t^2\right)t}$$

If the array [0.05,.0,0.005] would be replaced by [0,0,0] then one would get the current discount factor function. Hence to plot the current discount factor function and the one that would result after such a change, i.e., an addition of $05 + 0t^1 + 0.005 t^2$ to the current term structure, one would execute:

```
> plot([DisGC(t,[0,0,0]),DisGC(t,[0.05,.0,0.005])],
t=0..6,colour=[green,red]);
```

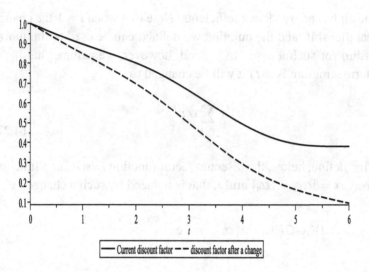

| Current discount factor — — discount factor after a change |

To plot the current term structure and the one that would result after such a change, i.e., an addition of $05 + 0t^1 + 0.005t^2$ to the current term structure, one would execute:

```
> plot([-ln(DisGC(t,[0,0,0]))/t,
-ln(DisGC(t,[0.05,.0,0.005]))/t],
t=0..6,colour=[green,red]);
```

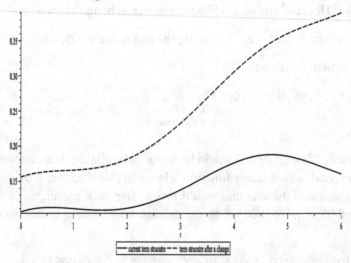

| current term structure — — term structure after a change |

Note that indeed the changes we considered are not all feasible as we cannot have a non-decreasing discount factor function. However, our immunization strategy will not be adversely influenced by such an assumption (although it is not as efficient as it could have been).

Generalizing the possible changes to the term structure, of course, has its influence on the immunization strategy. When only a parallel shift in the term structure was considered, there was only one measure of duration, $\sum_{t=1}^{n} w(t)t$. In the generalized model described above there are many measures of durations that are defined similarly.

The next additional measure of duration is one that takes care of changes to the term structure that are induced by α_2, an addition of a linear function. This measure is $\sum_{t=1}^{n} w(t)t^2$ or the convexity as defined by equation (4.10). Consequently, if the current term structure is $R(t)$ and after the change the term structure will be given in the form of $R(t) + \sum_{i=1}^{2} \alpha_i t^{(i-1)}$ immunization will require that the first order duration, $\sum_{t=1}^{n} w(t)t$, of the asset and the liability will be the same and also the second order duration $\sum_{t=1}^{n} w(t)t^2$ (referred to as convexity) of the asset and the liability will be the same.

Allowing a more realistic change to the term, i.e., considering a larger n in $\sum_{i=1}^{n} \alpha_i t^{(i-1)}$, requires more duration constraints to be satisfied. In general one must satisfy n duration constraints, of the form $\sum_{t=1}^{n} w(t)t^n$ that insure that the nth order duration of the asset and the liability are the same.

This might not always be possible and second best solutions are sometimes utilized. When short sales are allowed, more degrees of freedom are introduced and it might be possible to meet the duration constraints that are not feasible with long positions only.

To help us in the calculation we have defined the following function that calculates the kth order duration of a bond with a coupon rate of c where the discount function is d and the maturity of the bond is n units of time (measured in years); **GenDur(c,d,n,k)**. For simplicity this function assumes that coupons are paid annually. Thus the first order duration of a bond with a coupon rate of 10%, a discount factor function named Dis and maturity of three years is given by executing:

```
>  GenDur(0.10,Dis,3,1);
```

$$2.711204142$$

The table below demonstrates the value of the different duration order.

	A	B	C	D	E	F	G
				Durations of Diffrent Orders			
1	"Maturity in Years"	1	2	3	4	5	6
2	"First order duration"	1	1.907707413	2.711204142	3.364812028	3.915903938	4.516020886
3	"Second Order Duration"	1	3.723122239	7.755596263	12.44873409	17.58790758	24.03840039
4	"Third Order Durtion"	1	7.353951890	22.71033201	47.86395115	83.35321223	136.0590903
5	"Discount Factor"	0.8952380952	0.8004329004	0.6614317781	0.4938850868	0.3948203473	0.3815354079

4.4 Immunization strategies with and without short sales

This section illustrates the mechanics of immunization and highlights a few strategies. At the outset it is important to realize that an immunization strategy is not a static but a dynamic strategy. As time passes, the duration of both assets and liabilities change. The term structure of interest rates may change and will thus affect the duration of both assets and liabilities. Consequently, the conditions which were satisfied when the portfolio was constructed, may be violated by the passage of time as well as due to the maturity of some bonds in the portfolio. Therefore there is a need to revise the portfolio and reshuffle it so that the duration of the liabilities and the assets will be equal again.

The main goal, as we have already seen, is to match the duration of the liabilities and the assets. This matching may not be feasible, depending of course, on the order of durations one wants to match, short sales restrictions and the availability of bonds in the market. Obviously, when short sales are not allowed, infeasibility is more likely to occur. In any event one must decide how to address the infeasibilities. A way of addressing the infeasibilities is suggested by the optimization problem below.

Consider a market with N bonds. Define an $O \times N$ matrix A such that a_{ij} is the ith duration of the jth bond, $i = 1, \ldots, N$, $j = 1, \ldots, O$ (where O is the largest duration order used). Similarly, we can define an $O \times 1$

vector $L = (L_1, \ldots, L_O)$ such that its ith component is the ith duration of the liabilities.

Let C be the amount invested in the bond portfolio that is constructed in order to immunize the liabilities. We assume C to be the present value of the total liabilities. Let c_i be the amount invested in bond i (positive or negative), and x_i be defined as $\frac{c_i}{C}$, thus x_i is the percentage of the portfolio invested in bond i. Hence , $\sum_{i=1}^{N} x_i = 1$ and if short sales are not allowed, $x_i \geq 0$ for $i = 1, \ldots, N$.

The duration of a portfolio is the weighted average of the durations of the bonds in the portfolio. The weights are the values invested in a bond, divided by the value of the portfolio, e.g., the weight of bond i is x_i. We therefore use the vector $x = (x_1, \ldots, x_N)$ to denote the portfolio. A portfolio x matches the O durations of the liability if

$$Ax = L \tag{4.29}$$

or if

$$\sum_{j=1}^{N} x_j a_{ij} = L_i, \quad \text{for} \quad i = 1, \ldots, O$$

If short sales are not allowed, the above system of equations with the constraint $x_i \geq 0$ for $i = 1, \ldots, N$ should be satisfied for the durations of the liabilities and the assets to match. In this illustration we adopt the rule that if the duration constraints, i.e., $Ax = L$ cannot be satisfied, a second best solution will be used instead. The second best concept used here is that of a minimization of the sum of absolute deviations from the constraints. We used the absolute deviations concept of a second best solution as it allows us to formulate the optimization problem as a linear programming problem.

Let us define the two vectors $\varepsilon^{+} = \left(\varepsilon_1^{+}, \ldots, \varepsilon_O^{+}\right), \varepsilon^{-} = \left(\varepsilon_1^{-}, \ldots, \varepsilon_O^{-}\right)$ and the minimization problem below:

$$Min \sum_{i=1}^{O} \left(\varepsilon_i^{+} + \varepsilon_i^{-}\right)$$
$$\text{s.t. } Ax - L = \varepsilon^{+} - \varepsilon^{-}$$
$$\varepsilon^{+} \geq 0 \quad \varepsilon^{-} \geq 0 \tag{4.30}$$

where if short sales are not allowed, the constraint $x \geq 0$ should be added.

The constraints of the problem in a scalar form are written as

$$\sum_{j=N}^{N} x_j a_{ij} = L_i + \varepsilon_i^+ - \varepsilon_i^-$$
$$\textbf{for} \quad i = 1, \ldots, O$$
$$\varepsilon_i^+ \geq 0 \quad \varepsilon_i^- \geq 0.$$

Based on the properties of a linear programming problem, it is possible to show that the above minimizes the sum of absolute deviations from the duration constraints, i.e., it minimizes $\sum_{i=1}^{O} |Ax - L|_i$. The optimal value of this problem is zero, i.e., $\varepsilon^+ = 0$, $\varepsilon^- = 0$, if and only if, it was feasible to satisfy all the duration constraints. The optimal solution, in case it is not possible to satisfy the constraint, is a second best solution.

The input arguments to the procedure that solves the optimization in (4.30) are:

- a list representing the payoff matrix from the bonds, where it is assumed that time is discretized and each column in the matrix corresponds to a time e.g., column 1 to time 1; column 2 to time 2; etc., and the period between each time is equal. For simplicity it is assumed to be a year and thus that thecoupons are paid annually.
- a list — representing the prices of the bonds.
- a list — representing the maturity of each bond.
- a scalar — representing the liability time (the procedure assumes a single liability).
- a scalar — the order of the duration to be matched in the immunization.
- a scalar — the order of the polynomial used in order to estimate the continuous discount factor function.

To illustrate the use of this procedure, consider a bond market with a payment matrix as defined below:

	A	B	C	D	E	F	G
1	"Bonds/Time"	1	2	3	4	"price"	"maturity time"
2	"bond 1"	5	105			67.5	2
3	"bond 2"	7	7	107		69.3	3
4	"bond 3"	0	0	0	100	40	4
5	"bond 4"	104				93.6	1

Assume a single liability, occurring at time 3, immunization based on duration of order of 2 and that the polynomial order for the discount factor is 16. Hence the input parameters to the procedure for this case are:

- the pay off matrix in the form of [[5,105,0,0], [7,7,107,0], [0,0,0,100], [104,0,0,0]]
- the vector of bonds' prices as [67.5,69.3,40,93.6]
- the maturity times of the bonds as [2,3,4,1]
- the scalar representing the liability time, 3
- the scalar representing the order of duration, 2
- the scalar representing the polynomial order, 16
- name assigned by the user to keep the Duration matrix DM1 below where DM1[i,j] is the ith order duration of the jth bond.

Hence, the following command should be issued in order to find the immunized portfolio. The command is executed below and the meaning of the output is explained after the output is produced. As you can see most of it is self explanatory.

```
> Immunize([[5,105,0,0],[7,7,107,0],[0,0,0,100],
[104,0,0,0]],[67.5,69.3,40,93.6],[2,3,4,1],3,2,16,DM1);
```

The no-arbitrage condition is satisfied.
The discount factor for time, 1, is given by, 0.9000000000
The interest rate spanning the time interval, [0,1], is given by, 0.111
The discount factor for time, 2, is given by, 0.6000000000
The interest rate spanning the time interval, [0,2], is given by, 0.667
The discount factor for time, 3, is given by, 0.5495327103
The interest rate spanning the time interval, [0,3], is given by, 0.820
The discount factor for time, 4, is given by, 0.4000000000

The interest rate spanning the time interval, $[0,4]$, *is given by,* 1.500
The function Vdis ([c1,c2,..]), values the cashflow [c1,c2,..]
The continuous discount factor is given by the function, 'dis', (.)
The sum of absolute deviations for the TS estimation is, 0.
The optimal portfolio without short sales is,
$\{Neg1 = 0.08301880225,\ Neg2 = 0.,\ Pos1 = 0.,\ Pos2 = 0.,$
$x1 = 0.,\ x2 = 0.8716982142,\ x3 = 0.1283017858,\ x4 = 0.\}$
The optimal portfolio with short sales is, $\{Neg1 = 0.,\ Neg2 = 0.,$
$Pos1 = 0.,\ Pos2 = 0.,\ x1 = -0.07653053341,\ x2 = 1.178571240,$
$x3 = 0.,\ x4 = -0.1020407062\}$

The procedure first identifies if the no arbitrage condition is satisfied and reports the discrete discount factor for each period. Based on the discrete discount factors, a continuous approximation of the discount factor is obtained. If the no arbitrage condition is not satisfied, the second best solution for a set of discrete discount factors is solved for and a continuous approximation of a discount factor function is obtained. The continuous approximation of the discount factor is defined by the procedure as a function named 'dis'. Similarly a function that calculates the present value of cash flows across the discrete time period is defined as the 'Vdis' function. The final two lines, the set objects, are the optimal solutions, i.e., the portfolio composition, first for the case where short sales are not allowed, followed by the solution where short sales were allowed. The value of x_i is the proportion invested in bond i, hence the value of the xs in both cases is the portfolio composition. The variables Negi and Posi correspond to the epsilon in the optimization problem (4.30). Hence it is possible to deduct from these values the value of $\sum_{i=1}^{O} \left(\varepsilon_i^+ + \varepsilon_i^-\right)$ at the optimum, which is just the sum of the Negi and Posi variables. That is, if this sum is zero all the duration constraints were satisfied. If the sum is not zero, the Negi and Posi variables tell us the amount by which the duration constrained was above or below its required value. That is, if Negi is not zero, as is the case in the above output where short sales are not allowed, it means that the duration of the portfolio was below the required duration (the liability's duration) and vise versa. Hence, in the above case where $Neg1 = 0.08301880225$ it means that the first order duration of the liability exceeded the first order duration of the portfolio by 0.08301880225. Let us see how that works. The duration matrix A defined above can be displayed by executing the command below:

```
> print(DM1);
```

$$\begin{bmatrix} 1.933333334 & 2.757575977 & 3.999999999 & 1 \\ 3.800000001 & 7.969697900 & 16.00000000 & 1 \end{bmatrix}$$

That is, the (i,j) component of this matrix is the ith duration of the jth bond. e.g., the first duration of bond 1 is 1.933333334 and its second duration is 3.800000001. This can be versified as follows. The nonzero holding in the optimal portfolio when short sales were not allowed was $x2 = 0.8716982142$, $x3 = 0.1283017858$. The first order duration of bond 2 is 2.757575977 and that of bond 3 is 3.999999999. Hence the first order duration of the portfolio is

```
> 0.8716982142*2.757575977+0.1283017858*3.999999999;
```

$$2.916981198$$

Consequently, the first order duration of the portfolio minus that of the liability is

```
> %-3;
```

$$-0.083018802$$

The second order duration of the portfolio is

```
> 0.8716982142*7.969697900+0.1283017858*16.00000000;
```

$$9.0$$

which is the required duration as it equals the second order duration of the liability. Indeed in the optimal solution $Neg2 = 0$ **and** $Pos2 = 0$, i.e., the second constraint is satisfied.

In order to keep the value of the discount factor function, in the above market, and not overwrite it in our next calculation, we execute the commands below.

```
> dis1:=unapply(%,dis(t));
```

$$dis1 := t \rightarrow piecewise(0 \leq t \text{ and } t \leq 4, 1 - 1.272758999\,t^6$$
$$+2.987457807\,t^7 - 3.253732160\,t^8 + 2.159954896\,t^9 -$$
$$0.9678397583\,t^{10} + 0.3066317588\,t^{11} - 0.06996790708\,t^{12} +$$
$$0.01148341255\,t^{13} - 0.001327120506\,t^{14} + 0.0001027598697\,t^{15} -$$
$$0.000004791311324\,t^{16} + 1.015892386\,10^{-7}t^{17}, undefined)$$

The above command makes sure that the function dis, will be kept as 'dis1' and will not be affected by further calculations. The discount factor function 'dis1' is plotted below

```
> plot(dis1(t),t=0..4);
```

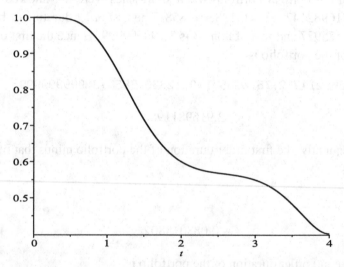

Next let us first see the change in the output if the no arbitrage condition is not satisfied . To this end we change the price of the first bond to be 57 instead of 67.5 and re-execute the procedure below.

```
> Immunize([[5,105,0,0],[7,7,107,0],[0,0,0,100],
[104,0,0,0]],[57,69.3,40,93.6],[2,3,4,1],3,2,16,DM2);
```

The no-arbitrage condition is not satisfied
An arbitrage portfolio is:
Buy, 1.085714286, *of Bond*, 1
Short, 1., *of Bond*, 2

Buy, 0.1500000000, *of Bond*, 3
Buy, 0.01510989011, *of Bond*, 4
Buying this portfolio produces income of, $-1.4 \, 10^{-8}$, *at time*, 0
This portfolio produces income of, $1. \, 10^{-9}$, *at time*, 1
This portfolio produces income of, 107.0000000, *at time*, 2
This portfolio produces income of, $-107.$, *at time*, 3
This portfolio produces income of, 15.00000000, *at time*, 4
The continuous discount factor is given by the function, 'dis', (.)
The sum of absolute deviations for the TS estimation is, 9.697834896
The optimal portfolio without short sales is,
{*Neg1* = 0.08286648154, *Neg2* = 0., *Pos1* = 0., *Pos2* = 0.,
x1 = 0., *x2* = 0.8721171648, *x3* = 0.1278828352, *x4* = 0.}
The optimal portfolio with short sales is, {*Neg1* = 0., *Neg2* = 0.,
Pos1 = 0., *Pos2* = 0., *x1* = −0.07555240082, *x2* = 1.177500482,
x3 = 0., *x4* = −0.1019480812}

```
> print(DM2);
```

$$\begin{bmatrix} 1.932531544 & 2.758347473 & 4.000000000 & 1 \\ 3.797594630 & 7.973555524 & 16.00000000 & 1 \end{bmatrix}$$

Observing the outputs we see that if the procedure determines that the no arbitrage condition is not satisfied, it reports it. It also identifies an arbitrage portfolio and the arbitrage profit. The rest of the output is the same. Note however that in this last output the reports says "The sum of absolute deviations for the TS estimation is, 9.697834896", which means that the sum of absolute deviations between the present value of the bonds and their prices is approximately 9.6.

We can visually compare the relation between the discount factor functions, in the case with and without arbitrage. It is done in the figure below where the solid graph is the discount factor function when arbitrage exists and the dash is when arbitrage does not exist:

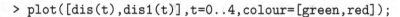

```
> plot([dis(t),dis1(t)],t=0..4,colour=[green,red]);
```

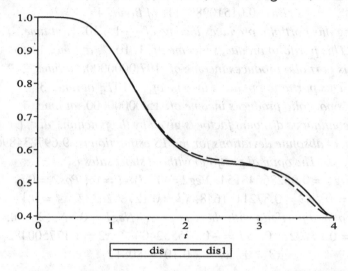

In order to illustrate the immunization technique, let us assume that we face a liability at time 3 in the market where the no arbitrage condition was satisfied (the first execution of the immunize procedure) and short sales were allowed. Assume further that the present value of the liability, due at time 3, is 10,000. Then its future value at time 3 is

```
> 10000*dis1(3)^(-1);
```

$$18197.03752$$

As seen from the output above, the portfolio was composed from investments in bond 2 and bond 3, where the percentage invested in bond 2 and 3 respectively are listed below:

$$x2 = 0.8824348082, \quad x3 = 0.1175651918.$$

In terms of the units of bonds purchased for each bond, the number of units of bond 2 in the portfolio is :

```
> (10000*0.8824348082)/69.3;
```

$$127.3354702$$

and the number of units of bond 3 in the portfolio is

```
> (10000*.1175651918)/40;
```

29.39129795

Assume that a year after the initial portfolio was composed (just after the coupon was paid) the prices of the bonds and their specifications are as given in the table below:

	A	B	C	D	E	F
			Spreadsheet(2)			
1	"Bonds/Time"	1	2	3	*Price*	
2	"bond 1"	105			94.5	
3	"bond 2"	7	107		91.9	
4	"bond 3"	0	0	100	75	

Thus the value of the portfolio (excluding the coupon paid) is now:

```
> 127.3354702*91.9+29.39129795*75.0;
```

13906.47706

A coupon payment of $7 for each unit of bond 2 was also received; hence the total from coupon payment is

```
> 7*127.3354702;
```

891.3482914

Consequently the total value that we have now for investment is:

```
> 13906.47706+891.3482914;
```

14797.82535

Note that now the liability time is time 2 (as it was initially time 3 and one year passed) and thus we need to update our portfolio. Also the input parameters should be changed accordingly and hence we should execute:

```
> Immunize([[105,0,0],[7,107,0],[0,0,100]],
[94.5,91.9,75],[1,2,3],2,2,16,DM3);
```

The no-arbitrage condition is satisfied.
The discount factor for time, 1, is given by, 0.9000000000
The interest rate spanning the time interval, [0,1], is given by, 0.111
The discount factor for time, 2, is given by, 0.8000000000
The interest rate spanning the time interval, [0,2], is given by, 0.250
The discount factor for time, 3, is given by, 0.7500000000
The interest rate spanning the time interval, [0,3], is given by, 0.333
The function Vdis ([c1,c2,..]), values the cashflow [c1,c2,..]
The continuous discount factor is given by the function, 'dis', (.)
The sum of absolute deviations for the TS estimation is, 0.
The optimal portfolio without short sales is,
{Neg1 = 0.02633779254, Neg2 = 0., Pos1 = 0., Pos2 = 0.,
x1 = 0., x2 = 0.9604933107, x3 = 0.03950668928}
The optimal portfolio with short sales is, {Neg1 = 0., Neg2 = 0.,
Pos1 = 0., Pos2 = 0., x1 = −0.07359813050, x2 = 1.073598130,
x3 = 5.399999994 10^{-10}

```
> print(DM3);
```

$$\begin{bmatrix} 1 & 1.931447225 & 3.000000000 \\ 1 & 3.794341674 & 9.000000000 \end{bmatrix}$$

We have now $14797.82535 to invest, the liability we have to meet in 2 years is 18196.87196 and its present value is

```
> 18196.87196*dis(2);
```

14557.49757

Hence, the present value of the amount dedicated to cover the liability exceeds the present value of the liability. This situation can also be expressed in terms of future values. The value of the portfolio we currently hold is 14797.82535 and its future value, at time 2, based on the current term structure is thus

```
> 18196.90408/dis(2);
```

22746.13010

which is more than twice the future value of the liability.

This is a result of favorable significant changes in the term structure. In order to visualize the change in the term structure, we graph below the initial discount factor function, dis1, with the current function, dis, and another function, dis1(t+1)/dis1(1). This last function is the discount factor function, assuming a deterministic term structure environment. This assumes no change occurred in the term structure and that the change is due only to the passage of time. That is, the discount factor calculated based on such an assumption is calculated from the forward rate as of the initial time, e.g., the discount factor function as of the current time based on the forward rate.

```
> plot([dis(t),dis1(t),dis1(t+1)/dis1(1)],t=0..3,
colour=[green,red,black]);
```

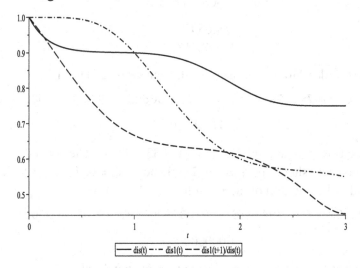

The current discount factor function is the solid curve. The discount factor function that would have resulted at this time, if there had been no changes to the term structure but the passage of time, is the dash curve. The dash dot curve is the discount factor function of a year ago. It is obvious that under the solid curve, the present value is much larger than under the dash curve. This is the reason there is so much surplus in the present value relative to the liability.

We have one more year to go and the optimal portfolio to hold for the last year, assuming short sales are not allowed, is given by:

$$x2 = 0.9604933107, x3 = 0.03950668928$$

Therefore we are going to invest

> 14797.82535*0.9604933107;

$$14213.21226$$

in bond 2 and

> 14797.82535*0.03950668928;

$$584.6130881$$

in bond 3. Hence the number of units purchased from bond 2 and 3, respectively are

> 14213.21226/91.9;584.6130881/75;

$$154.6595458$$
$$7.794841175$$

The first order duration of the portfolio cannot be 2, but it is

> 0.9604933107*1.931447225+0.03950668928*3.000000000;

$$1.973662208$$

as predicted by the value of Neg1 = 0.02633779254. The second order duration however should be 4 as Neg2 = 0 and Pos2 = 0. Let us calculate the second order duration of the portfolio

> 0.9604933107*3.794341674+0.03950668928*9.000000000;

$$4.000000000$$

Assume that after a year has passed, immediately after the coupons were paid, bond prices are as given as follows:

	A	B	C	D	E	F	G	H
		1	2	3	4			
1	"Bonds/Time"					"price"	"maturity time"	
2	"bond 1"	5	105			67.5	2	
3	"bond 2"	7	7	107		69.3	3	
4	"bond 3"	0	0	0	100	40	4	
5	"bond 4"	104				93.6	1	

Thus the value we have at hand to meet the liability is composed of two parts, the coupon payments and the value of the bonds: from bond 2 we receive a total of

```
> (7+80.25)*154.6595458;
```

$$13494.04537$$

and from bond 3 a total of

```
> 72*7.794841175;
```

$$561.2285646$$

Hence the total value we have at hand to meet the liability of 18196.87196 due now is

```
> 13494.04538+13494.04538;
```

$$26988.09076$$

The preceding example demonstrates the ingredients and process of immunization based on duration of order 2. The process will be carried out in the same manner for a higher order duration.

4.5 Concluding Remarks

In this chapter we introduce the concept of duration as a measure of sensitivity of bond prices to parallel shifts in the term structure of interest rate. The duration concept goes back to the 1930s. It has been used extensively as a tool in compiling portfolios of bonds that are targeted to meet a known liability in the future. The chapter also introduces the concept of generalized duration and demonstrates its use in immunization when short sales are allowed and when they are not allowed.

The current academic literature justifiably criticizes this definition of duration and its use, demonstrated above, as being inconsistent with the absence of arbitrage. On the other hand, practitioners testify that the technique has been used for a few decades by pension companies and alike to immunize their liabilities very successfully. An alternative definition of duration does exists but it depends on the stochastic process that governs the dynamic of the term structure; this topic is beyond the scope of this book.

4.6 Questions and Problems

Questions 1 - 11 refer to the market defined below:

Consider a bond market that includes 4 bonds paying coupons semiannually all with a face value of $100:

Bond 1: a 5% coupon bond maturing in 2 years (i.e., the first coupon of $2.5 will be paid in 6 months)

Bond 2: a 7% coupon bond maturing in 3 years (i.e., the first coupon of $3.5 will be paid in 6 months)

Bond 3: a 0 coupon bond maturing in 4 years

Bond 4: a 0 coupon bond maturing in one year

Note a 7% coupon bond with a face value of $100 maturing in 1 year when the term structure is flat at 7% and coupons are paid semiannually will not be priced at par. This is because $3.5 out of the $7, received over a year, are received after 6 months and not after a year. You may use the procedures Dur and BondPrice that assume semiannual coupon payments. For e.g., the price of the 7% coupon bond with a face value of $100 maturing in 1 year, when the term structure is flat at 7% is calculated as

```
> with(FixIncFun):BondPrice(0.07,0.07,1);
```

$$100.1125497$$

The price and duration of the 7% coupon bond with a face value of $100 maturing in 1 year when the term structure is flat at 5% is calculated as

```
> Dur(0.07,0.05,1,100);
```

$$0.9832544954$$

```
> BondPrice(0.07,0.05,1);
```

$$101.9870788$$

Assume that the current time is time 0, and that time 1 is 1 year after time 0, time 2 is 1 year after time 1 etc.

1. Without making any calculations based on the above introduction of the Duration concept, can you say what the durations of bond 4 and 3 are? (Hint: remember the interpretation of duration is a weighted average.)

2a. Prove that the duration of a portfolio is the weighted average of the duration of the bonds in the portfolio.

2b. If you buy a portfolio composed of bonds 3 and 4, what should be the proportion invested in each bond so that the portfolio will have a duration of 2.5?

3. Can you compose a portfolio of bonds 3 and 4 with a duration of 0.5?

4. Can you, without any calculations, find upper and lower bounds for the duration of bond 1?

5. Assume that the term structure in this market is flat at 7% and that coupons are paid paid semiannually;

   i. find the prices of the bonds
   ii. find the duration of each bond
   iii. Assume that there exists also a bond in this market that pays $6 at time 0.5, 1.5 and 2.5 and $106 at time 3.5, find the price and the duration of this bond at time 0.

6. Assume that the term structure in this market is flat at 8% and find the prices of the bonds.

7. Use the duration approximation to find the prices of the bonds based on their prices at 7% if the rate would increase to 8% and compare your results to 6 above. Repeat the above using both convexity and duration for the approximation.

8. Assume that the term structure is flat at 7%, calculate the duration of a coupon paying bond maturing at time 2 with a coupon of 2%, 3%, 6% and 7%. Can you generalize the results you obtained?

9. Assume that the term structure is flat at 6% and 9% and calculate the durations of the bonds. Can you generalize the results you obtained?

10. Assume a flat term structure of 7% and that you have a liability of

$1000 to pay at time 2.75. You have currently in your hand the present value of that liability. You invest it all in bond 2 (the 7% bond).

a. Assume also that an instant after you purchased bond 2, the interest rate was changed to a flat 8% and calculate the value of your portfolio as of time 2.75. Repeat the last calculation for the cases where the rate was changed to 9%, 5% and 4%. Did you manage to meet your liability in any case? Can you interpret the results?

b. Assume that 6 months after you purchased bond 2 (immediately after the coupon was paid) the interest rate was changed to a flat 8%.

 i. Identify the percentage invested in each bond for all the portfolios with a duration of 2.15.

 ii. How many units of bond 3 and bond 4 will be held in a portfolio with duration of 2.15 that is composed of only bond 3 and bond 4? What is the convexity of this portfolio?

 iii. Is it possible to compose a portfolio such that both the convexity of the portfolio and the duration of the portfolio are the same as the convexity and the duration of the liability? Use the following function to calculate the convexity (note this is an approximation as the convexity is calculated assuming a continuously compounded rate of return). Would your answer change if short sales were not allowed? Is there a portfolio with the same duration and convexity as of that of the liability if short sales were not allowed only for bonds 1, bond 2, and bond 3? If your answer is positive solve for the units of bonds 1, 2 and 4 that are being held in the portfolio, otherwise show that such a portfolio does not exist.

```
> Conv:=(c,r,n,F)->(F*(1+r)^(-n)*n^2+sum((1/4)
*F*c*(1+r)^(-(1/2)*i)*i^2, i = 1 .. 2*n))/
(F*(1+r)^(-n)+sum((1/2)*F*c*(1+r)^(-(1/2)*i), i =
1 .. 2*n));
```

$$Conv := (c,r,n,F) \to \frac{F(1+r)^{-n}n^2 + \sum_{i=1}^{2n} \frac{1}{4}Fc(1+r)^{-\frac{1}{2}i}i^2}{F(1+r)^{-n} + \sum_{i=1}^{2n} \frac{1}{2}Fc(1+r)^{-\frac{1}{2}i}}$$

```
> Conv(0.05,0.08,1.5,100);#E.g., for bond 1 the
conextiy is
```

$$2.252323613$$

11. Assume a flat term structure of 7% and

    i. Compose a portfolio of bonds 2 and 4 that costs as much as bond 1 does, and has the same duration as that of bond 1.

    ii. Suppose that an instant after you composed the portfolio, the interest rate changed from 7% to 8%. Find the effect on the price of the portfolio and the bonds.

    iii. How many portfolios that cost the same as bond 2 and have the same duration as bond 2, can you compose?

    iv. If short sales were not allowed would your answer to iii be different?

12. Consider a market which includes bonds with the following cash-flows:

"Bonds/Time"	1	2	3	4
"bond 1"	5	105		
"bond 2"	7	7	107	
"bond 3"	0	0	0	100
"bond 4"	104			

Assume that coupons are paid annually that the current time is time 0, that time 1 is 1 year after time 0, time 2 is 1 year after time 1 etc.

    a. Suppose the term structure is flat at 7% and that you have a liability of $1000 to pay at time 3. You have currently in your hand the present value of that liability. The only capital market open to you is the market above. To insure that you be able to meet your liability, you adopt the following investment strategy:

time 0: You compose a portfolio with duration of 3 and invest the present value of the 1000 in that portfolio.

time 1: After a year, you find out that the term structure is flat at 5%. You liquidate your portfolio and invest the money in a portfolio with duration of 2.

time 3: After 2 years, you find out that the term structure is flat at 6%. You liquidate your portfolio and invest the money in a portfolio with a duration of 1.

time 4: After 3 years, you find out that the term structure is flat at 4%. You liquidate your portfolio and compare it to the 1000 you have to pay.

b. Repeat the above assuming that after a year, you find out that the term structure is flat at 8%, after 2 years it is flat at 9%, and after 3 years it is flat at 10%.

13. Assume the following market in which coupons are paid annually, the current time is time 0, that time 1 is 1 year after time 0, time 2 is 1 year after time 1 etc.:

Spreadsheet(1)						
	A	B	C	D	E	F
1	"Bonds/Time"	1	2	3	4	Price
2	"bond 1"	0	105			67.5
3	"bond 2"	7	7	107		69.3
4	"bond 3"	0	0	0	100	40
5	"bond 4"	104				93.6

Estimate the discount function and the term structure to fit the prices of the bonds exactly and verify that the term structure is not flat. Assume that you have a liability of $1000 to pay at time 3. You have currently in your hand the present value of that liability. The only capital market open to you is the market above. To insure that you be able to meet your liability an immunization strategy is carried out:

a. with respect to the first order duration, and

b. with respect to first and second order durations.

Try to avoid short positions unless it is not possible to immunize without them. If immunization is not possible even with short positions, suggest second best solutions.

Assume that the bonds and prices after a year are given by:

	A	B	C	D	E
		Spreadsheet(2)			
1	"Bonds/Time"	1	2	3	Price
2	"bond 1"	105			94.5
3	"bond 2"	7	107		91.9
4	"bond 3"	0	0	100	75

after two years they are given by:

	A	B	C	D	E
		Spreadsheet(3)			
1	"Bonds/Time"	1	2	Price	
2	"bond 2"	107		80.25	
3	"bond 3"	0	100	72	

after three years they are given by:

	A	B	C	D	E
		Spreadsheet(4)			
1	"Bonds/Time"	1	3	Price	
2	"bond 2"	maturing			
3	"bond 3"	100		95	

Chapter 5

Forwards, Eurodollars, and Futures

In Chapter 1 we introduced the concepts of forward contracts in the realm of a one period model. The current chapter investigates contracts that depend on the term structure of interest rates in the framework of a multiperiod model. In this framework the chapter takes a second and more realistic look at forwards and introduces futures and Eurodollar contracts.

We also examine the difference between forward contracts and futures contracts, a difference that was moot in the setting of a one-period model. We still suppress the effect of possible default on the valuation of these contracts since we focus on the fundamental concepts. As we will see, given the structure of the two contracts, the default issue is of greater concern in the case of a forward contract than in the case of a futures contract.

This multiperiod setting also allows the value of a forward contract to be investigated at some point in time after the initiation of the contract and before its maturity. The investigation of a multiperiod scenario facilitates the analysis of the pricing of forward contracts on assets that pay known cash flows during the life of the contract. A very similar argument allows us to find the forward price of a stock that pays a known and fixed dividend yield during the life of the contract. This chapter will also investigate forward rate agreements as they are very similar to forward contracts.

5.1 Forward Contracts: A Second Look

Section 1.2 introduced forward contracts in the setting of a one-period model. The payoff, at maturity, of such a contract depends on the realization of the security or commodity on which the contract is written at the maturity time. Consider for example a forward contract written on a security XXY, whereby one party pays the other $110 and in return receives the security.

Recall that the $110 is obtained by multiplying the security price at the initiation time by $(1+r)$, where r is the interest rate in the market from the initiation time to the maturity (delivery) time of the security. Hence if at the delivery time the price of the security is above $110, the party with the obligation to purchase it for $110 profits and the net cash flow to this party is the price of the security — $110. If at the delivery time the price of the security is below $110 this party loses. Thus the payoff (the cash flow) to the party with the obligation to purchase the security (referred to as the party with the long position in the contract) for $110 can be depicted in a graph as follows.

```
> plot( x-110,x=50..150,labels=['stock
price','payoff']);
```

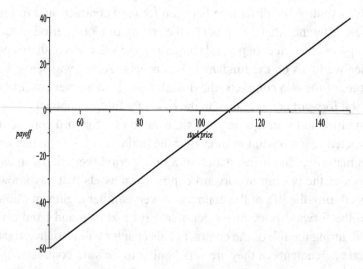

In order to prepare ourselves for the study of other types of contracts, e.g., Futures and Swaps, where the payoff from the contract is obtained not only at one point of time but at multiple points of time, we cast the forward contract in a multipeirod setting.

From a conceptual perspective, a forward contract in a multiperiod setting is not much different from a forward contract in a one-period setting.

We can think about the multiperiod as one long time period. We are only concerned with the spot price of the asset on which the contract is written and the price of that same asset on the maturity date of the contract. Thus, if we think about the time until the maturity of the contract as one (longer) time period we can still apply the results obtained in Section 1.2. Namely, the forward price is equal to the future value of the asset. The forward price can be written as $e^{(r(t)t)}S(0)$ or as $\dfrac{S(0)}{d(t)}$, where $S(0)$ is the spot price of the asset, t is the time to maturity, and $r(t)$ and $d(t)$ are, respectively, the risk-free rate and the discount factor spanning the time interval $[0,t]$. We see that we perceive the forward price as the future value of the asset, based on the term structure and the spot price of the asset.

We can visualize the payoff from a forward contract in a multiperiod setting in the following way. Let us consider a forward contract in which one party is committed to deliver a certain good (or a financial asset) at some future time T for a price of FF agreed upon now and to be paid at time T. Assume that the current time is 0, the forward contract matures at time one, and the forward price is \$7. We consider the payoff from the point of view of the party with a long position in the contract. The cash flow resultant from this contract occurs only at time $T = 1$ and will be $S(T) - FF$ where $S(T)$ is the spot price at time T.

At any other time, of course, the cash flow from this contract is zero. Hence, if we visualize the cash flows from this forward contract in the time span zero to six, the result will be as in the following figure, where the black linear graph represents the payoff from the contract. The procedure **PlotForPyf** generates the payoff. The parameters for **PlotForPyf** are, in order, the maturity time of the contract, the forward price, and the right end point of the time span to be displayed in the graph.

```
> PlotForPyf(1,7,6);
```

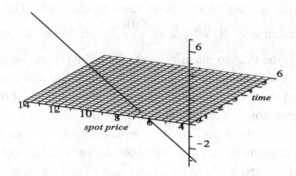

The reader can experiment with different values of the parameters and drag the graph to look at it from different perspectives in the online version. This should convey to the reader that considering the forward contract in a multiperiod setting really does not change any of its characteristics relative to a forward contract in a one-period model.

At any point in time prior to the maturity of the contract, the cash flow from the forward contract, as seen in the preceding figure, is zero. Of course, the contract still has some value. This value can be positive or negative, depending on the spot price of the asset and on the term structure (or equivalently on the discount factor function) at that point in time. Examining forward contracts in a multiperiod setting facilitates the investigation of their value prior to maturity, which is our next topic.

5.2   Valuation of Forward Contracts Prior to Maturity

Consider a forward contract requiring the delivery of a certain asset at time T. We assume that the current time is zero; hence the contract matures in T units of time. At the time the contract is written its value is zero. Indeed this is how the forward price is calculated. We will refer to this contract as the "old" forward contract. Suppose that some time has passed, say t

units of time, and the time to maturity of the old contract is $T - t$. If a forward contract on the same asset maturing in $T - t$ units of time were written now, its value would be zero. The new forward price may differ (and most likely would) from the price the holder (long) of the old contract pays in order to take delivery of the underlying asset. The current value of the "old" contract, however, is not necessarily zero. The "old" forward price specified on the "old" contract, the *delivery price*, does not reflect the circumstances of the market today. The distinction between a forward price and a delivery price was moot in the setting of a one-period model.

Each forward contract specifies the price to be paid on the delivery date for the asset in question, the underlying asset. The delivery price is equal to the forward price on the date the forward contract is initiated. The forward price is set up in such a way that the initial value of the contract is zero. As market conditions evolve, the spot price changes and so does the forward price. The forward price, which is the future value of the spot price of the asset, changes also, while the delivery price remains the same. Hence, the forward price and the delivery price, though identical on the initiation date of the contract, need not be identical at any other point in time over the life of the forward contract.

Let us now get back to the question of the value of the "old" contract. This contract obligates the one who holds it short to deliver the underlying asset in $T - t$ units of time. Thus it is equivalent to paying out the price of the asset $S(T)$, in $T - t$ units of time, and receiving the delivery price, which we denote by $F0$. Hence, holding a short position in the forward contract is equivalent to the cash flow $F0 - S(T)$ in $T - t$ units of time. Therefore, following the same guidelines as in the one-period model, we have to discount this cash flow to the present time to obtain its price.

The value of $S(T)$ is stochastic (random), and to get its current value we cannot use the discount factor to time T. However, we know the current price, $S(t)$, of the underlying asset and therefore, the current price $S(t)$ must be the present value of $S(T)$. That the present value of $S(T)$ is the spot price of the asset can also be explained in a slightly different way. Replicating $S(T)$ at time T costs $S(t)$ today (assuming the asset provides no income) since buying it now, guarantees having exactly $S(T)$ at time T. Suppressing default risk, the value of $F0$ is simply its present value based on the risk-free discount factor. Denoting the current time by t, and the discount factor function by d we arrive at equation (5.1) for the value of the forward contract.

$$S(t) - d(T-t)F0 \tag{5.1}$$

Given a discount factor function and the delivery price we can visualize the value of the forward contract as a function of time and of the spot price in a three-dimensional graph. Assume a forward contract that was initiated in the past with a delivery price of \$70 and which matures in three units of time. Let us generate a discount factor function **disf** by running **NarbitB** for a certain market. We will suppress the graphing of the discount factor function by adding a fifth input parameter and setting it equal to zero.

```
> NarbitB([[110,0,0],[8,108,0],[6,6,106]],[90,80,75],
3,disf,0);
```

The no-arbitrage condition is satisfied.
The discount factor for time, 1, is given by, $\frac{9}{11}$
The interest rate spanning the time interval, $[0,1]$, *is given by,* 0.2222
The discount factor for time, 2, is given by, $\frac{202}{297}$
The interest rate spanning the time interval, $[0,2]$, *is given by,* 0.4703
The discount factor for time, 3, is given by, $\frac{6535}{10494}$
The interest rate spanning the time interval, $[0,3]$, *is given by,* 0.6058
The function Vdis ([c1,c2,..]), values the cashflow [c1,c2,..]
The continuous discount factor is given by the function, 'disf', (.)

If we were interested in checking the goodness-of-fit of our continuous approximation, we would just need to inquire about the value of the variable **SumAbsDiv** that is defined by the procedure.

```
> SumAbsDiv;
```

0

A value of zero means that the continuous approximation coincides with the value of the discount factors on the payment dates of the bonds.

The following figure, produced by the procedure **ForVal**, demonstrates the value of the forward contract as a function of the time to maturity and of the spot price. The parameters for this procedure are, in order, the discount factor function, the range of the time to maturity in the plot, the range of the spot price in the plot, and the delivery price. The horizontal plane defines the *Value* $= 0$ plane. The other manifold is the value of the forward contract for different combinations of the spot price and the time to maturity. The emphasized line is the intersection of the plane and the manifold. It emphasizes the locus of points *(SpotPrice, TimeToMaturity)* at which the value of the forward contract is zero. Note of course, that when the time to maturity is zero, the forward contract has a zero value if the spot price and the delivery price coincide (at $70). At some time t prior to maturity the forward contract will have a value of zero if $70\, disf\,(t) = SpotPrice$. Thus the line, the intersection of the plane and the manifold, is the graph of the function $SpotPrice = 70\, dif\,(t)$ in the *Spot Price – Time To Maturity* plane.

```
> ForValue(disf,0..3,30..80,70);
```

forward's value as a function of spot price & time to maturity

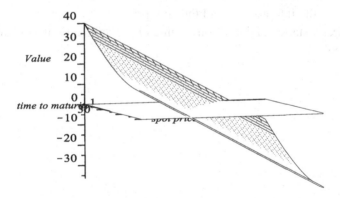

Each point on the emphasized line represents a combination of its coordinates — t, time to maturity, and S, spot price — at which the value of the forward contract is zero. Hence, it is the combination at which a forward contract, on the same asset, with a forward price of $70 would be issued if the time to maturity were t and the spot price were S. If the delivery price of the "old" forward contract happens to coincide with the forward price in the market, then the value of the "old" forward contract is zero.

The exercises at the end of the chapter ask the reader to demonstrate this algebraically. Note that when the time to maturity is zero, the value of the forward contract is zero if the delivery price equals the spot price. In our case, that spot price is $70.

In the following figure, we study the value of the forward contract for a given discount factor function as the time to maturity approaches the current time. Once the discount factor function has been assumed, the only source of uncertainty regarding the value of the contract is the spot price. It would be more realistic to visualize the evolution of the value of the forward contract as time moves forward and the current time approaches the maturity time. In doing so, however, there is another source of uncertainty besides the spot price that has to be considered. This is the interest rate that will prevail in the market from the current time to the maturity of the contract. Therefore, the state of nature is summarized by two numbers: the spot price and the interest rate.

We assume, as before, a forward contract with a delivery price of $70 and maturity in three units of time. A three-dimensional animation can be utilized to visualize the evolution of the value of the forward contract as a function of the interest rate and the spot price, as time approaches to maturity time. A static version of one frame of the animation is depicted in figure below

```
> plots[animate3d]({70*exp(-r*t)-Spt,0},r=0.01..0.18,
Spt=30..100,t=0..3,axes=normal,title='Value of Forwards
That Mature in t Units of Time as a Function of Spot
Price and Interest Rate.',labels=['rate','spot
price',Value],orientation=[-24,66],
titlefont=[TIMES,BOLD,10],
style=PATCHCONTOUR,axes=framed);
```

Value of Forwards That Mature in t Units of Time as a Function of Spot Price and Interest Rate.

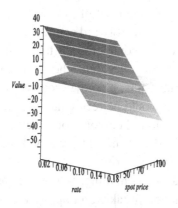

Note that when the time to maturity is zero (the last frame in the animation), the value of the forward contract is independent of the rate of interest.

In equation (5.1) the value of an "old" forward contract at time t, maturing in $T - t$ units of time, was stipulated in terms of the spot price of the asset $S(t)$, the delivery price, and the discount factor as $S(t) - d(T - t)F0$. Let us denote the forward price of a forward contract written on the same asset today, at time t, and maturing in $T - t$ units of time by $F(t)$. We can substitute for the spot price $S(t)$ in terms of the discount factor and the forward price of a contract maturing in t units of time. According to our derivation the forward price $F(t)$ is $\dfrac{S(t)}{d(T-t)}$. Hence, $S(t) = F(t)d(T-t)$ and we arrive at another expression, equation (5.2), for the value of an "old" forward contract at time t.

$$d(T - t)(F(t) - F0). \tag{5.2}$$

Thus the value of the "old" contract today is the present value of the difference between the delivery price of the "new" and "old" contracts. It could be positive or negative, depending on whether the forward price today is smaller or larger than the forward price in the past. We therefore see that the value of the contract is positive if the delivery price is smaller than the forward price, i.e., $F0 < F(t)$ and vice versa.

As in most cases, there is more to the result in equation (5.2) than just a mechanical substitution. An exercise at the end of this chapter elaborates on this, and points out some insights and certain financial courses of action open to an investor who wants to get out of a forward contract. Suppose you have a long position in an "old" forward contract on a particular asset. If you enter an opposite forward contract now (take a short position) on the same asset with the same maturity date, then you no longer need to deliver the asset. To understand this, note that you had a long position in the contract which meant you would be receiving the asset at the maturity date. If you hold a short position, then you would be obligated to deliver what you would have received. At maturity, you will be paying the old forward price and receiving the new forward price.

To enter a forward contract costs nothing. Hence, the cash flow which is a consequence of the transaction of taking an opposite position in another forward contract is the difference between the two forward prices. This cash flow, however, will be transacted at the maturity time of the opposing contracts. The value of this cash flow now is, thus, the discounted value of the difference between the two forward prices. Hence, the value of the "old" forward contract is given by equation (5.2).

The investigation of a multiperiod scenario facilitates an analysis of pricing forward contracts on assets that pay known cash flows during the life of the contract. A very similar argument allows us to find the forward price of a stock that pays a known and fixed dividend yield during the life of the contract. These topics are examined next, starting with a forward contract on a coupon-paying bond, where we also use the opportunity to exemplify the value of a forward contract prior to maturity.

5.3   Forward Price of Assets That Pay Known Cash Flows

Consider the bond market outlined in Table 5.1.

We use this market as an example through which we will explain the effect of the cash flows obtained from the asset during the life of the forward contract. The setting of the bond market is also as specified below by **NarbitB**. We use five approximating functions to estimate the term structure and define the discount function as **dis**.

Table 5.1 A Simple Bond Market Specification.

Price/Time	1	2	3	Security
$94	$105	$0	$0	B1
$97	$10	$110	$0	B2
$85	$8	$8	$108	B3

```
> NarbitB([[105,0,0],[10,110,0],[8,8,108]],[94,97,85],
5,dis);
```

The no-arbitrage condition is satisfied.

The discount factor for time, 1, *is given by,* $\dfrac{94}{105}$

The interest rate spanning the time interval, $[0,1]$, *is given by,* 0.1170

The discount factor for time, 2, *is given by,* $\dfrac{1849}{2310}$

The interest rate spanning the time interval, $[0,2]$, *is given by,* 0.2493

The discount factor for time, 3, *is given by,* $\dfrac{82507}{124740}$

The interest rate spanning the time interval, $[0,3]$, *is given by,* 0.5119

The function Vdis ([c1,c2,..]), values the cashflow [c1,c2,..]

The continuous discount factor is given by the function, 'dis', (.)

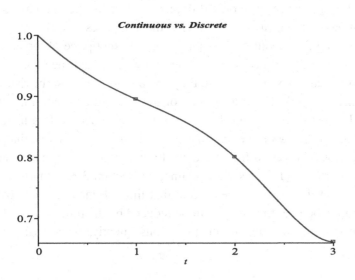

Continuous vs. Discrete

182

Fixed Income Fundamentals

As we can see from **NarbitB**, there are no arbitrage opportunities. As well, the continuous discount factor function, as seen in the previous figure, fits perfectly with the discrete discount factors. In this market there are three time periods and three different bonds. For simplicity one may think about the time period segments as years, that the current time, time zero, is a year prior to the first coupon payment and that the bonds make annual coupon payments.

Consider a forward contract written at time zero specifying delivery of bond three at time two, immediately *after* the second coupon is paid. Bond three's cash flows are (8, 8, 108). According to the contract, the party with a long position will pay the forward price, F, at time two and will receive an instrument similar to a zero-coupon bond that will pay \$108 at time three. Hence, we can calculate the forward price based on the present value of the cash flow $(0, -F, 108)$ being equal to zero. Once we have solved for F we can also graph the payoff, as of time two, from such a contract. We leave this derivation as an exercise for the reader.

Recall our discussion using the cost-of-carry model to calculate the forward price. The idea was to buy the asset now, hold it until maturity, and deliver it at that time. The purchase of the asset was financed by a loan and hence (at the delivery time) the loan had to be repaid. The amount of money borrowed was equal to the spot price of the asset, and hence the amount to be repaid was the future value of the spot price. Consequently, a forward price, to avoid arbitrage opportunities, must be equal to the future value of the spot price. The only difference is that for the purchase of an asset that pays known cash flows, buying the asset does not require taking a loan for the full amount of the spot price. The spot price of the bond is \$85, but the bond pays a coupon of \$8 at time one and at time two.

When the coupons are received, they can be re-invested at the risk-free rate of interest until the maturity time of the forward contract, time two. Hence, the cost of delivering the bond at time two will be less than the future value of the spot price. At time zero we can secure the rate that will be paid on the \$8 invested from time one to time two. This will be exactly the forward rate $r_0(1,2)$, as we explained in Section 3.3. Similarly, the \$8 obtained at time two can be used at that time. Hence, the net cost of delivering the bond at time three will be reduced by the future value of the \$8 obtained at time one and at time two. Consequently, the cost will be

$$\frac{85}{dis(2)} - 8(1 + r_0(1,2)) - 8. \tag{5.3}$$

We have already mentioned that, in general,

$$1 + r_0(t1, t2) = \frac{dis(t1)}{dis(t2)}.$$

Thus, (5.3) can be rewritten in terms of the function **dis** by applying this substitution. However, we wish to reinterpret this relationship here. This will also be useful in understanding how to derive these types of relationships.

One should always remember that a particular cash flow has two characteristics: its magnitude and its timing. The discount factors allow us to move cash flows through time, converting[1] cash of one time period to that of another. A useful methodology when converting cash in this manner is to "move" all the cash flows involved to a mutual point in time, and then to "move" this amount to the required point in time.

Proceeding in this manner, to find the cost of delivering the bond at time two, we first calculate the cost as of time zero. The bond costs \$85 at time zero but pays \$8 at times one and two. The \$8 paid at time one is worth \$8$d \cdot (1)$ at time zero. Similarly, the \$8 paid at time two is worth \$8$d \cdot (2)$ at time zero. Hence, the total cost of delivering the bond at time two

$$85 - 8 \cdot dis(1) - 8 \cdot dis(2) \tag{5.4}$$

in terms of dollars at time zero. In our case this will be

```
> 85-8*dis(1)-8*dis(2);
```

$$\frac{82507}{1155}$$

Therefore, the cost of delivering the bond at time two, in terms of dollars of time two, will be the future value of this amount, i.e.,

---

[1]One can conceptualize two different points in time as two different markets, similar to a foreign market. For example, there is a market at time t_1 and a market at time t_2 with different currencies much the same as the U.S. and Canadian dollar. In the foreign market situation the exchange rate is the factor that allows us to convert from one currency to another. Similarly, the discount factor allows us to convert dollars of time t_1 to dollars of time t_2.

$\dfrac{85 - 8\,dis(1) - 8\,dis(2)}{d(2)}$. However this is exactly equation (5.3). In our example we calculate it as follows:

```
> (85-8*dis(1)-8*dis(2))/dis(2);
```

$$\frac{165014}{1849}$$

Or in a decimal form,

```
> evalf(%);
```

$$89.24499730$$

Therefore, we can make a general statement about the forward price of a forward contract on an asset that pays a known cash flow throughout the life of the contract. The forward price is the future value of the spot price, minus the future value, as of time zero, of the cash flow obtained during the life of the contract.

Let $S(0)$ be the spot price of the asset and T the maturity of the contract, and assume that the asset pays a cash flow of $c(t)$ at time t. Let the discount factor for time t be denoted as $d(t)$. The general result for the future price F is thus

$$F = \frac{S(0)}{d(T)} - \frac{\sum_{t=1}^{T} c(t)\,d(t)}{d(T)}, \tag{5.5}$$

or in terms of the forward rates in equation (5.6),

$$F = S(0)(1 + r(T)) - \sum_{t=1}^{T} c(t)(1 + r_0(t,T)). \tag{5.6}$$

We can see that a positive cash flow obtained during the life of the contract reduces the forward price. It is best understood utilizing the cost-of-carry model. If the deliverable good produces positive cash flows, these cash flows can help with financing the purchase of the good in the spot market. Hence the amount of money borrowed to buy the good on the spot is reduced by the present value of the cash flow produced by the good to be delivered. In the foreign currency case, the positive cash flow was due to the interest earned on the currency in the foreign market.

In the case of a commodity, the cash flow produced (or its equivalent) can be positive or negative depending on the storage cost and the convenience yield. A similar argument applies to a forward contract on a stock that pays a fixed dividend yield. To cement the ideas explored in the last two sections we investigate in the next section the forward price, prior to maturity, of assets that pay a known cash flow — a coupon-paying bond.

5.3.1 *Forward Contracts, Prior to Maturity, of Assets That Pay Known Cash Flows*

Consider the same forward contract as in Section 5.3. Let us see what the forward price will be if the delivery time is $t = 1.5$ instead of time $t = 2$. The maturity date of this contract does not coincide with any cash flow payment date of the asset. Indeed, there is no conceptual change. One needs only to be careful with the timing and the specification of the cash flows. In our example, we can apply equation (5.5) to obtain the forward price as

```
> (85-8*dis(1))/dis(15/10);
```

$$\frac{14292419328}{157492693}$$

or in decimal form

```
> (85-8*dis(1))/dis(1.5);
```

$$90.74972976$$

Suppose that a year has passed and we take another snapshot of the same market. The first bond has matured and we will assume that no new bonds have been issued. The second bond will mature in a year and will pay $110. The third bond will mature in two years and will pay $8 in one year, and $108 in two years. The prices of these two outstanding bonds are now assumed to be different than they were one year ago. They are $90 and $80, respectively. We run **NarbitB** based on this specification to get an estimate of the term structure. The current time zero is of course time one of the last model. (We suppress the graph by adding a fifth parameter and assigning it a zero value.) If you would like to see the graph of the discount factor function, rerun **NarbitB** as below but without the zero as the last input parameter.

```
> NarbitB([[110,0],[8,108]],[90,80],3,dis1,0);
```

> *The no-arbitrage condition is satisfied.*
> *The discount factor for time,* 1, *is given by,* $\frac{9}{11}$
> *The interest rate spanning the time interval,* $[0,1]$, *is given by,* 0.2222
> *The discount factor for time,* 2, *is given by,* $\frac{202}{297}$
> *The interest rate spanning the time interval,* $[0,2]$, *is given by,* 0.4703
> *The function Vdis ([c1,c2,..]), values the cashflow [c1,c2,..]*
> *The continuous discount factor is given by the function, 'dis1', (.)*

We name the current discount factor as **dis1** and we use three estimating functions for the continuous approximation of the discount function. As before, we see that there are no arbitrage opportunities and we obtain a perfect fit for the estimation.

Consider the forward contract discussed above. We will refer to this contract as the "old" forward contract. The holder of the short position of this contract needs to deliver the 8 percent bond in one year, immediately after the coupon payment. The value of the short position in the "old" forward contract is no longer zero. The value of the long position in the same contract is not zero either: it is the negative of the value to the party with the short position. The short position in the forward contract obligates the investor to deliver the specified bond for $\$\frac{165014}{1849}$. We can use the function **dis1** to calculate the cash flows which are consequent from this contract, and so derive the value of this contract today.

In other words, the party with the long position in the bond will receive the bond. This is equivalent to obtaining $108 in two years and paying out $\$\frac{165014}{1849} = 89.24499730$ in one year. Hence the value of the cash flow $[-89.24499730, 108]$ can be calculated as

```
> dis1(1)*(-89.24499730)+dis1(2)*108;
```

$$0.43591130$$

The value is not zero because the "old" forward price of the contract, the delivery price, does not reflect the circumstances of the market today.

Let us see what the value of the forward contract on that bond would be if the contract were issued today. Following the same arguments as above, equation (5.5), we can find the forward price as

```
> (80/dis1(1))-8;
```

$$\frac{808}{9}$$

or alternatively as

```
> (108*dis1(2))/dis1(1);
```

$$\frac{808}{9}$$

```
> 808/9.0;
```

Can you explain this alternative way? We leave this explanation as an exercise. This idea is also explored in the end-of-chapter exercises.

We know already from equation (5.2) the relation which holds between the forward price of the "old" and "new" contracts. We repeat the explanation here with reference to the contracts we are examining. We calculate the difference in the forward prices of the two contracts.

```
> (808/9)-(165014/1849);
```

$$\frac{8866}{16641}$$

If an investor holds a short position now in the "new" contract, and a long position in the "old" contract, it is equivalent to the cash flow of $\frac{8866}{16641}$ one year from now. Consider why this is the case. The long position in the "old" contract obligates the investor to pay $\frac{165014}{1849}$ in a year and receive the bond. The short position in the "new" contract obligates the investor to deliver the bond (which the investor received as a consequence of the "old" contract) and to receive $\frac{808}{9}$. Therefore, the portfolio composed of a long position in the "old" contract and a short position in the "new" contract amounts to the above cash flow received in one year. Thus, the value of this portfolio today will be given by

```
> dis1(1)*((808/9)-(165014/1849));
```

$$\frac{806}{1849}$$

This value happens to be the value of the "old" forward contract now. This result is not a coincidence, but rather a general result as we have seen before. It is a consequence of the fact that the price of the portfolio will be the value of the old forward contract since the value of the new contract is now zero.

5.3.2   *Forward Price of a Stock That Pays a Known Dividend Yield*

Consider a stock that pays a fixed and known dividend yield. Usually we assume that the dividend is paid in a continuous manner, at every instant of time. The dividend is a certain percentage of the stock's value. Thus, if the stock price at time t is denoted by $S(t)$, the dividend payment at the time of payment, at every instant t, is $y \cdot S(t)$. We use y to denote the continuous dividend yield — the percentage of the stock price that is paid as dividends. As the argument depicted below shows, the case of the forward contract on a stock which pays a fixed dividend yield follows an already known derivation. It is in the same spirit and uses the same logic as utilized in the calculation of the future value based on the continuously compounded rate of interest.

As usual, let time zero denote the current time and assume a forward contract obligating the holder of the short position to deliver one unit of the stock at time T. We would like to apply the cost-of-carry model to calculate the forward price of the stock as of time zero. The asset, the stock in this case, produces income between now and time T. Therefore, we do not have to borrow $S(0)$, the spot price of the stock, in order to purchase one unit of the stock. We can take advantage of the income stream.

There is, however, a slight difference between this case and the other cases of assets that produce income streams. In this case the income stream at time t is not known. The stock price at time t, $S(t)$, is a random variable. This is in contrast to the example of a coupon-paying bond for which the income is known with certainty.

Nevertheless, we can still analyze this case without assuming the price process or making any other assumptions regarding the random nature of the price process. The forward contract commits the party with the short position to deliver one unit of the stock. If there is a certain (nonrandom) strategy that will produce a unit of the stock at time T and for which the cost of the strategy is known now, then the future value of that cost must be the forward price. If this were not true, arbitrage opportunities would exist.

The key idea is to have an investment strategy which is certain to produce one unit of the stock at time T. We do not actually care about the value of the stock at time T, or at any time t prior to time T. As long as our strategy has a known cost and is certain to produce one unit of the stock at time T, that is what we require.

Consequently, we are looking for an investment vehicle for which the value of the portfolio is perfectly correlated with (or mimics exactly) the movement of the stock price. If such an investment strategy can be found (and followed by the party with the short position in the forward contract), then there is no further need to be concerned about the value of the stock price. The commitment of the party with the short position is to deliver one unit of the stock, not a specified dollar value of stock.

Let us now examine if we can find such a strategy, given the structure of the problem. Assume that at time zero we buy X units of the stock. The writer of the contract is obligated to deliver a unit of the stock at time T and is guaranteed an income in the form of dividends from the stock. Hence, applying a variant of the cost-of-carry model, the writer should buy less than a unit of the stock, i.e., $X < 1$, and use the dividend income to purchase more units of the stock along the way.

The main point is the fact that the dividend is a certain fixed percentage of the stock value. Hence, regardless of the value of the stock, if at time zero X units of the stock are purchased and the dividends are immediately re-invested in the stock, the holding of stock (number of units, not value) at time t becomes deterministic.

Assuming that the above strategy is followed, let $X(t)$ be the holding of the stock at time t, so $X(0) = X$. At each time t the growth rate of $X(t)$ is y. This very much resembles the notion of continuous compounding at a known risk-free rate. In fact it is exactly the same situation. We know, therefore, that at time T the holding of the stock will be $X(T) = X(0)e^{yT}$, and thus for $X(T)$ to be $1, X(0)$ should be $e^{(-yT)}$. Thus, if the investor purchases $e^{(-yT)}$ units of the stock at time $t = 0$ at a cost of $e^{(-yT)}S(0)$ and follows the above strategy, the investor is guaranteed to have a unit of the stock at time T.

Consequently, applying the usual arguments of the cost-of-carry model, which indeed is the pricing by replication argument, the writer of the contract can borrow $e^{(-yT)}S(0)$, to be paid back at time T, and can buy the stock. Following this strategy, the writer will have a unit of the stock at time t and will have to repay the loan. The loan repayment will be $e^{(-yT)}S(0)e^{(r(T)T)}$, where $r(T)$ is the continuously compounded interest rate from time zero to time T. Hence, to avoid arbitrage opportunities, the forward price must be the future value of $e^{(-yT)}S(0)$, which is

$$e^{(-yT)}S(0)e^{rT} = e^{((r-y)T)}S(0). \tag{5.7}$$

5.4 Eurodollar Contracts

A *Eurodollar* is a U.S.-dollar-denominated deposit in banks outside the USA. Eurodollars are similar to *Treasury bills* or *zero-coupon bonds*, as they are discount instruments. The interest rate earned on a Eurodollar deposit is higher than the Treasury bill rate. The Eurodollar is not a risk-free instrument since it is invested with a bank and not backed by a government. Thus, it should offer a higher rate than government bonds in order to compensate for the risk. The interest rate associated with a Eurodollar is known as *LIBOR*, or **London Interbank Offer Rate**, as it is the rate earned by one bank on Eurodollars deposited with another bank.

As the term LIBOR implies, most Eurodollar deposits are issued in London. A LIBOR term structure of interest rate can be estimated and used to value Eurodollars belonging to a different risk category than government bonds. This is much the same as the explanation regarding a term structure for municipal or corporate bonds offered in Section 3.5.

5.4.1 *Forward Rate Agreements*

A *forward rate agreement* (FRA) is a contract very similar to the swap explained in Section 1.2. It can be perceived as a swap of a variable return for a fixed return on some future period. The FRA is a contract obligating one who holds it short to pay the LIBOR rate at time t_2, on a notional principal invested from some future time t_1 to time t_2, where zero is the current time and $0 < t_1 < t_2$.

The one who holds the contract long pays at time t_2 a fixed return on the notional principal, but the return is agreed upon at time zero. This return is referred to as the FRA rate. As with other forward contracts, no cash changes hands at time zero. The FRA rate is determined so that the value of the contract at time zero, the initiation date, is zero.

The underlying asset in this contract is usually the LIBOR rate. The contract will be realized to be profitable to the one who holds it short, if the LIBOR rate spanning the time interval (t_1, t_2) will be smaller than the FRA rate. The payoff to the long holder at time t_2 is thus

$$N\left(L_{t_1}\left(t_1, t_2\right) - F\right), \tag{5.8}$$

where N is the notional principal, F is the FRA rate and $L_{t_1}\left(t_1, t_2\right)$ is the LIBOR rate,[2] as of time t_1, spanning the time interval t_1 to t_2. Note that the rate $L_{t_1}\left(t1, t2\right)$ is known at time t_1, but not at time zero (when the parties enter the contract). Hence, in this situation F plays the role of a forward price, which is a rate in this case.[3] In order to value F we proceed with seeking a portfolio replicating the LIBOR return from time t_1 to time t_2. We have, in fact, seen how this is done before in Section 1.5. Here, however, the return is on some future period. We have to be careful about the

---

[2]The LIBOR term structure is actually estimated based on FRA agreements. The FRA data conveys the forward rate in the LIBOR market. Hence, in order to estimate the term structure of LIBOR, we have to utilize equation (4.8) to derive the term structure from the forward rate. In our discussion regarding the forward rate in the government bond market, we derive the forward rate from the term structure. In the LIBOR market we have to do the reverse, as demonstrated by an exercise at the end of this chapter.

[3]These agreements are usually settled in cash on the initiation of the forward period. For example, if the agreement is signed on date t_0 for a forward rate from date t_1 to t_2, it is settled on date t_1 in cash. That is, the payoff to the holder of the short position is the present value of (5.8), namely, $\dfrac{N\left(L_{t_1}\left(t_1, t_2\right) - F\right)}{L_{t_1}\left(t_1, t_2\right)}$.

If the FRA is done with respect to the term structure of government bonds and both parties are federal agencies with no risk of default, the rate of the FRA must be the forward rate implied in the term structure. The reader is asked, in the end-of-chapter exercises, to prove this in two ways — through replication and through valuation by discount factors.

two types of risk categories involved. If we would like to have no risk in replicating the LIBOR rate from time t_1 to time t_2, we should use risk-free instruments to insure having $\$N$ to invest at time t_1 at the LIBOR rate.

Let us apply a cost-of-carry-like model which, as we mentioned before, is really the replication argument. We will approach the replication from the point of view of the short seller and set up a portfolio with cash flow only at time t_2. As explained above, in order to have $\$N$ with no risk of default at time t_1, one needs to have $\$\dfrac{N}{1+r(t_1)}$ at time zero, where $r(t_1)$ is the risk-free interest rate, the spot rate, from time zero to t_1.

Investing $\$\dfrac{N}{1+r(t_1)}$ at the risk-free rate from time zero to time t_1 will give rise to $\$N$ at time t_1, which will be invested at the LIBOR rate to time t_2. Hence, at time t_2, the holder of the short position will have $N(1+L_{t_1}(t_1,t_2))$, will deliver $NL_{t_1}(t_1,t_2)$, and will receive NF. The remaining issue (which is a bit sticky) is how to finance having $\$\dfrac{N}{1+r(t_1)}$ at time zero. But let us look first at the current pattern of cash flow. We define the following array in Maple where the first component is the cash flows at time zero, the second at time t_1, and the third at time t_2 (for simplicity we omit the subindex t_1 in the calculations below).

```
> r:='r';
```

$$r := r$$

```
> [time0=-N/(1+r(t1)),timet1=0,timet2=N*(1+L(t1,t2))
-N*L(t1,t2)+N*F];
```

$$[time0 = -\frac{N}{1+r(t1)}, timet1 = 0,$$
$$timet2 = N(1+L(t1,t2)) - NL(t1,t2) + NF]$$

We simplify it and then collect terms based on N.

```
> simplify(%);
```

$$[time0 = -\frac{N}{1+r(t1)}, timet1 = 0, timet2 = N+NF]$$

```
> collect(%,N);
```

$$[\textit{time0} = -\frac{N}{1+r(t1)}, \textit{timet1} = 0, \textit{timet2} = (1+F)N]$$

For the value of the contract to be zero at the initiation time, F should be chosen such that the present value as of time zero, of $N(1+F)$ obtained at time t_2 will be $\frac{N}{1+r(t_1)}$. It is apparent now that without loss of generality N can be set to one. Let us substitute $N = 1$ in the above equation and investigate the issue further.

```
> subs(N=1,%);
```

$$[\textit{time0} = -\frac{1}{1+r(t1)}, \textit{timet1} = 0, \textit{timet2} = 1+F]$$

To solve for F we need to know how to value either $1+F$ at time zero or $\frac{1}{1+r(t1)}$ at time t_2. Consider the $1+F$ obtained at time t_2. The issue of how to value it at time zero amounts to a question of determining its risk category. Should we discount it with the risk-free rate or with the LIBOR rate?

In our investigation above, we suppress the default risk by one of the parties and assume that they are in the same risk category. Since the holder of the short position of the contract pays interest on Eurodollars at time t_2, we should treat $1+F$ as being in the same risk category. Hence, moving the $1+F$ to time zero amounts to discounting it at the LIBOR rate. Consequently, F should satisfy equation (5.9) since entering the contract costs nothing.

$$-\frac{1}{1+r(t1)} + \frac{1+F}{1+L_0(0,t_2)} = 0 \qquad (5.9)$$

We can call upon Maple to solve for F as below.

```
> solve (-1/(1+r(t1))+(1+F)/(1+L[0](0,t2))=0,F);
```

$$-\frac{-L_0(0,t2)+r(t1)}{1+r(t1)}$$

Alternatively, we can determine how to finance the $\frac{1}{1+r(t1)}$ needed at time zero. This amounts to valuing it at time t_2. Again, we consider the issue of what its risk category is. Since we want to have N at time t_1

with no default risk we must invest it at the risk-free rate from time zero to time t_1. However, if we assume that both parties to the contract are in the LIBOR risk category, the commitment of the one who holds the contract short to pay $NL_{t_1}(t_1, t_2)$ should also be replicated based on the Eurodollar risk category. Therefore the alternative way is to finance the funds needed at time zero by borrowing (or taking a deposit of) Eurodollars at time zero to be held until time t_2. By arbitrage arguments the cash flow at time t_2 should also be zero, which gives rise to equation (5.10).

$$1 + F = \frac{1 + L_0(0, t_2)}{1 + r(t_1)} \tag{5.10}$$

Namely, what is being received from holding the contract long should equal the loan repayment taken to create this position. Clearly, equation (5.10) yields the same value for F as does equation (5.9).

5.5 Futures Contracts: A Second Look

Futures contracts are very similar instruments to forward contracts. There are nevertheless some important distinctions between the two instruments. We have outlined some of these features below, particularly those essential for the valuation of futures contracts. A description of the institutional details surrounding futures contracts can be found in the website of the Chicago Mercantile Exchange (CME).

A futures contract is exchange traded and is consequently a highly standardized instrument. It is easier to get out of a certain position in a futures contract than the same position in a forward contract, making use of the strategy outlined in Section 5.2 after equation (5.2). Taking the opposite position to a currently held position is relatively straight forward to accomplish in the futures market.

Conversely, getting out of a forward contract position is potentially much more difficult since it is generally the case that forward contracts are tailor-made for a particular client. As a result of this tailoring, it may be difficult to find a party with whom to establish the opposite position to that originally taken.

In order to reduce the risk of default implicit in these types of contracts (a point which we have ignored thus far in our discussion) and to protect the exchange, certain procedures are followed. Profit or loss from a particular position in a futures contract is calculated and settled for each investor's account at the end of each trading day. This process is called *marking to market*, and will be explained shortly.

By virtue of marking to market, the consequent cash flows from a futures contract are a series of cash flows. These occur every trading day from the day the position is initiated until its maturity (or until the contract position is closed out). In contrast, the consequent cash flows of a forward contract occur only at one point in time, the maturity date.

A futures contract commits two parties to an exchange of a certain good or financial asset (the underlying asset) at a certain agreed-upon date at a certain agreed-upon price. This price is called the *futures price*. In this respect, a futures contract is parallel to a forward contract. Also, as in the case of forward contracts, the futures price is decided on the initiation date in such a way that the value of the contract at that time vanishes.

The mechanism of marking to market may be thought of as writing a new futures contract at the end of each trading day. The new contract has a new futures price which makes the value of the contract zero as of that day. The difference between the futures price from the previous day and the new one is paid to the party whose position has positive value that day. It is subtracted from the account of the party whose position had negative value that day. The two values perfectly offset each other since the net value of the two positions must be zero.

If the futures price today is higher than the futures price yesterday, the party with the long position profits as the contract requires a higher price in order to take delivery of the underlying asset. The value of this futures contract today is positive. The party with the short position pays the difference between the futures price of yesterday and that of today to the holder of the long position. The direction of cash flows is reversed if the futures price today is lower than that of yesterday.

In any event, unless there is no change in the futures price, money changes hands and a new futures contract with the same details as the original except for a different price, is written each day. This process repeats itself every trading day until the maturity date of the contract. At maturity, the party with the long position pays the writer (the party with the short position) of the contract the spot price of the underlying asset and takes possession of the security.[4]

Let us consider a symbolic example to clarify the description. We will examine the cash flows from the point of view of the party with a long position in the futures contract. A negative cash flow therefore means that the party with the long position is making a payment to the party with a short position. Let us denote the futures price of the underlying security on date t by $fr(t)$. The payment on day t to the party with the long position in the futures contract is therefore $fr(t) - fr(t-1)$. Let us generate a sequence of futures prices from day 1 to day 9, assuming that the futures contract matures on day 10. The futures prices for each day are noted below. The **seq** command generates what is referred to in Maple as an expression sequence.

```
> seq(fr(i),i=1..10);
```

$$fr(1), fr(2), fr(3), fr(4), fr(5), fr(6), fr(7), fr(8), fr(9), fr(10)$$

On the maturity day of the contract, $t = 10$, the futures price is the spot price of the security $s(10)$, that is,

```
> fr(10):=s(10);
```

$$fr(10) := s(10)$$

On day one, the party with the long position enters the contract and no cash changes hands since the value of the contract to both parties on that date is zero. On the second trading day, the party with the long position receives payment of $fr(2) - fr(1)$, and the futures price of the contract is changed to $fr(2)$. We denote the payment to the party with the long position of the futures contract on day i, for $i = 2, \ldots, 10$, by **PayDay(i)** and define this in Maple. The value of PayDay(1) is zero so we just omit it from the discussion. This is done via the **do** command below.

```
> for i from 2 to 10 do;
> PayDay(i):=fr(i)-fr(i-1);
> od;
```

---

[4]Very few futures contracts end in delivery of the underlying asset at maturity. Most futures contracts are settled in cash by the investors close to or prior to maturity.

$$PayDay(2) := fr(2) - fr(1)$$
$$PayDay(3) := fr(3) - fr(2)$$
$$PayDay(4) := fr(4) - fr(3)$$
$$PayDay(5) := fr(5) - fr(4)$$
$$PayDay(6) := fr(6) - fr(5)$$
$$PayDay(7) := fr(7) - fr(6)$$
$$PayDay(8) := fr(8) - fr(7)$$
$$PayDay(9) := fr(9) - fr(8)$$
$$PayDay(10) := s(10) - fr(9)$$

On the maturity date of the futures contract, the holder of the contract (the party with the long position) pays the party with the short position the futures price of yesterday, $fr(9)$, and receives the underlying security. The cash flow on the date on which the futures contract matures is thus $s(10) - fr(9)$. We ignore for a moment the concern of time value of money. Hence, we sum up the payments received by the party with the long position in the futures contract on each trading day between the initiation of the contract and its maturity. This is done with the next Maple command.

```
> sum('PayDay(i)','i'=2..10);
```

$$-fr(1) + s(10)$$

So we see that, ignoring the time value of money, the party with the long position in the futures contract pays $fr(1)$, the futures price agreed upon on the day the contract was written, and in exchange receives the underlying security. This exchange is identical to that of a forward contract written on the same underlying asset and maturing on the same date. The cash flows from a forward contract and from a futures contract are, of course, not the same since we have ignored the time value of money.

Note also that the prices $fr(i)$ of the futures contract are not known with certainty on the date the futures contract is initiated. Nevertheless, ignoring the time value of money, the result is always that the cash flows of a futures contract are like those of a forward contract. As we have mentioned already, if there is one time period before the expiration of the futures contract (i.e. one trading day), then, ignoring the institutional details of forward and futures contracts, they are identical.

Due to the different cash flow profiles which result from a forward contract and a futures contract, the forward price is not generally equal to the futures price. In order to calculate the value of a futures contract and the futures price, some assumptions regarding the evolution of the term structure must be delineated. The calculation of the futures price and the valuation of a futures contract is simpler, however, when we assume that the term structure is deterministic. In fact in such an environment, forward and futures prices are equal if the default risk is assumed away. We thus first explain what is meant by a deterministic term structure, and then proceed to prove this equality in such an environment.

5.6   Deterministic Term Structure (DTS)

In a market where the term structure is deterministic, one knows with certainty the spot interest rate which will prevail in the market from any future time t_1 to time t_2, $0 < t_1$. As usual, we assume that time zero is the current time. Of course, one always knows the prevailing term structure at the current time. It turns out that this certainty assumption, together with the absence of arbitrage opportunities, means that the spot interest rate for future time periods must be equal to the forward interest rate $r_0(t_1, t_2)$. The reader is asked in an exercise at the end of the chapter to show that this must be the case in a market with a deterministic term structure.

Graphically, we can visualize the evolution of the term structure or the discount factor function as follows. We first recalculate the discount factor function for a new market and define it to be **dis**(.). This is done by rerunning **NarbitB**.

```
> NarbitB([[105,0,0],[5,105,0],[4,4,104]],[94,97,85],
10,dis,0);
```

The no-arbitrage condition is satisfied.
The discount factor for time, 1, is given by, $\frac{94}{105}$
The interest rate spanning the time interval, $[0,1]$*, is given by,* 0.1170
The discount factor for time, 2, is given by, $\frac{1943}{2205}$
The interest rate spanning the time interval, $[0,2]$*, is given by,* 0.1348
The discount factor for time, 3, is given by, $\frac{171757}{229320}$
The interest rate spanning the time interval, $[0,3]$*, is given by,* 0.3351

The function Vdis ([c1,c2,..]), values the cashflow [c1,c2,..]
The continuous discount factor is given by the function, 'dis', (.)

```
> SumAbsDiv;
```

$$0$$

The reader may note that we have chosen 10 approximating functions and that the discount function **dis** perfectly fits the discount factors of times one, two, and three. If that term structure is deterministic, then the discount factor function which will prevail from time t_1 to time t, $t_1 < t$, must be given by

$$d(t_1,t) = \frac{dis(t)}{dis(t_1)}.$$

$$(5.11)$$

The reader should recognize that (5.11) is a consequence of perceiving the discount factors as factors which convert dollars from one time period to dollars of another. The value at time zero of one dollar to be obtained at time t is $d(t)$. The conversion in equation (5.11) can be perceived as being composed of two separate steps. First, convert a dollar from time t to its value in terms of dollars of time t_1, where $0 < t_1$ and $t_1 < t$, using the discount factor (conversion factor) $d(t_1,t)$. Then convert that dollar value at time t_1 to a dollar value at time zero. If there are no arbitrage opportunities, the equality

$$d(t) = d(t_1)d(t_1,t)$$

$$(5.12)$$

must hold. Consequently, the discount factor as of time t_1, $d(t_1,t)$, which converts dollars received at time t to dollars of time t_1, is given by (5.11).

We can now graph the evolution of the discount factor function. The original discount function is displayed (i.e., the discounted dollar of any time period t at time zero) in the figure that follows. The bottom graph represents the discount factor function as of time $t = 0$, the middle graph represents the discount factor function as of time $t = 0.3$, and the top graph represents the discount factor function as of time $t = 0.5$.

```
> plot([dis(t),dis(t)/dis(.3),dis(t)/dis(.5)],t=0.5..2,
colour=[red,green,blue],thickness=2,labels=[time, 'disc.
fac.'], title='The Discount Factor Functions for
t=0,t=0.3 and t=0.5',titlefont = [TIMES,BOLD,10]);
```

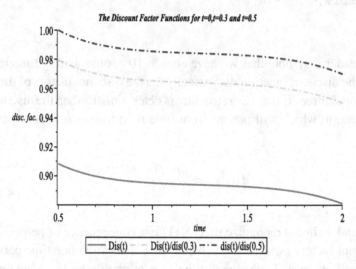

The same idea can be viewed in three dimensions, as shown in the following figure.

```
> plot3d(dis(t)/dis(t0),t0=0..3,t=t0..3, title='The
Discount Factor as of Time t0,for
t0=0,...,3',axes=normal,orientation=[61,48],
labels=['Time t0','Time t','disc
fac.'],axes=frame,style=patch, titlefont =
[TIMES,BOLD,10],axes=framed);
```

The Discount Factor as of Time t0, for t0=0,...,3

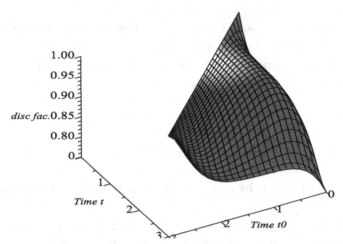

5.7 Futures Contracts in a DTS Environment

Futures and forward contracts are different. A futures contract, due to the market-to-market process, generates cash flows during its life while a forward contract does not. The cash flow from a forward contract is obtained only at the maturity of the contract. What can be said about the relationship between a futures contract and a forward contract in a deterministic term structure environment? We present two approaches to answer this question: an approach that is built on valuation utilizing the discount factors and an approach that is built on the replication approach. The former will be presented first. Both approaches are essentially built on arbitrage arguments. Both approaches will be demonstrated assuming that there are three days to the expiration of the contracts. The generalization to a longer period is self-explanatory. Hence in the first approach below we start by calculating the future price in a contract that has three days to expiration and we compare it to a forward price.

The Discount Factor Approach

Assume that we take a long position in a forward contract that matures in two days. As before, let F denote the forward price of the contract, $S(i)$

the spot price of the asset at date i, and $fr(i)$ the futures price at date i. Let time 1 be the current time, the first day of the contract.

The discount factor function is known and deterministic, where $dis(i)$ is the discount factor from time 1 to time i. Hence, assuming a deterministic term structure environment we know at time 1 the one-day spot rate at time 1 and 2 and they are given by

$$1 + r_1(1,2) = \frac{1}{dis(2)}, \text{ and}$$

$$1 + r_2(2,3) = \frac{dis(2)}{dis(3)}.$$

Recall that we denote by $r_i(jk)$ the spot rate prevailing at time i spanning the time interval $[j,k]$.

Let us start by calculating the futures price, $fr(2)$ of a contract written at time 2 for delivery at time 3. In this case there is one day to the expiration of the futures contract and, as already explained, the futures price is the forward price. Hence,

$$fr(2) = (1 + r_2(2,3)) \cdot S(2)$$

and thus

$$fr(2) = \frac{S(2) \cdot dis(2)}{dis(3)}.$$

Now we are in a position to calculate the futures price of a contract written at time 1 for delivery at time 3. The (market to market) cashflow (assuming a long position in the contract) as a result of such a contract is:

time 1 0
time 2 $fr(2) - fr(1)$
time 3 $S(3) - fr(2)$.

Since the value of the contract at time 1 is zero, the present value of the cash flow should also be zero.

The present value of $S(3) - fr(2)$ as of time 2 is zero. This is because the present value of

$$fr(2) = (1 + r_2(2,3)) \cdot S(2)$$

obtained at time 3 as of time 2 is $\dfrac{fr(2)}{1+r_2(2,3)} = S(2)$ and the present value
of $S(3)$, obtained at time 3, as of time 2 is also $S(2)$.

Thus, $fr(1)$ is solved for by requiring that the present value of $fr(2) - fr(1)$ (obtained at time 2) as of time 1 is zero.

The present value of $fr(1)$ is

$$\frac{fr(1)}{1+r_1(1,2)}.$$

In order to find the present value of $fr(2) = (1+r_2(2,3)) \cdot S(2)$, note that $(1+r_2(2,3)) \cdot S(2)$ obtained at time 2, as of time 1, is a risky cash flow. At time 1 we do not know what the spot price of S will be at time 2, but due to our assumption of a DTS environment we do know at time 1 the value of $1+r_2(2,3)$. Hence, one should think about $(1+r_2(2,3)) \cdot S(2)$ as having $1+r_2(2,3)$ units of the asset. Normally (in reality) one does not know at time 1 the spot rate that will prevail in the market at time 2, but here we assumed it to be known. Hence we know that the present value of $1+r_2(2,3)$ unit of S at time 2 is simply $1+r_2(2,3)$ units of the asset at time 1, namely, $(1+r_2(2,3)) \cdot S(1)$. Thus, we can calculate $fr(1)$ by requiring that

$$(1+r_2(2,3))S(1) - \frac{fr(1)}{1+r_1(1,2)} = 0$$

and thus

$$fr(1) = (1+r_1(1,2))(1+(r_2(2,3))S(1)$$

or since

$$(1+r_1(1,2))((1+r_2(2,3)) = 1+r_1(1,3)$$

it can be written as,

$$fr(1) = (1+r_1(1,3))S(1).$$

Hence, the futures price is the same as the forward price even in this case.

Finally we can analyze the futures price $fr(0)$ of a contract written at time 0 for delivery at time 3. The cashflow (assuming a long position in the contract) as a result of such a contract is:

time 0 0
time 1 fr (1) $-fr$ (0)
time 2 fr (2) $-fr$ (1)
time 3 $S(3) -fr$ (2)

By the same argument as above, the present value, as of time 2 of the cash flow at time 3 is zero, and hence its present value at time 0 is also zero.

The cash flow at time 2 is

$$fr(2) - fr(1) = (1 + (r_2(2,3)) \cdot S(2) - (1 + r_1(1,3)) \cdot S(1)$$

and its present value as of time 1 is

$$(1 + r_2(2,3)) \cdot S(1) - \frac{(1 + r_1(1,3)) \cdot S(1)}{1 + r_1(1,2)} =$$
$$(1 + r_2(2,3)) \cdot S(1) - (1 + r_2(2,3)) \cdot S(1).$$

Note again that the present value of $S(2)$ is $S(1)$ since at time one, $S(2)$ is not known and that the present value of $(1 + r_1(1,3))S(1)$ is obtained by discounting it by the risk free rate (since $S(1)$ at time one is known). Thus, the present value of the cash flow obtained at time 2, as of time 1, is also zero. Thus $fr(0)$ is obtained from the fact that the present value of the cash flow obtained at time 1, as of time zero, is also zero, namely from

$$(1 + r_1(1,3))S(0) - \frac{fr(0)}{1 + r_0(0,1)} = 0.$$

Hence,

$$fr(0) = (1 + r_1(1,3))(1 + r_0(0,1))S(0)$$

or putting it differently,

$$fr(0) = (1 + r_0(0,3))S(0).$$

Hence, in a DTS environment the futures price is the same as the forward price.

The Replication approach

The main idea in this approach is mimicking a forward contract using futures contracts, by investing the cash flow obtained during the life of the futures contract until its maturity date. The required result is deduced via arbitrage arguments.

We maintain the notation of $S(t)$ for the price of the underlying asset at time t, T as the maturity time, $t = 1$ as the day on which the contract is initiated, and F as the forward price. As we demonstrated above (ignoring the time value of money), the cash flow from the futures contract to the party with the short position in the contract is $fr(1) - S(T)$. The forward contract generates a cash flow of $S(T) - F$ to the party with the long position in the contract, only at T.

Since we have assumed that the term structure is deterministic, perhaps we will be able to devise a strategy whereby at each marking to market time an investment in a futures contract is also possible, together with investing and borrowing at the risk-free rate of interest. Our aim will be to find an investment strategy that offsets the cash flow from the marking to market by investing those cash flows at the risk-free rate until the maturity time of the contract. Because the term structure is deterministic, we know the interest rate that will prevail in the market in the future. This knowledge may allow us to re-enter the futures contract, knowing how many units of the original contract to buy so as to offset the payoff at maturity from the investment made at the risk-free rate. Since entering a futures or forward contract requires no cash up front, we are aiming to generate an investment strategy that results in a cash flow only on the maturity date of the futures contract. We would like to see if we can generate the same cash flow that is obtained from holding a futures contract short, still ignoring time value of money considerations. In other words, we would like to have a portfolio and an investment strategy involving the futures contract and the risk-free rate so that the cash flow during the time interval $[1, T]$ is obtained only at time T and is equal to $-fr(1) + S(T)$. This is the same cash flow that is obtained from the futures contract if the time value of money is ignored.

Since entering into a futures contract costs nothing (as is also the case for a forward contract), does this mean that if we find a portfolio of futures contracts such as described above we can conclude that equation (5.13) is true?

$$F - S(T) - fr(1) + S(T) = 0. \qquad (5.13)$$

This must be the case, since equation (5.13) will be the cash flow from a long position in a forward contract and from the portfolio we found above. Neither entering a forward contract nor entering the portfolio found above costs anything. Hence, the resultant cash flows from these portfolios must also be zero on the date on which they are initiated. Otherwise arbitrage opportunities exist. Equation (5.13), however, leads to the conclusion that the futures price and the forward price are equal in this deterministic interest rate environment.

Assume that we take a long position in a forward contract that matures two days from today. As before, let F denote the forward price of the contract, $S(i)$ the spot price of the asset at date i, $fr(i)$ the futures price at date i. Let time one be the current time, the first day of the contract. The discount factor function is known and deterministic, where $d(i)$ is the discount factor from time one to time i. Our method is simply to try and work backward.

Consider an example where a contract is initiated on day one and thus there is no marking to market for the futures contract on this day. On day two marking to market occurs. The contract matures on day three.

We will work through this example carefully to demonstrate the marking to market process. A long position in the forward contract gives rise to a payoff of $S(3) - F$ on day three. Our aim is to try and find a portfolio consisting of futures contracts and risk-free investments that will cost nothing to establish and will produce a cash flow of $fr(1) - S(3)$ only on day three. Suppose on day one we take a position in x_1 futures contracts. As usual, our notation convention is that a positive value of x_1 stands for a long position while a negative value of x_1 refers to a short position. The first marking to market occurs a day later, at the end of day two, and we have the cash flow of $x_1 (fr(2) - fr(1))$. We define this object in Maple as **PayDay(2)**.

```
> PayDay(2):= x1*(fr(2)-fr(1));
```

$$PayDay(2) := x1\,(fr(2) - fr(1))$$

If $fr(2)$ is greater than $fr(1)$, there is a positive cash flow to the party with the long position and vice versa. In any event, we invest this amount at the risk-free rate of interest. That is, we borrow if the cash flow of our position is negative and we lend if the cash flow of our position is positive. We do this immediately to accomplish our goal of having actual cash flows happen only at the end of day three.

We can also enter, at the end of this day (day two), into a futures contract that matures one day later (day three). We may need it to offset some cash flow. Suppose we took a position in x_2 units of a futures contract on the same underlying asset. This costs zero and hence does not alter the cash flow at the end of day two.[5]

Now consider the cash flow at the end of day three. The original contract (for the one who holds it long), entered into on day one, requires delivering $x_1 S(3)$ of the underlying asset and receiving $x_1 fr(2)$. The original contract, entered into on day one, requires receiving $x_1 S(3)$ of the underlying asset and delivering $x_1 fr(2)$. We also took x_2 positions in a futures contract on day two which results in a cash flow of $x_2 (S(3) - fr(2))$. Finally, the amount invested at the risk-free rate on day two will have grown to $x_1 (fr(2) - fr(1)) (1 + r_2(2,3))$. Note that in a DTS environment $r_2(2,3)$ is known as of day one and equals $\dfrac{dt(2)}{dt(3)}$. However, for the time being we will continue using $1 + r_2(2,3)$.

In the upcoming calculations we will further simplify this expression as $1 + r$. We revert to the substitution as in (5.13) at the end of our argument. This will emphasize the need for the assumption of a deterministic term structure.

In total, therefore, the cash flow at day three is as defined below by **PayDay(3)**.

```
> PayDay(3):=x1*(S(3)-fr(2))+x2*(S(3)-fr(2))
+x1*(fr(2)-fr(1))*(1+r);
```

$$PayDay(3) := x1\,(S(3) - fr(2)) + x2\,(S(3) - fr(2))$$
$$+ x1\,(fr(2) - fr(1))(1 + r)$$

---

[5]"Day" does not necessarily refer to a calendar day. Instead, it should be interpreted as the time period that elapses between consecutive marking to markets.

Since we try to have an end cash flow of $fr(1) - S(3)$, we simplify it and collect the terms in the above expression with respect to $fr(2)$. Later we will equate to zero the coefficient of $fr(2)$. Hence, collecting the coefficients yields

```
> PayDay(3):=collect(simplify(PayDay(3)),fr(2));
```

$$PayDay(3) := (-x2 + x1\, r)fr(2) + x1\, S(3) + x2\, S(3) - x1fr(1) - x1fr(1)r$$

Since our aim is to **not have** $fr(2)$ appearing as part of the cash flow at the end of day two, we will try to purchase futures contracts in quantities x_1 and x_2 such that the coefficient of $fr(2)$ is zero. The coefficient of $fr(2)$ in the expression **PayDay(3)** is

```
> coeff(PayDay(3),fr(2));
```

$$-x2 + x1\, r$$

Hence x_1 and x_2 should satisfy equation (5.14)

$$x_1 = \frac{x_2}{r}. \tag{5.14}$$

We thus substitute it in the expression **PayDay(3)** and obtain the following new expression for **PayDay(3)**:

```
> PayDay(3):=subs(-x2+x1*r=0,PayDay(3));
```

$$PayDay(3) := x1\, S(3) + x2\, S(3) - x1fr(1) - x1fr(1)\, r.$$

The following Maple command solves for x_1 in terms of x_2 and r, and substitutes the solution based on equation (5.14) to reach a new expression for **PayDay(3)**.

```
> PayDay(3):=subs(x1=solve(-x2+x1*r=0,x1),PayDay(3));
```

$$PayDay(3) := \frac{x2\, S(3)}{r} + x2\, S(3) - \frac{x2fr(1)}{r} - x2fr(1).$$

Finally we see if the expression **PayDay(3)** can be factored.

```
> PayDay(3):=factor(PayDay(3));
```

$$PayDay(3) := \frac{x2\,(1+r)\,(S(3) - fr(1))}{r}.$$

Thus, we see that in order to have a cash flow of $fr(1) - S(3)$ at the end of day three, we need to choose x_2 such that the coefficient of $fr(1) - S(3)$ is one. Hence we extract the coefficient of $fr(1) - S(3)$ in the Maple command

```
> coeff(PayDay(3),fr(1)-S(3));
```
$$0$$

and solve for x_2:

```
> solve(%=1,x2);
```

Consequently, we should choose x_2 to satisfy equation (5.15),

$$x_2 = -\frac{r}{1+r}, \qquad (5.15)$$

and since by equation (5.15) $x_1 = \dfrac{x_2}{r}$, x_1 should satisfy

$$x_1 = -\frac{r}{1+r}. \qquad (5.16)$$

In order to confirm the receipt of the required cash flow at the end of day three we substitute the value of x_2, based on equation (5.16), in **PayDay(3)**. This is performed in the next command.

```
> subs(x2=-r/(1+r),PayDay(3));
```
$$fr(1) - S(3)$$

Therefore we see that by shorting (since x_1 and x_2 are negative) $\dfrac{1}{1+r}$ futures contracts on day one and $\dfrac{r}{1+r}$ futures contracts on day two, the required cash flow as far as magnitude and timing are concerned, is obtained. As explained at the outset of these arguments, we would like to examine this portfolio and the investment strategy described more closely. At time one, we take a long position in a forward contract and we short $\dfrac{1}{1+r}$ futures contracts. On the next trading day, the proceeds from the marking to market process are invested at the risk-free rate and we take a short position in $\dfrac{r}{1+r}$ of the futures contract. We have no intermediate cash flows and the cash flow at time three (at the end of the third trading day) from the forward contract and the futures contracts is

$$fr(1) - S(2) + S(2) - F. \tag{5.17}$$

However, the combined cost of this portfolio and of the investment strategy is zero. Hence, to avoid arbitrage opportunities the payoff must be zero as well; thus,

$$fr(1) - F = 0. \tag{5.18}$$

Consequently, the futures price $fr(1)$ is equal to the forward price F.

There is only one small problem: on day one, how can we short $\dfrac{1}{1+r}$ futures contracts when r, the spot rate from day two to day three, is not known on day one?[6] Indeed this is why we need the assumption of the term structure being deterministic. As explained above, in such an environment the spot rate $r_2(2,3)$ (we used r in the Maple calculation) is known on day one and is given by

$$1 + r_2(2,3) = \frac{d_2}{d_3}. \tag{5.19}$$

Hence x_1 is given by $-\dfrac{d_3}{d_2}$ and x_2 is given by

```
> simplify((-(d2/d3)-1)/(d3/d2));
```

$$-\frac{(d2 + d3)\,d2}{d3^2}$$

Our example considered a forward and a futures contract with two days to maturity. It will work for any arbitrary number of days until maturity. The reader is asked in an exercise to develop a similar template for finding an investment strategy — a strategy which will demonstrate the same relationship between the forward price and the futures price for a pair of contracts with n days until maturity.

---

[6]We cannot instruct an investor to buy x futures contracts, where x is the interest rate that will prevail in the market from tomorrow to the day after tomorrow. The information the investor has now does not include the value of this rate unless the term structure is deterministic. In a more technical notation, this issue is related to measurability.

The argument presented here (and its proof or a slight modification of it) will reappear in several other situations related to valuation. The idea of solving for the required position by working backward (in a recursive manner) one period at a time, is reminiscent of a concept known as *dynamic programming*.

Given a sequential decision problem, one starts with penultimate decisions to be made, assuming that an optimal decision was taken at every previous step. An optimal strategy is solved for as a function of the decision taken a step before. In the example above we assumed that at the initial time an optimal number of futures contracts x were purchased.

We then solved for the optimal decision, x_2, a day prior to maturity assuming that x_1 was optimal, thereby receiving the equation for the payoff at maturity as a function of x_1 and x_2. This payoff was then equated to the required payoff and the values of x_1 and x_2 were solved for.

5.8   Concluding Remarks

This chapter takes a second look at forward contracts. These contracts were analyzed in Chapter 1 in the framework of a one-period model. Here they are investigated in a multiperiod model in which the differences between forward and futures contracts that remain indistinguishable in a one-period model can be shown. The chapter investigates Eurodollar contracts and forward rate agreements, as well as the effect of known cash flows paid by an asset on its forward price.

There is a common feature of financial assets considered in this chapter. They can be priced knowing only the realization of the current term structure and do not require a specification of the evolution, across time, of the term structure. The chapter concludes by proving the equivalency between forward and futures contracts in a DTS environment. The technique used to demonstrate this equivalency paves the ground for the numerical valuation of interest rate options, American options that are attended to in a later chapter. The next chapter takes a second look at swaps, the pricing of which again requires knowledge only of the current term structure, and not of its evolution through time. We will only touch upon some assets, the valuation of which necessitates the specifications of the evolution of the term structure of interest rates.

5.9   Questions and Problems

Problem 1

Consider a forward contract that was issued some time ago for a delivery at time T with the forward price of $\$F$. Suppose it is now time t $(t < T)$ and the conditions in the market are such that the forward price of the same underlying asset for delivery at time T is also $\$F$

(1) Assuming that the continuously compounded risk-free interest rate prevailing in the market is r, recover the price of the underlying asset today.
(2) What is the current value of the forward contract that was issued some time ago for a delivery at time T with the forward price of $\$F$?

Problem 2

Assume the bond market outlined in Table 5.1

Price/Time	1	2	3	Security
$94	$105	$0		B1
$97	$10	$110	$0	B2
$85	$8	$8	$108	B3

Consider a forward contract written at time zero specifying delivery of bond three at time two (immediately after the second coupon is paid). According to the contract, the party holding it long will pay the forward price F, at time two, and will receive an instrument similar to a zero-coupon bond that will pay $108 at time three.

(1) Calculate the the forward price F using the replication approach and the discount factor approach (with the Vdis function).

(2) What is the value of $\dfrac{108 \cdot d(3)}{d(2)}$, where d is the discount factor in this market.

(3) Compare the value of F calculated in part 1 and the value of the expression in part 2. What is your conclusion and why? Hint (See problem 3)

(4) Graph the payoff from such a contract as of time 2, as a function, of the spot rate $r_2(2,3)$.

Problem 3

Suppose you have a bond market where bonds pay an annual coupon. Assume further that the discount factor function is known and is denoted by $d(t)$. Consider a bond with a face value of $100 that just paid its coupon, $C, maturing in two years with a current price of P. The remaining cash flows from this bond are $C in a year from now and $(100+C)$ in two years from now.

As it has been discussed in the text, the forward price, F, of this bond, for delivery in one year from now (just after the coupon is being paid), can be found utilizing equation (5.5) and is given by

$$F = \frac{P}{d(1)} - C,$$

where P is the current price of the bond. Show that, alternatively, the forward price of this bond can be found as

$$F = \frac{(100+C)d(2)}{d(1)}$$

Interpret these results.

Problem 4

Assume that the current term structure of interest rates is known. Show that a forward price, F, of a coupon-paying bond that matures in n units of time from now and has n coupon payments remaining for a delivery in $m(m < n)$ units of time, immediately after a coupon payment at time m can be determined as

$$F = \left[\frac{1}{d(m)}\right]\left(\sum_{i=m+1}^{n} Cd(i) + FVd(n)\right),$$

where $d(i)$ is the discount factor for time i, FV is the face value of the bond, and C is a coupon payment. How would this result have to be modified if the delivery would occur just before the coupon payment at time m?

Problem 5

The LIBOR term structure is actually estimated based on FRA agreements. The FRA data convey to us the forward rate in the LIBOR market. Hence in order to estimate the term structure of LIBOR we have to utilize equation (5.8) to derive the term structure from the forward rate. In our discussion regarding the forward rate, in the government bond market, we derive the forward rate from the term structure. In the LIBOR market we have to do the reverse. Delineate the steps of extracting the term structure from the forward rate structure, where the spot rate at time 0 for a year is 11.1111111%, the forward rate, as of time 0, from year one to two is 12.5000000%, and the forward rate as of year zero, from year two to three is 14.2857143%. Generate a continuous estimation of the term structure by using the NarbitB procedure.

Problem 6

Consider a FRA in which the underlying rate is the risk-free rate, the rate implied by government bonds. Assume that both parties are federal agencies with no risk of default. Prove that the rate of the FRA must be the forward rate implied in the term structure. Prove this statement in two ways — through replication and through valuation by discount factors.

Problem 7

Assume a market with a deterministic term structure and that time zero is the current time; that is, the spot interest rate which will prevail in the market from any future time t_1 to time $t_2 (0 < t_1 < t_2)$ is known with certainty. Show that in such a market the spot interest rate for future time periods must be equal to the forward interest rate $r_0(t_1, t_2)$ — otherwise arbitrage opportunities would exist.

Problem 8

Assume a market with a deterministic term structure. Find an investment strategy which will demonstrate that the forward price and the futures price are the same for a pair of contracts with $3 < n$ days until maturity.

Problem 9

Assume that the bond market outlined in Table 5.1 has a deterministic term structure. Calculate the cash flow at times 1, 2 and 3 from a future contract on a stock (that pays no dividends) to be delivered at time 3, with a price of \$100 at time 0.

Chapter 6

Swaps: A Second Look

We have already been introduced to swaps in Chapter 1 where they were investigated in the framework of a one-period model. Here we take a second look at swaps in a more realistic multiperiod setting for which we have a continuum of states of nature in each period. This setting allows the investigation of one of the most common forms of swaps that could not been analyzed in Chapter 1. It will be followed by revisiting currency and equity swaps in a multiperiod setting. As before, the risk of default by the parties is ignored.

6.1 A Fixed-for-Float Swap

One of the most common swaps is a "fixed-for-float" swap. In this type of swap, one party pays a fixed rate of interest on a certain principal every period, e.g., semiannually. The other party pays a floating rate of interest, commonly LIBOR, according to the rate that prevails in the market at that time. The parties do not swap the principal and hence it is termed a notional principal.

Assume a *notional* principal of N, and assume that the parties enter into the swap agreement at time t_0, and that the payment dates are at times $t_1, \ldots, t_n$. Thus, for example, at time t_1, the party who pays the fixed rate, r, pays the amount Nr. The party who pays the floating rate pays the amount $Nr_{t_0}(t_0, t_1)$ at time t_1. The rate $r_{t_0}(t_0, t_1)$ is the prevailing rate in the market from time t_0 to t_1 and is known at time t_0. At time t_i, this party will pay the amount $Nrt_{i-1}(t_{i-1}, t_i)i = 1, \ldots, n-1$. At time t_0 the value of $r_{t_0}(t_0, t_1)$ is known but the other rates are not. These rates will be known only at the beginning of the period to which they apply; e.g., the rate $r_{t_2}(t_2,t_3)$ will be known at time t_2. In practice, the payments are netted and only the difference is paid to the appropriate party. If we look at the swap from the point of view of the party who pays the fixed rate, for example, at time t_1, this party pays (or, if the expression in (5.1) is negative, receives)

$$Nr - Nr_{t_0}(t_0,t_1).$$

(6.1)

Consider the swap at its initiation time. We would like to find the fixed rate that will make this swap fair. We are ignoring the credit risk of the parties in order to simplify our discussion. Therefore, on the initiation date of the contract, the fixed cash flows are nearly those of a regular bond. The only difference is that at maturity the principal is not paid. The floating cash flows are like those of a floating (variable) rate bond, but again the principal is not paid at maturity. As we have already seen the value of a variable rate bond immediately after a coupon payment is its face value — the principal. Hence, in our case, the value of the floating payments will be N minus the present value of N, the notional principal.

Let $d(t)$ be the discount factor for time t, where time is measured in years, and assume that the payment dates are $t = \dfrac{1}{2}, \dfrac{2}{2}, \dfrac{3}{2}, \ldots, \dfrac{2T}{2}$, i.e., payments are made semiannually and the current time is $t = 0$. The value of the floating payments today is

$$N - Nd(T).$$

(6.2)

The value of the fixed payments is the present value of the future cash flows. We assume that the payments are made semi-annually and that the rate[1] is reported as an annual rate based on semiannual compounding. The value of the fixed payments is thus given by equation (6.3).

$$\sum_{t=1}^{2T} N\frac{r}{2}d\left(\frac{t}{2}\right)$$

(6.3)

Therefore, the value of the swap to the party who pays the fixed rate is

---

[1] In practice the rates are reported annually but based on the number of days in each period. Hence instead of having $\dfrac{r}{2}$ we will actually have $r\left[\dfrac{number\_of\_days\_in\_the\_period}{365}\right]$.

$$N - Nd(T) - \sum_{t=1}^{2T} N\frac{r}{2}d\left(\frac{t}{2}\right). \tag{6.4}$$

We say that the swap is a "fair" deal if the present value of the fixed payments equal that of the variable payments. The value of r which makes the swap a fair deal, i.e., makes the expression in equation (6.4) vanish, is given by

$$r = 2\frac{1 - d(T)}{\sum\limits_{t=1}^{2T} d\left(\frac{t}{2}\right)}. \tag{6.5}$$

This is confirmed by Maple as below. First let us make sure that the variables, N, T, r, t, and d, are not assigned any value.

```
> N:='N':d:='d':T:='T':r:='r':
> solve(N-N*d(T)-sum('N*(r/2)*d(t/2)','t'=1..2* T)=0,r);
```

$$-\frac{2(d(T) - 1)}{\sum\limits_{t=1}^{2T} d\left(\frac{1}{2}t\right)}$$

The procedure **FxFlswap** values a swap at its initiation from the point of view of the party who pays the fixed rate. The input parameters, in order, are the notional principal, the discount factor function, the number of payments until the swap matures, and the fixed rate of interest at which the swap was initiated. (We maintain the assumption that the payments are made semiannually.) Given the values of N, the notional principal, and of $d(t), t = \frac{1}{2}, \frac{2}{2}, \frac{3}{3}, \dots, \frac{2T}{2}$, where $2T$ is the number of payments and T is the maturity date (we assume that the swap is initiated at time zero), the procedure **FxFlswap** can be utilized to solve, symbolically, for the fixed rate r. This is shown in the command below.

```
> solve(FxFlswap(N,d,T,r)=0,r);
```

$$-\frac{2(d(T) - 1)}{\sum\limits_{t=1}^{2T} d\left(\frac{1}{2}t\right)}$$

Now let us look at a structure of a bond market as defined by **NarbitB** below and name the discount factor function $d(t)$. This allows the execution of the procedure **FxFlswap** in order to find the value of r. Consider the market outlined in **NarbitB** below in which, for simplicity, we assume that[2] coupons are paid annually. (We add the zero parameter at the end to suppress the graph of the discount factor. If you would like to see it, rerun **NarbitB** and omit the last parameter.)

```
> NarbitB([[5,5,5,105],[3,103,0,0],[6,6,106,0],
[110,0,0,0]], [60,90,85,101],7,d,0);
```

The no-arbitrage condition is satisfied.

The discount factor for time, 1, *is given by,* $\dfrac{101}{110}$

The interest rate spanning the time interval, $[0,1]$, *is given by,* 0.08911

The discount factor for time, 2, *is given by,* $\dfrac{9597}{11330}$

The interest rate spanning the time interval, $[0,2]$, *is given by,* 0.1806

The discount factor for time, 3, *is given by,* $\dfrac{84305}{120098}$

The interest rate spanning the time interval, $[0,3]$, *is given by,* 0.4246

The discount factor for time, 4, *is given by,* $\dfrac{163553}{360294}$

The interest rate spanning the time interval, $[0,4]$, *is given by,* 1.203

The function Vdis ([c1,c2,..]), values the cashflow [c1,c2,..]

The continuous discount factor is given by the function, 'd', (.)

Assume a fixed-for-float swap initiated at time zero that matures in four years. Since the payments are semiannual the swap will have eight payments. To solve for the value of the fixed rate we should execute the command below:

---

[2]The reader may try to run **NarbitB** for a smaller number of approximating functions to see that a perfect fit is not possible with a smaller number of approximating functions. The first time that the absolute deviations are reported to be zero is for seven approximating functions. Each time you run **NarbitB** it defines a local variable **SumAbsDiv**. If its value is zero it means that a perfect fit has been achieved. To versify the value of **SumAbsDiv** just issue the command **SumAbsDiv**; on the command line. If a coupon would have been paid semi-annually we would have had to take another step prior to the valuation of the swap. Since our unit of time is a year and **NarbitB**, in such a market, uses half a year as the unit of time, we first need to scale the function d(t) to conform to the time unit of a year. This is done by issuing the command **d:=unapply(d(t/2),t):**.

```
> evalf(solve(FxFlswap(N,d,4,r)=0,r));
```

$$0.1786534908$$

Note that the value of r is independent of N. Indeed, this is easily verified by equating the value of the swap, equation (5.4), to zero. The fixed rate that will make this swap a fair deal is about 17.8%.

The annual interest rate that applies to a loan given from time zero to time i, based on semiannual compounding, in decimal form, is the ith element of the array below.

```
> [seq(evalf((((1/d(i/2)^(1/i))-1)*2),i=1..4)];
```

$$[0.09072998555, 0.087207618, 0.085611491, 0.084748161]$$

The fixed rate determined by **FxFlswap**, given the discount factor function $d(t)$, is only a function of T, namely, the maturity time of the swap. We can calculate, as in the array below, the fixed rate that will apply to a swap with maturity dates of T, $T = 1, \ldots, 4$. This is the Tth element of the following array.

```
> [seq(evalf(solve(FxFlswap(N,d,T,r)=0,r)),T=1..4)];
```

$$[0.08728271246, 0.08488946465, 0.1168241028, 0.1786534908]$$

We therefore see the relation between the fixed rate that applies to the swap and the term structure of interest rates in the market. In fact, we can further analyze this relation utilizing the connection among forward rates, the term structure of interest rates, forward rate agreements and swaps.

A fixed-for-float swap can be broken down into some basic building blocks. The first block is the exchange of cash at time t_1, which is exactly identical to the case of the swap investigated in a one-period setting. The remaining blocks are much the same as the forward rate agreement (FRA) dealt with in Section 5.4.1. At time t_0 one party agrees to pay the other the return on N dollars invested from, for example, time t_1 to t_2 in terms of LI-BOR. In exchange, the other party pays a fixed rate at that time. Similarly the exchange of cash at time t_3 and so on can be thought of in the same way. Indeed, the fact that a swap is built from basic building blocks is a generic property of most types of swaps. The idea can be visualized using a three-dimensional graph.

Based on what we already know from the section dealing with FRAs, Section 5.4.1, we are in a position to calculate the fixed rate that should apply to each of these building blocks. The catch, though, is that in a swap agreement such as this, the same fixed rate should apply to all the building blocks. Hence, the value of each block may not be zero, but the value of the blocks in aggregate is zero if the swap is fair. The exercise at the end of the chapter will return to this point and will ask the student to analyze this relation further.

Of course the **FxFlswap** procedure can also value a swap that is initiated at some fixed value r. For example, consider a swap that matures in two years where the notional principal is \$10,000 and the fixed rate is initially set at 15 percent. Since we already know that the fair fixed rate should be 8.468322068%, the value of such a swap should be negative to the party who pays the fixed rate. This is confirmed below.

```
> FxFlswap(10000,d,2,.15);
```

$$-1173.183981$$

Occasionally, a customer will ask for a swap in which the fixed rate is below the fair fixed rate. This is referred to as a *buy-down swap*. Such a customer (who pays fixed and receives LIBOR) will have to pay a certain amount at the initiation of the swap. The reverse situation is called a *buy-up swap*. Both of these situations are referred to in the exercises at the end of the chapter. A swap in which the value of the fixed cash flow equals that of the floating cash flow is called a *par swap*. After the initiation time, the situation in the market may (and usually does) change and a new term structure of interest rates should be used to value the swap.

You may like to try and change the structure of the market and re-run the commands above to investigate the sensitivity of the fixed rate to the structure of the market and the implied term structure. You however, must be careful and first unassign the values of the variable by operating the command $T := 'T'$, etc. If we value the swap after its initiation at some point in time between two consecutive payment dates, we must pay attention to the timing. This is done in the same manner as valuing a variable rate bond between two consecutive payments. The next subsection deals with valuing an existing swap.

6.1.1 *Valuing an Existing Swap*

Consider an existing swap. Assume that the current time is zero and that the length of time until the next payment is v. The value of an outstanding variable bond immediately after a payment, say, at time v, is N. Thus, the value of such a bond at time zero is $(N + \imath N)d(v)$, where $\imath N$ is the payment at time v. In other words, $\imath$ is the interest rate applicable to the payment at time v. However, the floating payment in a swap does not include the payment of the principal on the last payment date. Hence, we should subtract the present value of the principal in order to arrive at the value of the floating payment in a swap. If we assume that the maturity date is T and, as before, that the units of time are years, then the value of the floating payments is given by equation (6.6) below.

$$(N + \imath N)d(v) - Nd(T). \tag{6.6}$$

One must remember that the discount factor we use is the one in effect at the current time, time zero. The value of the fixed payments will be given by

$$\sum_{t=0}^{2(T-v)} N\frac{r}{2}d\left(v + \frac{t}{2}\right). \tag{6.7}$$

In equation (6.7) r is the fixed rate agreed upon at the initiation of the swap. The value of the swap to the party who pays the fixed interest is given by equation (6.8) below.

$$(N + \imath N)d(v) - Nd(T) - \sum_{t=0}^{2(T-v)} N\frac{r}{2}d\left(v + \frac{t}{2}\right). \tag{6.8}$$

The procedure **FxFlswap** is also capable of valuing a swap already in existence.[3] As before we value it from the point of view of the party that pays the fixed rate. The input parameters, in order, are the notional principal, the discount factor function, the maturity date of the swap, the fixed

---

[3]It is easy to see that, as for the par swap, the value of a swap after its initiation with a notional principal of N is also N times the value of a swap with a notional principal of $1. That is, the value of the swap is a homogeneous (of degree one) function of N. Hence we could have programmed the procedure **FxFlswap** to value a swap of a $1 notional principal.

rate of interest at which the swap was initiated, the time until the next payment (measured in units of a year), and the variable rate applicable to the first payment. Consider the swap we valued above. Now assume that we keep the same parameters as before but, that the swap was initiated prior to the current time. The time until the next payment is $\frac{3}{12}$ (i.e., 3 months) and the floating rate applicable to the next payment is 7 percent. The value of such a swap will be given by executing the command below.

```
> FxFlswap(10000,d,21/12,.15,3/12,0.07);
```

$$-960.9600240$$

Let us look at another example in a market with a different structure. In order to define a term structure we run **NarbitB** for another market[4] structure. Suppose we look at the market specified by **NarbitB** below, where **coupons are paid annually**, and we define the discount factors to be the function **Dis**.

```
> NarbitB([[5,5,105],[8,108,0],[6,6,106]],
[90,102,95],2,Dis,0);
```

The no-arbitrage condition is not satisfied
An arbitrage portfolio is:
$$Buy, \frac{348}{335}, of Bond, 1$$
$$Buy, \frac{1}{134}, of Bond, 2$$
Short, 1, of Bond, 3
Buying this portfolio produces income of, $\frac{50}{67}$, at time, 0
This portfolio produces income of, $-\frac{50}{67}$, at time, 1
This portfolio produces income of, 0, at time, 2

---

[4]Note that the no-arbitrage condition is not satisfied here, but we are using an estimation of the term structure which is "best" in a certain sense. This is usually the case in real markets since the prices of the bonds include some "noise". Moreover, note that the arbitrage portfolio generates a negative cash flow, $-\$\frac{50}{67}$, at time one and the same amount of positive cash flow is produced at time zero. The arbitrage profit is thus due only to the interest earned investing $\$\frac{50}{67}$ from time zero to time one.

$$\textit{This portfolio produces income of, } \frac{206}{67}, \textit{ at time, } 3$$
The continuous discount factor is given by the function, 'Dis', (.)

Consider a swap in existence where the notional principal is \$10,000, the discount factor is the function **Dis**, the maturity time is $\frac{13}{12}$ years, the fixed rate of the swap is 12 percent, the time until the next payment is one month, and the rate of the next floating payment is 10 percent. The value of the swap is calculated below:

```
> FxFlswap(10000,Dis,13/12,.12,1/12,.10);
```

$$-146.1283520$$

Such a swap, if it had been initiated today (with six months until the next payment), would have had a different fixed rate. We can actually solve for the rate that would apply if such a swap were initiated today, by executing the next command.

```
> solve(FxFlswap(10000,Dis,1.5,r)=0);
```

$$0.07259337189$$

We can also utilize the **FxFlswap** procedure in the case where a swap is renegotiated. Consider a swap in existence and assume that the parties would like to change the fixed rate of the swap so that the value of the swap will be zero. This of course would trigger some cash transfer. Such a transaction might be motivated by tax reasons. Consider the swap we just valued at −\$146.1283520. Suppose the parties would like to change the fixed rate so that the swap value will be zero. This is solved for by the command below.

```
> solve(FxFlswap(10000,Dis,13/12,r,1/12,.10)=0,r);
```

$$0.1099852543$$

Thus, the party who pays the fixed rate should now pay \$146.1283520 and in the future pay a fixed rate of 10.99852543% instead of the 12 percent at which the swap was initiated. We can verify this result via the command below.

```
> FxFlswap(100,Dis,13/12,.1099852543,1/12,.10);
```

0.

The value of the fixed rate of interest that will make the value of the existing swap, equation (5.8), zero is given in equation (6.9) below.

$$\frac{2((1+\iota)d(v))-d(T)}{\displaystyle\sum_{t=0}^{2(T-v)} d\left(v+\tfrac{t}{2}\right)}. \tag{6.9}$$

This is confirmed by solving for r such that the expression in equation (5.9) is zero. We first make sure the variables have no assigned values.

```
> N:='N':d:='d':T:='T':r:='r':v:='v':tau:='tau':
```

```
> solve(((N+tau*N)*d(v)-N*d(T)-sum('N*(r/2)*d(v+t/2)',
't'=0..2*(T-v))=0,r));
```

$$\frac{2(d(v)\tau+d(v)-d(T))}{\displaystyle\sum_{t=0}^{2T-2v} d\left(v+\tfrac{1}{2}t\right)}.$$

6.2   Currency Swaps

In Chapter 1, we investigated a swap, albeit in the setting of a one-period model. The situation in a multiperiod environment is very similar. The vast majority of these types of swaps involve swapping not only interest payments, but also the principals. It is therefore essentially a situation where a company, in a domestic market, agrees to swap two cash flows. It exchanges a cash flow identical to the one resulting from issuing a foreign bond in a foreign market for a cash flow identical to one resulting from issuing a domestic bond in the domestic market.

For the sake of consistency, we keep the same notation as in Chapter 1. Hence, we consider a domestic firm which receives an amount N_1 of foreign currency now (at time zero) and is required to pay an amount of foreign currency N_1R_1 at time $t = 1,\ldots,T-1$, and $N_1(1+R_1)$ at time T, where T is the maturity time. This cash flow profile could be a loan repayment for a loan that the firm obtained in the foreign market at a rate R_1 and N_1 would then be the principal amount of the loan. This cash flow is being swapped with a cash flow of a foreign firm that receives an amount N_0 of domestic currency at the current time, and pays N_0r_0 at time $t =$

$1, \ldots, T-1$, and $N_0(1+r_0)$ at time T. Again, this could be a loan payment on a loan obtained in the domestic market at a rate r_0, where N_0 is the principal amount.

In practice, the swap might be arranged for the domestic firm by a financial institution. The institution either finds a foreign firm like above or "warehouses" this cash flow until it finds an optimal match for it. In certain cases, the institution must assume some risk as a result of the absence of an exact matching. Hence, it requires a fee, a "finder's fee", as well as compensation for the risk taken. This fee is usually obtained in terms of an increase in the rate, r_0, that the domestic firm is asked to pay. (The end-of-chapter exercises ask the reader to analyze such a situation.) The motivation for entering into such a swap is as it was in the case of the one-period model and, as before, we still ignore the risk of default by the parties involved.

Given the exogenous circumstances, i.e., the domestic term structure, the foreign term structure, and the spot exchange rate, valuing such a swap is a straightforward matter. Assume that the domestic discount factor is given by the function $disL(t)$, and that the foreign discount factor function is given by $disF(t)$. The present value, in terms of the local currency, of the domestic cash flow is like the present value of the cash flow from a bond and is thus given by equation (6.10) below.

$$N_0 - \sum_{t=1}^{T} N_0(r_0)disL(t) - N_0 disL(T) \tag{6.10}$$

The present value of the foreign cash flow in terms of the foreign currency is, by the same token, given by equation (6.11) below.

$$N_1 - \sum_{t=1}^{T} N_1 R_1 disF(t) - N_1 disF(T) \tag{6.11}$$

We denote the cost of one unit of the foreign currency in terms of units of the domestic currency by $F0$. Hence the spot exchange rate of one unit of the domestic currency is $\dfrac{1}{F0}$ units of the foreign currency. At the initiation of the swap, the domestic firm receives the domestic currency N_0 and pays out the foreign currency, N_1. At each coupon payment time the domestic firm pays the domestic coupon, $N_0 r_0$, and receives the foreign coupon, $N_1 r_1$. At the maturity date of the swap, the principals are swapped back: the domestic firm pays out N_0, the domestic principal, and receives back N_1, the foreign principal. Therefore the value of the swap, from the point of view of the domestic firm in the domestic currency, is given by

$$N_0 - \sum_{t=1}^{T} N_0 r_0 disL(t) - N_0 disL(T) -$$

$$\left(N_1 - \sum_{t=1}^{T} N_1 R_1 disF(t) - N_1 disF(T) \right) F0. \tag{6.12}$$

There is another way of valuing this type of a swap. Rather than discounting the foreign cash flow to the current time period and then converting it to the local currency via the spot exchange rate, we can convert each component of the future foreign cash flow at the time it occurs. This requires the use of a series of forward contracts. We essentially repeat the same argument as was employed for the one-period model. This time, however, we think of each time period $[0, t_1]$, $[0, t_2]$, etc., as a separate one-period model. Thus, if we denote the forward exchange rate for time t, as of time zero, by $FF(t)$, applying this argument separately to each time period yields equation (6.13) below.

$$FF(t) = \frac{F0\, disF(t)}{disL(t)} \tag{6.13}$$

$FF(t)$, so defined, is the forward price of one unit of the foregin currency in terms of the domestic currency.[5] The foreign discount factors function can be written in terms of the domestic discount factor function and the spot exchange rate, as in equation (6.14).

$$disF(t) = \frac{FF(t)\, disL(t)}{F0} \tag{6.14}$$

Substituting equation (6.14) into equation (6.12) results in the relation (6.15).

---

[5]The reader may recall that equation (6.13) is a consequence of the replication argument, that in this context is referred to as the *cost-of-carry model*. To guarantee a unit of a foreign currency at time t the investor can buy the present value, as of time zero, of a unit of a foreign currency obtainable at time t. In terms of the local currency this will cost $disF(t)F0$, which must equal the present value of the forward exchange rate.

$$N_0 \left(1 - disL\left(T\right)\right) - \sum_{t=1}^{T} N_0 r_0 disL\left(t\right) - N_1 \left(F0 - FF\left(T\right) disL\left(T\right)\right) - $$

$$\sum_{t=1}^{T} N_1 R_1 FF\left(t\right) disL\left(t\right).$$

$$(6.15)$$

Clearly, this substitution is more than just the pure mathematical operation. It actually points out to us the building blocks of foreign currency swaps. One can actually "engineer" a homemade foreign currency swap by entering into a sequence of forward contracts, maturing at times $t = 1, \ldots, T$. If the investors had a liability of $N_1 R_1$ units of foreign currency at time t, they can enter into a forward agreement to receive that amount at time t. In exchange, the investor would then pay the amount $N_1 R_1 FF\left(t\right)$ in local currency at time t. Thus, the present value, as of time zero, of the $N_1 R_1$ units of the foreign currency obtainable at time t is $N_1 R_1 FF\left(t\right) disL\left(t\right)$ in terms of the domestic currency.

Equation (6.15) follows directly from this argument and can also be presented in a manner that relates more closely to this interpretation, i.e., as equation (6.16):

$$\sum_{t=1}^{T} \left(N_1 R_1 FF\left(t\right) - N_0 r_0\right) disL\left(t\right) + \left(N_1 FF\left(T\right) - N_0\right) disL\left(T\right) - N_1 F0 + N_0.$$

$$(6.16)$$

Let us look at an example to clarify this idea and to see the interrelation between the parameters involved in this valuation. To this end we make use of the procedure **FXswap** that values a currency swap from the point of view of the domestic firm in the domestic currency. The input parameters to the procedure **FXswap** are, in order, N_0, r_0, $disL$, N_1, R_1, $disF$, and $F0$ as defined in equation (6.12). These are followed by the parameters, T, and *per*, where T is the time to the last payment and *per* is the payment period (usually semiannual). Solving symbolically for the value of the swap produces the expression below, which is a generalized version of equation (6.16).

```
> FXswap(N0,r0,disL,N1,R1,disF,F0,T,per);
```

$$NO - NI\,FO - \left(\sum_{t=1}^{\frac{T}{per}} NO\,r0\,disL(tper) \right) - NO\,disL(T)$$

$$+ \left(\sum_{t=1}^{\frac{T}{per}} NI\,RI\,disF(tper) + NI\,disF(T) \right) FO$$

It is also possible to generate the symbolic relation between r_0 and the other parameters by running **FXswap** as below.

```
> solve(FXswap(N0,r0,disL,N1,R1,disF,F0,T,per)=0,r0);
```

$$\frac{NO - NI\,FO - NO\,disL(T) + FONI\,RI\left(\sum_{t=1}^{\frac{T}{per}} disF(tper) \right) + FONI\,disF(T)}{NO\left(\sum_{t=1}^{\frac{T}{per}} disL(tper) \right)}$$

Let us consider now a numerical example. Assume a foreign exchange swap in a market where the domestic term structure is solved for by the **NarbitB** procedure below and is defined to be **disL**. For simplicity, we assume that in this market coupons are paid annually, and hence the units of time are years. The following figure depicts the continuous approximation of the discount factor in this market.

```
> NarbitB([[107,0,0,0],[5,5,5,105],[8,108,0,0],
[6,6,106,0]],[97,90,102,95],8,disL);
```

The no-arbitrage condition is satisfied.

The discount factor for time, 1, *is given by,* $\dfrac{97}{107}$

The interest rate spanning the time interval, $[0,1]$, *is given by,* 0.1031

The discount factor for time, 2, *is given by,* $\dfrac{5069}{5778}$

The interest rate spanning the time interval, $[0,2]$, *is given by,* 0.1399

The discount factor for time, 3, *is given by,* $\dfrac{40589}{51039}$

The interest rate spanning the time interval, $[0,3]$, *is given by,* 0.2575

The discount factor for time, 4, *is given by,* $\dfrac{4722407}{6430914}$

The interest rate spanning the time interval, $[0,4]$, *is given by,* 0.3618

The function Vdis ([c1,c2,..]), values the cashflow [c1,c2,..]
The continuous discount factor is given by the function, 'disL', (.)

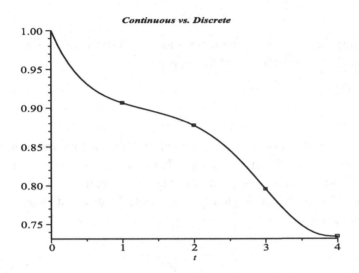

The Graph of the Function *DisL*

Let us also assume that the spot exchange rate is *F0* and is assigned the numerical value of $\frac{11}{10}$, and that the term structure of forward exchange rates is given as below:

```
> F0:=11/10;
```

$$F0 := \frac{11}{10}$$

We use the **do** command to generate the term structure of forward exchange rates.

```
> for i from 1 to 4 do;
> FF(i):=F0-i/7;
> od;
```

$$FF(1) := \frac{67}{70}$$
$$FF(2) := \frac{57}{70}$$

$$FF(3) := \frac{47}{70}$$
$$FF(4) := \frac{37}{70}$$

The purpose of the next command is to un-assign the value of i, which is still equal to 5 from the end of the loop above.

```
> i:=evaln(i);
```

$$i := i$$

Hence, $F0$ is the spot exchange rate and $FF(i)$ is the forward exchange rate for time i, as of the current time. That is, an investor can enter into a forward contract now to buy a unit of the foreign currency at time i for the price of $FF(i)$. According to equation (6.14) the discount factor in the foreign market is given by

$$disF(t) = \frac{FF(t)\,disL(t)}{F0}. \tag{6.17}$$

The numerical value of the foreign discount factor **disF** at times one, two, and three is evaluated below based on equation (6.14).[6]

```
> FF(1)*disL(1)/F0;
```

$$\frac{6499}{8239}$$

```
> FF(2)*disL(2)/F0;
```

$$\frac{96311}{148302}$$

```
> FF(3)*disL(3)/F0;
```

$$\frac{1907683}{3930003}$$

---

[6]Alternatively we could value it by the command

```
> seq(FF(i)*disL(i)/F0,i=1..3);
```

$$\frac{6499}{8239}, \frac{96311}{148302}, \frac{1907683}{3930003}$$

We can utilize **NarbitB** to generate a continuous estimation of the discount factors in the foreign market in the following way. Consider an artificial foreign market populated only by four zero-coupon bonds with a face value of one unit that mature at the same time as the bonds in the domestic market. The prices of such bonds must be the value of the discount factor for their maturity time. Thus running **NarbitB** as below will produce **disF**.

```
> NarbitB([[1,0,0,0],[0,1,0,0],[0,0,1,0],[0,0,0,1]],
[FF(1)*disL(1)/F0,FF(2)*disL(2)/F0,FF(3)*disL(3)/F0,
FF(4)*disL(4)/F0],5,disF,0);
```

The no-arbitrage condition is satisfied.
The discount factor for time, 1, is given by, $\frac{6499}{8239}$
The interest rate spanning the time interval, $[0,1]$, *is given by,* 0.2677
The discount factor for time, 2, is given by, $\frac{96311}{148302}$
The interest rate spanning the time interval, $[0,2]$, *is given by,* 0.5398
The discount factor for time, 3, is given by, $\frac{1907683}{3930003}$
The interest rate spanning the time interval, $[0,3]$, *is given by,* 1.060
The discount factor for time, 4, is given by, $\frac{174729059}{495180378}$
The interest rate spanning the time interval, $[0,4]$, *is given by,* 1.834
The function Vdis ([c1,c2,..]), values the cashflow [c1,c2,..]
The continuous discount factor is given by the function, 'disF', (.)

```
> SumAbsDiv;
```

$$0$$

We can now value a foreign exchange swap. The two term structures of interest rates and the term structure of forward exchange rates are shown in the figure below. The two graphs starting from one are the foreign and domestic term structures, where the domestic graph is above the foreign graph. The third graph is that of the forward exchange rate.

```
> plot([disL(t),disF(t),disF(t)*(11/10)/disL(t)],t=0..4,
colour=[green,red,black],thickness=2, title='TS of
Foreign and Domestic Interest Rates and TS of Forward
```

```
Exchange Rate',labels=[time,rates],
titlefont=[TIMES,BOLD,10]);
```

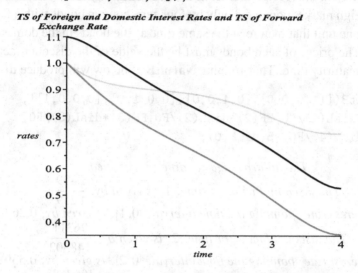

TS of Foreign and Domestic Interest Rates and TS of Forward
Exchange Rate

Consider a foreign currency swap in which both principals are $10,000, the foreign rate of interest is 15 percent, and the domestic rate is 6 percent. Assume that the swap is initiated at the current time with maturity in four years, that the spot exchange rate is $\frac{11}{10}$, and that the payments are made semiannually. The procedure **FXswap** values such a swap as demonstrated below. **The time parameters**, i.e., the maturity of the swap, the length of the period between payments, and the time to the first payment, **must be entered as fractions**. Maple checks that the number of periods is an integer and a decimal parameter will trigger an error message.

```
> FXswap(10000,.06,disL,10000,.15,disF,11/10,4,1/2);
```

$$-504.74288$$

It is possible to solve numerically for some of the parameters, given values for others. Consider a two-year swap at initiation with 10,000 units of domestic principal, 11,000 units of foreign principal, payments that are made semiannually, a foreign interest rate of 13 percent, and a spot exchange rate of 0.6. Given the above, the domestic rate can be solved for as below. Remember that if the unit of time is a year then the time to maturity will be 4 and the period will be $\dfrac{1}{2}$ for semiannual payments.

```
> solve({FXswap(10000,r,disL,11000,.13,disF,.6,4,
1/2)=0},{r});
```

$${r = 0.03778479136}$$

Alternatively, one can solve for the possible R and r given the exogenous circumstances as below.

```
> solve({FXswap(10000,r,disL,11000,R,disF,.6,4
,1/2)=0},{r});
```

$${r = -0.02398221366 + 0.4751308078 R}$$

The reader may try different combinations of parameters and different settings of foreign and domestic markets.

The **FXswap** procedure can also be used if, instead of the two term structures, the domestic term structure and the term structure of forward exchange rates are supplied. A direct substitution in the **FXswap** procedure will generate the value of a foreign exchange swap. Given the term structure of forward exchange rates and the foreign term structure, one should proceed in a similar manner as in the text above. Utilizing equation (6.13), the domestic term structure can be input and substituted in the procedure **FXswap** to value a foreign exchange swap. Such an exercise appears at the end of the chapter.

In the other swaps investigated in this chapter, no principal was exchanged at the time the swap was initiated. Therefore, when the additional parameter was added to the procedures, in order to value an existing swap, it actually allowed one to value a *deferred swap*. In other words, this is a swap that is agreed upon now and that will start at some specified time in the future. The future time is not necessarily a starting point that coincides with the beginning of a payment period. (See the exercises at the end of the book which elaborate on deferred swaps.) This is not the case for a foreign currency swap.

The value of an existing foreign currency swap does not (**and should not**) take into account cash flows that were exchanged in the past. When valuing an existing foreign currency swap, only the principals that will be exchanged at maturity and all of the future regular cash flows ("coupons") should be considered. Hence, the procedure that values an existing foreign currency swap cannot be applied to value a deferred foreign currency swap. Fortunately, there is a way of valuing such a swap, as is explained in the end-of-chapter exercises.

Consider a foreign exchange swap where the principals are 11,000, the domestic interest rate is 0.03, the foreign rate is 0.13, and the spot exchange rate is 0.6. The swap matures in $\frac{18}{12}$ years and payment occurs semiannually. The value of such a swap is calculated as below:

```
> FXswap(11000,0.03,disL,11000,.13,disF,.6, 3/2,1/2);
```

$$439.021982$$

Assume that 2 months passed $\left(\frac{2}{12} \text{ units of time}\right)$ from the initiation of the swap and that the exchange rate and the discount factor functions stayed the same. Thus, the exchange of interest payments will occur in $\frac{4}{12}$, $\frac{10}{12}$, and $\frac{16}{12}$ years, and in $\frac{16}{12}$ years the principals will be exchanged. Let us value this existing swap step by step and then verify the result by running the procedure **FXswap**.

```
> FXswap(11000,.03,disL,11000,0.130,disF,.6,
16/12,1/2,4/12);
```

$$-3787.703394$$

One should remember that at the initiation of the swap the principals are exchanged, and then they are exchanged again at the maturity of the swap. The present value of the domestic interest and principal payments is calculated below and assigned to the variable **Dome**.

```
> Dome:=add(11000*.03*disL(4/12+i/2),i=0..2)
+11000*disL(16/12);
```

$$Dome := 10787.79198$$

The present value of the foreign interest and principal currency (in terms of the foreign currency) is calculated below and assigned to the variable **Fore**.

```
> Fore:=add(11000*.13*disF(4/12+i/2),i=0..2)
+11000*disF(16/12);
```

$$Fore := 11666.81431$$

Thus, the value the foreign payment in terms of the domestic currency is

```
> Fore*0.6;
```

$$7000.088586$$

and hence the value of the swap (to the domestic firm) is given below.

```
> Fore*0.6-Dome;
```

$$-3787.703394$$

If we use our procedure to calculate the swap's value, we have to execute the procedure with an additional parameter at the end. This parameter is the time until the first payment: $\frac{4}{12}$ years in our case. The time to maturity of the swap, now that 2 months have passed since its initiation, is $\frac{16}{12}$ years instead of $\frac{18}{12}$ years.

```
> FXswap(11000,.03,disL,11000,0.13,disF,0.6,
16/12,1/2,4/12);
```

$$-3787.703394$$

Indeed we have confirmed that the same result is produced.

6.3 Commodity and Equity Swaps

Commodity and equity swaps follow the same basic structure as the other swaps we have investigated. One party agrees to pay another the spot price of a certain underlying asset and receives, in return, a fixed price agreed upon at the initiation of the swap.

In case of a commodity swap the parties agree on the quantity, referred to as the *notional quantity*, and on the time schedule $t = t_1, t_2, \ldots, t_k$, where t_k is the maturity time of the swap and k is the number of exchanges. For example, the notional quantity could be a number N of barrels of oil. The payments exchanged at time t are $S(t)N$ and FpN where the spot price of a barrel of oil at time t is $S(t)$ and the fixed price agreed upon is Fp. The net payment at time t, to the party who pays the fixed rate, is therefore

$$S(t)N - FpN. \tag{6.18}$$

The present value of $S(t)$, which is the value at time zero of having $S(t)$ at time t, is of course the spot price at time zero, $S(0)$: buying the good at time zero and holding it until time t will produce $S(t)$ at time t. This is just another way of looking at the cost-of-carry model through the present value concept. Hence, the present value of equation (6.18) is

$$S(0)N - d(t)FpN, \tag{6.19}$$

where $d(t)$ is the discount factor for time t.

There is another way of explaining the discounting of this cash flow. The investor can remove the uncertainty from $S(t)$ and can fix today the price of a barrel of oil at time t by entering into a forward contract. Hence, the investor knows that paying the forward price as of today, $Fr(t)$, at time t ensures the delivery of the oil. We can therefore replace $S(t)$, which is a random variable, with the certain (or deterministic) amount $Fr(t)$. This in turn allows us to calculate the value of the contract by simply discounting the net cash flow based on the current term structure of interest rates. Therefore, the value of the commodity swap is equation (6.20).

$$\sum_{i=1}^{k} (d(t_i))(Fr(t_i)N - FpN) \tag{6.20}$$

It is easy to see that each element in the summation of equation (6.20) is equal to equation (6.19). To this end, one simply needs to substitute for $Fr(t)$ its value in terms of $S(0)$ and $d(t)$. Since the forward price of an asset is the future value of its spot price $Fr(t)$ can be replaced with $\dfrac{S(0)}{d(t)}$. Hence, the value of the swap can also be written as in equation (6.21) below.

$$\sum_{i=1}^{k} (S(0)N - FpNd(t_i)) = kS(0)N - \sum_{i=1}^{k} FpNd(t_i) \tag{6.21}$$

Given N, $d(t)$, and $S(0)$ we can solve for the numerical value of Fp at which the value of the swap is zero. This is done in the command below where we also make sure that d is unassigned. However, we assume, as is generally the case, that for a swap at its initiation the payment schedule is equally spaced from the current time (time zero) to time k.

```
> d:='d':solve(sum(S(0)*N-d(t[i])*Fp*N,i=1..k)=0,Fp);
```

$$\frac{kS(0)}{\sum\limits_{i=1}^{k} d(t_i)}$$

Hence, Fp, as in equation (6.22), will indeed be the value agreed upon by the two parties.

$$Fp = \frac{kS(0)}{\sum\limits_{i=1}^{k} d(t_i)} \tag{6.22}$$

Valuing a swap at some time other than its initiation follows the same argument as discussed in Section 6.1.1. One should remember to make sure that $d(t)$ is the current term structure and that the time until the first payment may be different than the length of the time period between two consecutive payments.

The procedure **COmswap** values a commodity swap from the point of view of the party who pays the fixed price. The input parameters for this procedure are, in order, N, Fp, dis, $S(0)$, T, and per. T is the maturity time of the swap and per is the time between each consecutive payment. The rest of the parameters are as defined for equation (6.21). We can use the procedure in a symbolic way to solve for the value of the fixed rate given the rest of the parameters, as below.

```
> solve(COmswap(N,Fp,d,S0,T,per)=0,Fp);
```

$$\frac{T S0}{\left(\sum\limits_{t=1}^{\frac{T}{per}} d(pert) \right) per}$$

We can also use the procedure to value an equity swap at its initiation or to solve for the fixed price. Suppose we would like to find the fixed price that makes the value of a swap zero. Consider a swap of 1000 barrels of oil to be delivered (received) every 6 months for a period of 2 years when the spot price per barrel is $15. We first solve for the discount factor d utilizing **NarbitB** in a market where *coupons are paid semiannually.* Using **NarbitB** in this manner means that we keep a time unit of 6 months.

```
> NarbitB([[107,0,0,0],[5,5,5,105],[3,103,0,0],
[6,6,106,0]], [97,90,95,94],16,d,0);
```

The no-arbitrage condition is satisfied.
The discount factor for time, 1, is given by, $\frac{97}{107}$
The interest rate spanning the time interval, $[0,1]$, is given by, 0.1031
The discount factor for time, 2, is given by, $\frac{9874}{11021}$
The interest rate spanning the time interval, $[0,2]$, is given by, 0.1162
The discount factor for time, 3, is given by, $\frac{458392}{584113}$
The interest rate spanning the time interval, $[0,3]$, is given by, 0.2743
The discount factor for time, 4, is given by, $\frac{9002797}{12266373}$
The interest rate spanning the time interval, $[0,4]$, is given by, 0.3625
The function Vdis ([c1,c2,..]), values the cashflow [c1,c2,..]
The continuous discount factor is given by the function, 'd', (.)

```
> SumAbsDiv;
```
$$0$$

Since we maintain a time period of six months, the maturity of the swap will be at time 4 and payments will be exchanged every one unit of time. The price of a barrel of oil for this swap is solved for below:

```
> evalf(solve(COmswap(1000,Fp,d,15,4,1)=0,Fp));
```
$$18.06589418$$

Consider the same swap but with a fixed price of $18; its value in this case is calculated by the next command.

```
> evalf(COmswap(1000,18,d,15,4,1));
```
$$218.8461088$$

The procedure **COmswap** is also capable of valuing a swap after its initiation. Suppose we would like to value the above swap but that the time until the first payment is three months from initiation, rather than six. The only parameter we add to the procedure, as the last parameter, is the length of time until the next payment. Hence, the swap above, three months after its initiation, will be valued as below.

```
> evalf(COmswap(1000,18,d,7/2,1,1/2));
```
$$-25802.64847$$

The fixed price that makes this swap a fair deal is given below.

```
> evalf(solve(COmswap(1000,Fp,d,7/2,1,1/2)=0 ,Fp));
```
$$3.841153256$$

In the above valuation we assumed that the discount factor function **d** has the same structure as at the initiation time. If one would like to value the swap for a different structure one needs to run **NarbitB** again with the new data of the bond market.

In the commodity swap cases, and in the equity swap case as we will see below, the valuation makes use of the replication argument. In the commodity swap case, this replication argument is nothing more than the cost-of-carry model.

6.3.1 *Equity Swaps*

In case of an equity swap, the party agrees on a notional principal and on an index to which the floating rate is linked. At times, $t = 1,\ldots,k$ one party pays the other a fixed rate of interest on the notional principal N. In exchange, the party receives, at time t, the return on N invested in the index (including dividends if such are paid out) over the period $[t-1,t]$. An equity swap is thus essentially a fixed-for-float swap where the floating rate is linked to an index, e.g., the S&P 500 index, rather than to a variable interest rate. The net payment at time t to the party who receives the fixed rate is thus

$$FRN - I(t)N, \tag{6.23}$$

where $I(t)$ is the return on the index over the time period from $t-1$ to t, and FR is the fixed rate agreed upon at the initiation time $t=0$.

The valuation of the equity swap follows the same guidelines as that of the commodity swap. We first need to find the current value (present value) of $I(t)N$. In Section 2.5.2 we explained how we were able to arrive at the required value. Using the replication argument, we repeat it here for convenience. We borrow, at the current time, an amount $Nd(t-1)$ to be repaid at time t. This amount is invested at the risk-free rate of interest until time $t-1$, at which point it will be worth N. At time $t-1$, the amount N is invested in the index for one period until time t. Let us denote the value of this investment at time t (including the dividend paid at that time) by $V(t)$. At time t the loan needs to be paid back. The amount to be paid back is $N\dfrac{d(t-1)}{d(t)}$. However, since we only need to replicate the return on the index, which is $V(t) - N$, we can use N to subsidize the loan repayment. Hence, replicating the return on the index results in a certain (deterministic) payment equal to $\dfrac{Nd(t-1)}{d(t)} - N$ at time t. Therefore, we can replace the random quantity $NI(t)N$ in equation (6.24) with the deterministic quantity $N\dfrac{d(t-1)}{d(t)} - N$, arriving at equation (6.26) for the net payment at time.

$$FRN - N\left(\frac{d(t-1)}{d(t)}\right) + N$$

$$(6.24)$$

Equation (6.24) does not involve random quantities and hence its present value can be calculated by discounting it using the risk-free rate of interest. The value of this swap is then the summation, as in equation (6.25), of the present value of the net payments across $t = 1, \ldots, k$

$$\sum_{t=1}^{k} (FRNd(t) - Nd(t-1) + Nd(t)).$$

$$(6.25)$$

The value of $d(0)$ is one and since the terms $Nd(t-1) + Nd(t)$ cancel each other for t such that $1 < t$ and $t < k$, we arrive at equation (11.26) for the value of the swap

$$\sum_{t=1}^{k} FRNd(t) - N(1 - d(k)).$$

(6.26)

We can therefore solve for the numerical value of FR which makes the swap value zero. The next command uses *dis* for the discount factor as d is assigned a value and we would soon like to use it for numerical calculations.

```
> dis:='dis';
```

$$dis := dis$$

```
> solve(sum(FR*N*dis(t),t=1..k)-N*(1-dis(k))=0,FR);
```

$$-\frac{-1 + dis(k)}{\sum_{t=1}^{k} dis(t)}$$

At the initiation time, the value of the swap is zero and the parties will agree on FR such that

$$FR = \frac{1 - d(k)}{\sum_{t=1}^{k} d(t)}.$$

(6.27)

The procedure EQswap values an equity swap (from the perspective of the party paying the return on the equity).

The input parameters to this procedure are, in order, N, FR, and d, as defined in equation (6.26), T the maturity of the swap and *per* the length of the period e.g., every 6 months. We can verify the solution for FR by executing the command below:

```
> solve(EQswap(N,Fp,dis,T,per),Fp);
```

$$-\frac{1.(-1. + dis(T))}{\sum_{t=1}^{\frac{T}{per}} dis(pert)}$$

We can make use of the procedure **EQswap** to value an equity swap at its initiation and to value an equity swap which is already in existence. The numerical value of FR, the fixed rate of interest, that will make the value of the swap vanish is independent of the particular index to which the variable return is pegged. What matters is only the term structure of interest rates. Equivalently, what matters is the discount factor function. We already have explained that phenomenon at the end of Chapter 2 in Section 2.5.2. The reader may wish to review the strategy which replicates the return on the index, making sure to verify that the return is independent of the actual index being replicated. This is the driving force behind this phenomenon.

Consider a swap at its initiation with a maturity of two years for which payments are exchanged once each year. The fixed rate of interest is 8 percent and the notional principal is $1000. The discount factor function is d, as defined above.

Since the units of time in the term structure estimation are half-years, to value such a swap we execute the command with maturity time $T = 4$ and a period of two, i.e., $per = 2$.

```
> EQswap(1000,.08,d,4,2);
```

$$-135.6693849$$

The fixed rate that will make the value of this swap zero is given by

```
> evalf(solve(EQswap(1000,Fp,d,4,2)=0,Fp));
```

$$0.1632395332$$

If this swap had been in existence for six months, the next payment would occur in six months and its value would be calculated by simply adding another input parameter. This parameter would be the time until the next payment. The value would then be calculated by executing the command below.

```
> EQswap(1000,.070741961591,d,4,2,1);
```

$$-201.9281975$$

This calculation, of course assumes that in six months from now the discount factor is still $d(t)$. In reality one would move to reestimate the discount factor.

Consider a swap with the same parameters as above but for which the first exchange of payments will be in one month, rather than in one year.

The fixed rate of interest that would make this swap a fair deal for both parties is found by executing the Maple command below.

```
> evalf(solve(EQswap(1000,Fp,d,4,2,1/6)=0,Fp));
```

$$0.2795584893$$

Note that when we changed the time until the first payment we effectively altered the present value calculation in equation (6.25). We can investigate the sensitivity of the fixed rate of interest to the time until the first payment via the Maple command below. In this command, the time until the next payment is allowed to range from $\frac{1}{10}$ to 1, in increments of $\frac{1}{10}$. The sequence is a variety of fixed rates of interest that that would make the value of the swap zero.

```
> seq(evalf(solve(EQswap(1000,Fp,d,4,2,i/10)=0,Fp)),
i=1..10);
```

$$0.2750803910, 0.2814148287, 0.2857386019, 0.2886232037,$$
$$0.2905119336, 0.2917294868, 0.2925041995, 0.2929919153,$$
$$0.2932967488, 0.2934874990$$

The last section of this chapter visualizes the relation between swaps and forwards.

6.4 Forwards and Swaps: A Visualization

A swap can actually be thought of as a portfolio of forward contracts. We have already alluded to this relation before when we discussed fixed-for-float swaps. We can visualize this interpretation with the aid of the three-dimensional graphing capability of Maple. We examine the payoff structure which is a consequence of a forward contract, and then demonstrate that the aggregate of these payoffs across time is equivalent to the payoff structure of a swap contract. We examine the commodity swap in our example, but any of the other swaps would serve the purpose equally as well.

Let us consider a swap contract in which one party is committed to swap a barrel of oil at some future times $t = t1, t2, \ldots, tk$, for a price of F_p agreed upon now and payable at those times. Assume that the current time is zero, that $ti = i$ for $i = 1, \ldots, 4$ and that Fp is \$7. We consider the payoff from the point of view of the party who pays the fixed price for the barrel of oil. The cash flows resultant from this contract occur at times $t = 1, 2, 3,$ and 4, and are equal to $S(t) - FF$, where $S(t)$ is the spot price at time t. At any other time, of course, the cash flow from this contract is zero. We visualize the cash flow from this swap contract by executing the procedure **PlotSwPyf**. The parameters for this procedure are, in order, the sequence of time at which a swap payment occurs and the price agreed upon for the swap. The points in time are entered into the procedure in the form $[t1, t2, \ldots, tk]$, or, in our example, as [1,2,3,4].

Executing the command **PlotSwpyf**([1,2,3,4],7) will generate the graph in following figure. The reader can and is encouraged to, experiment with different values of the parameters and change the viewing perspective of the graph by dragging it in the online version.

```
> PlotSwPyf([1,2,3,4],7);
```

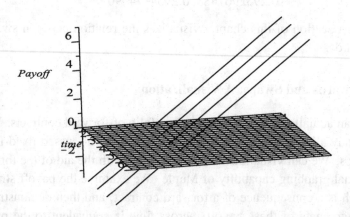

Swaps' Building Blocks

It is now visually apparent that the cash flows from a swap are like the cash flows from four forward contracts with a forward price of \$7 and maturity dates of 1, 2, 3, and 4. Economically, the swap is a portfolio composed of the forward contracts. To visualize this phenomenon we can instruct Maple to plot the cash flows of these four forward contracts over the time span [0,6], on the same set of axes, and then examine the resultant graphs. This is done with the next Maple command.

```
> plots[display](seq(PlotForPyf(k,7,6),k=1..4));
```

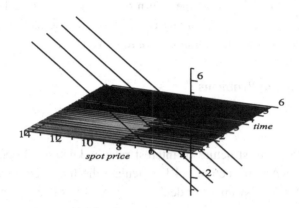

Forward's Payoff

6.5 Concluding Remarks

This chapter takes a second look at swaps. Swaps can be categorized as assets, the valuation of which does not require knowledge of the evolution of the term structure over time. The setting used in this second look is characterized by a multiperiod time with a continuum of states of nature. It is shown here that swaps can be viewed as a portfolio of forward contracts and thereby a link is established to the analysis of swaps in the setting of a one-period model in Chapter 1.

The key idea in the valuation of swaps is essentially the calculation of the net present values of the swapped cash flows. The present values are calculated utilizing the discount factor function estimated from the prices of the bonds in the market. At the initiation of the swap, its parameters are set so the values of the swapped cash flows offset each other. For example, the fixed-for-float swap is set in such a way that the value of the swap is zero at initiation. After initiation of the swap, market conditions usually change and the value of the swap is no longer zero. The value of a swap, either at initiation or later, is the difference between the current value of the swapped cash flows.

The investigation of equity swaps highlights the effect of the absence of arbitrage opportunities in a market. Such a market "prices" the risk embedded in each asset by adjusting the returns on the different assets available in the market. Hence, the return on one dollar invested in asset A should be worth the same as the return on one dollar invested in asset B. Thus swapping the returns on any two assets, as long as the amounts invested in them are the same, should be a fair swap.

6.6 Questions and Problems

Problem 1

Assume that the term structure of interest rates is known. Based on the discussion of FRAs, in Section 6.4.1, calculate the fixed rate that would make a fixed-for-float swap a fair deal. (*Hint*: As it has been discussed in the text, the swap can be broken down into building blocks that are similar to the FRAs. The catch, though, is that in a swap the same fixed rate should apply to all the building blocks. Hence, the value of each block may not be zero, but the value of the blocks in aggregate is zero if the swap is fair.)

Problem 2

Consider the data of the fixed-for-float swap in Section 6.1. Suppose a customer would like to enter into a *buy down fixed-for-float swap* and would like to pay a fixed rate of $r - \Delta$, where r is the fixed rate that would make an otherwise equivalent regular swap a fair deal. Determine the amount that this customer would have to pay at the initiation of the swap if $\Delta = 1\%$.

Problem 3

Consider the data of the fixed-for-float swap in Section 6.1. Suppose a customer would like to enter into a *buy up fixed-for-float swap* and would like to pay a fixed rate of $r + \Delta$, where r is the fixed rate that would make an otherwise equivalent regular swap a fair deal. Determine the amount that this customer would have to pay at the initiation of the swap if $\Delta = 1\%$.

Problem 4

In practice, a currency swap might be arranged for a domestic firm by a financial institution. The institution either finds a foreign firm or "warehouses" this cash flow until it finds an optimal match for it. In certain cases, the institution must assume some risk as a result of the absence of an exact match. Hence, it requires a fee, a "finder's fee", as well as compensation for the risk taken. This fee is usually obtained in terms of an increase in the rate, r_0 , that the domestic firm is asked to pay. Consider the swap in the example in Section 6.2. Assume that a financial institution agrees to arrange this swap for a domestic firm but requires the firm to pay $r_0 = 0.047$ instead of 0.03777664666 which makes the value of the swap zero. What is the "finder's fee" that the institution charged the firm?

Problem 5

The **FXswap** procedure can also be used if instead of the two term structures, the domestic term structure and the term structure of forward exchange rates are supplied. A direct substitution in the **FXswap** procedure will generate the value of a foreign exchange swap. Use the term structure of forward exchange rates and the foreign term structure given in the example of Section 6.2, to value the foreign exchange swap in Section 6.2.

Problem 6

The value of an existing foreign currency swap does not (**and should not**) take into account cash flows that were exchanged in the past. When valuing an existing foreign currency swap only the principals that will be exchanged at maturity and all of the future regular cash flows ("coupons") should be considered. Hence, the procedure **FXswap**, that values an existing foreign currency swap, cannot be applied to value a deferred foreign currency swap. However, valuing such a swap should not present a problem. One needs simply to value also the principals that will be exchanged at the future date, when the swap is initiated. This should be done in exactly the same manner the principals (of a regular swap) that are swapped at the termination time are valued. Consider the example of a foreign cur-

rency swap in Section 6.2 and value it, if it would have been a deferred
swap starting in six months.

Index

Printed in the United States
By Bookmasters